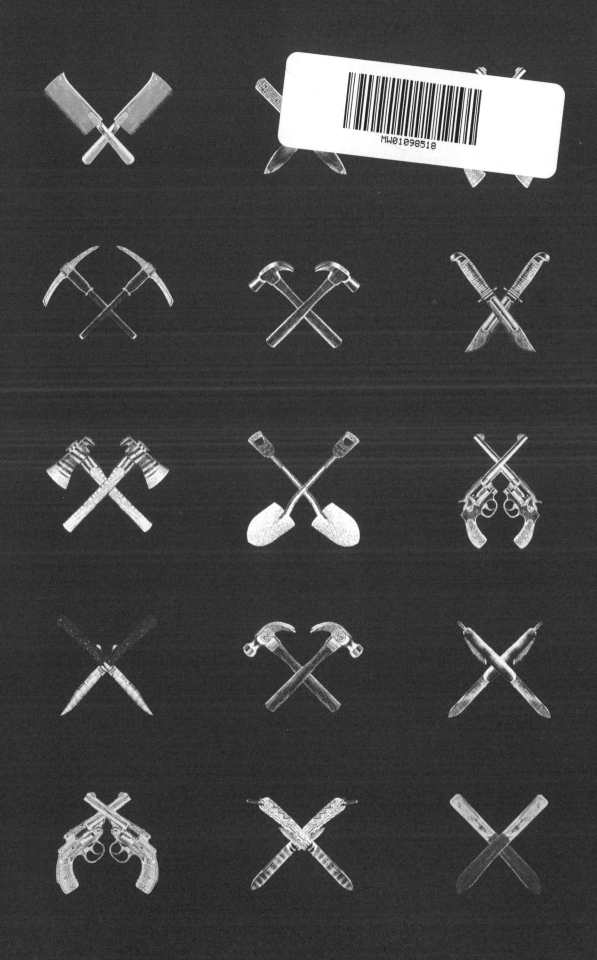

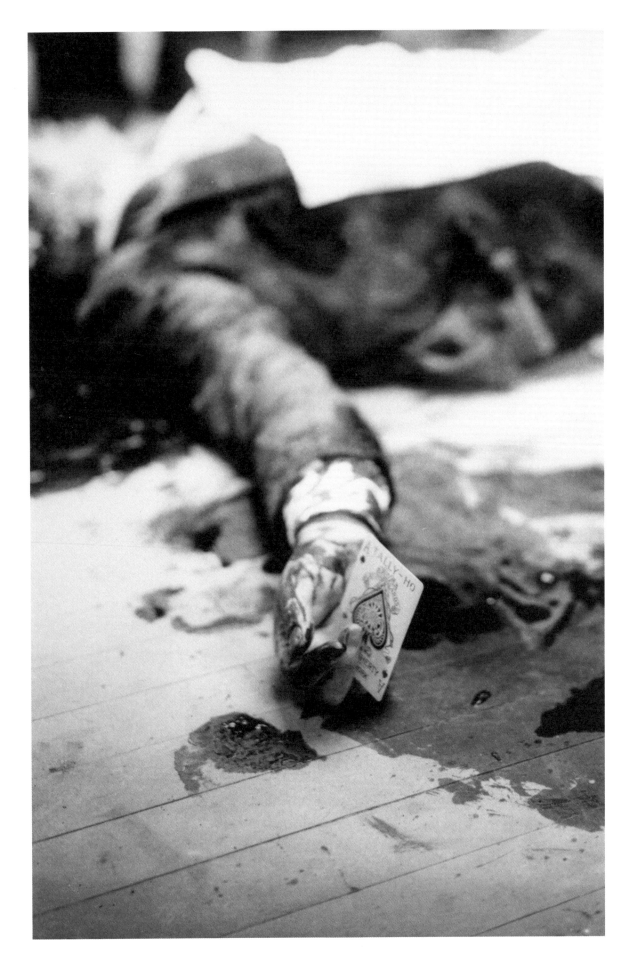

MURDER MAPS

USA

CRIME SCENES *REVISITED*

BLOODSTAINS TO BALLISTICS

CIVIL WAR TO WORLD WAR II
1865 ←——————————→ 1939

ADAM SELZER

CONTENTS

INTRODUCTION 6
FROM SUPERSTITION TO SCIENCE: THE SLOW BIRTH OF MODERN CRIMINOLOGY AND FORENSICS

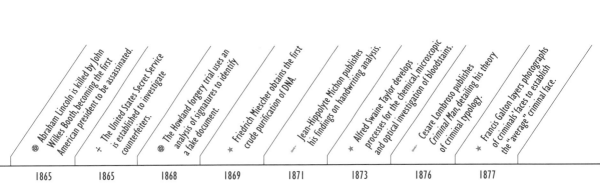

INTRODUCTION

FROM SUPERSTITION TO SCIENCE:
THE SLOW BIRTH OF MODERN CRIMINOLOGY AND FORENSICS

→ 1865 ←————————————————————→ 1939 ←

In 1859, workers at a dock in New York City noticed that a barrel that had been shipped into town smelled particularly foul and decided to open it up. The first thing that they saw when they prised the barrel open was a woman's face, detached from the body parts beneath, but still recognizably a face and, in some accounts, even still beautiful, despite the fact that the woman had been dead for several weeks.

The barrel was traced back to Henry Jumpertz, a barber in Chicago, and the body proved to be that of his girlfriend, Sophie Werner. In Jumpertz's own account, he had come home from his barbershop and found that Sophie had hanged herself. Fearful that he, as a Prussian immigrant, would be accused of murdering her, Jumpertz had dismembered the body, buried some of the innards on the nearby beach, and sealed the rest into a barrel that he kept next to his bed for the following two weeks. As he had been trained as a doctor in his home country, Jumpertz would have been reasonably accustomed to working with dead bodies. However, after a couple of weeks the general creepiness (and probably the smell) became too much for him, and he posted the barrel to New York.

An age-old proverb holds that "murder will out." The phrase appears in print, twice, in Geoffrey Chaucer's *The Canterbury Tales,* written in the late 14th century, but it is probably much older. Simply put, the proverb cautions that no one can get away with covering up a murder. The crime will always be discovered. A person might steal something and have the owner never realize it is gone, or tell a lie and never have it exposed, but the laws of nature dictate that a violation as abominable as murder cannot go undetected.

This seems like quaint and superstitious thinking today, when the news feeds us a steady diet of true crime stories, and even casual

OPPOSITE Investigators in the Lindbergh kidnapping case searching near where the body of Charles Lindbergh Jr. was found. They hoped to find a bullet that could be matched to the gun found in Richard Hauptmann's garage.

MILESTONES OF CRIMINAL INVESTIGATION, 1865–82

✴ INNOVATION

⊕ CASE

⊷ PUBLICATION

‡ INSTITUTION

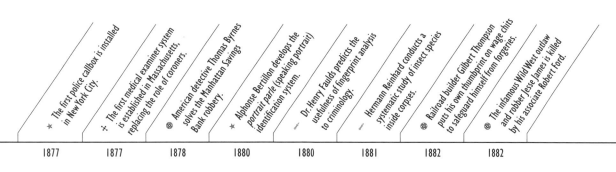

✴ The first police callbox is installed in New York City.
1877

‡ The first medical examiner system is established in Massachusetts, replacing the role of coroners.
1877

⊕ American detective Thomas Byrnes solves the Manhattan Savings Bank robbery.
1878

✴ Alphonse Bertillon develops the *portrait parlé* (speaking portrait) identification system.
1880

⊷ Dr. Henry Faulds predicts the usefulness of fingerprint analysis to criminology.
1880

⊷ Hermann Reinhard conducts a systematic study of insect species inside corpses.
1881

⊕ Railroad builder Gilbert Thompson puts his own thumbprint on wage chits to safeguard himself from forgeries.
1882

⊕ The infamous Wild West outlaw and robber Jesse James is killed by his associate Robert Ford.
1882

TV viewers can list any number of ways to dispose of a body. But the proverb was common well into the 19th century, when reporters would still ask investigators and criminals alike if they believed that "murder will out." By then, though, responses tended to be skeptical. Due to news traveling faster, stories spreading further, and the emphasis on rationality and reason ushered in by the Enlightenment, people no longer believed that a supernatural law would ensure that murder, of all crimes, was impossible to get away with.

By the late 19th century, advances in policing and criminology around the world were, in fact, bringing the proverb closer to truth than ever. However, progress was slow, as authorities seemed

MILESTONES OF CRIMINAL INVESTIGATION, 1883–95

✳ INNOVATION

⊕ CASE

➖ PUBLICATION

‡ INSTITUTION

reluctant to bring in experts and scientists to help investigate crimes. In as late as 1895, as authorities dug up the basement of the self-proclaimed serial killer H. H. Holmes's "Murder Castle" in Chicago, they were working blind. One witness described seeing police officers comparing bone fragments they had found to pictures in an anatomy book, desperately hoping to find a way to identify them as human remains. There were plenty of anthropologists in the city, but the police seemed to prefer to consult reporters. Experts were more apt to let facts get in the way of a good story. Police officers of the era still occasionally scoffed at "the theory of deduction" and held it cheap compared to "the plain methods of police work," which were often centered on beating suspects with a billy club until they confessed.

Police agencies in general hardly existed before the 19th century. Fifty years before the Holmes case, Chicago's police force consisted of a sheriff and two or three deputies. Moreover,

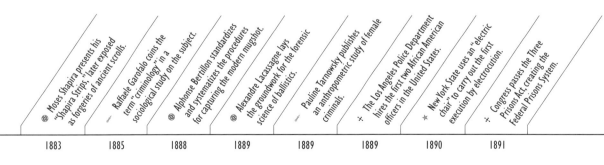

⊕ Moses Shapira presents his "Shapira Strips," later exposed as forgeries of ancient scrolls.	➖ Raffaele Garofalo coins the term "criminology" in a sociological study on the subject.	⊕ Alphonse Bertillon standardizes and systematizes the procedures for capturing the modern mugshot.	⊕ Alexandre Lacassagne lays the groundwork for the forensic science of ballistics.	➖ Pauline Tarnowsky publishes an anthropometric study of female criminals.	‡ The Los Angeles Police Department hires the first two African American officers in the United States.	✳ New York State uses an "electric chair" to carry out the first execution by electrocution.	‡ Congress passes the Three Prisons Act creating the Federal Prisons System.
1883	1885	1888	1889	1889	1889	1890	1891

in those days, city mayors only served a single-year term and each new mayor shook the department up. Allan Pinkerton formed his famed private detective service in the 1850s largely because he realized that local law enforcement was too subject to political influence.

In the same city, and in the same decade, a new form of forensics emerged: handwriting analysis. This turned out to be the saving grace for Henry Jumpertz, whom the press had labeled the "barrel murderer" (though he was one of countless people to earn that title over the years). Just as Jumpertz had expected, nearly everyone assumed that he had murdered Sophie, and probably would have made the same assumption even if he had not dismembered and concealed the body. The story became a sensation. A full book on Jumpertz was published—one of

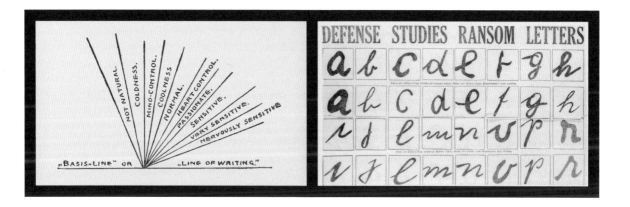

the young city's first true crime publications. Reporters flocked to watch as Jumpertz was convicted, sentenced to hang, and sent to prison to await his fate. A model prisoner, he even helped design the gallows on which he would be hanged.

However, the state supreme court ruled that there had been an error in the trial, and he was given a re-trial. In the first trial, Jumpertz claimed that he had lost a suicide note Sophie had written, but he was able to produce some letters in which she spoke of "renouncing the world," making it clear that she was suicidal. But the prosecution had argued that they were forgeries written by Henry himself.

During the second trial, though, the court decided that the hand-writing really was Sophie's, and Jumpertz was acquitted.

Neither side at the time offered any expert analysis of the handwriting, as such expertise barely existed. And, in any case, introducing expert forensic analysis of any sort in court was not normal practice. However, witnesses were brought to testify to the letters' authenticity, and

ABOVE, LEFT A diagram featured in Hugo J. von Hagen, *Reading Character from Handwriting*, 1902, suggesting the characteristics that may be deduced about a person from the slant of their handwriting, from "not natural" from a heavy left slant, to "coolness" from a slight right slant, and "nervously sensitive" from a heavy right slant.

ABOVE, RIGHT A comparison of Richard Hauptmann's handwriting (second and bottom rows) and the ransom notes issued to the Lindberghs (top and third rows), used in the Lindbergh kidnapping case.

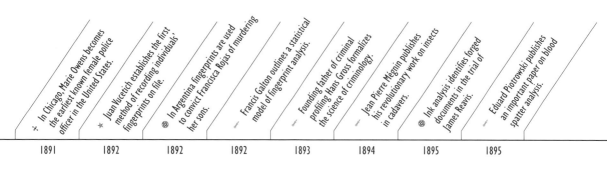

In Chicago, Marie Owens becomes the earliest known female police officer in the United States. — 1891

Juan Vucetich establishes the first method of recording individuals' fingerprints on file. — 1892

In Argentina fingerprints are used to convict Francisca Rojas of murdering her sons. — 1892

Francis Galton outlines a statistical model of fingerprint analysis. — 1892

Founding father of criminal profiling Hans Gross formalizes the science of criminology. — 1893

Jean Pierre Mégnin publishes his revolutionary work on insects in cadavers. — 1894

Ink analysis identifies forged documents in the trial of James Reavis. — 1895

Eduard Piotrowski publishes an important paper on blood spatter analysis. — 1895

documents written in both Sophie and Henry's hand admitted for comparison. People were beginning to understand that handwriting was unique, and could be used as evidence.

In the decades following the Jumpertz affair, forensic sciences began to advance at a rapid pace, as did the new field of "criminology."

The term "criminology" was first coined in 1885, and early texts on the discipline seem at best laughable, and at worst racist, when read now. Great emphasis was put on physical features and race. Arthur MacDonald, one of the earliest noted criminologists, invented a device called the kymographion, a sort of early polygraph that measured changes in physiological responses. His other gadgets measured things such as pain sensitivity in given body parts. These innovations were driven by the belief that minute analysis of the body could determine whether someone was a "criminal type." For instance, MacDonald believed that criminals were more sensitive to pain in their left hands than in their right.

As ridiculous as this all sounds today, beneath it was the revolutionary concept that science could fight crime. Though nearly everything that MacDonald wrote would soon be outdated, it was a step towards making the proverb "murder will out" closer to the truth.

For a criminal to disappear was, of course, far easier in those days. Changing one's name was a straightforward affair, and if one moved to another city, one could easily go undetected. Though photographs were common by the 1850s, it was not until the late 1880s that detectives began to use them in earnest.

Alphonse Bertillon, a French police officer born in 1853, is best remembered today for popularizing the use of what we now call "mugshots," though in this arena his main contribution was really just helping to standardize the process and style of photographs taken of criminals. His most important contribution was the development of anthropometry, the science of measuring the human body. As a young copyist in the Paris police department, Bertillon was frustrated by the casual approach of officers to making identifications based on the physical similarities of suspects compared to available photographs. Bertillon worked to supplement the photographic records by including measurements such as the length of the head, the size of the foot, the length of the middle finger, and other attributes that he insisted remained constant throughout a person's adult life. Though neither the police nor the prisoners he measured thought much of the idea at the time, and his method was only designed to work on men who had short hair and had reached full maturity, it became common practice throughout the Western world by the 20th century.

OPPOSITE Members of the New York City Police Department practicing taking measurements for the Bertillon method of identification in 1908. In late 19th-century France, Alphonse Bertillon pioneered a system for taking precise measurements of criminals to enable more accurate identifications. The system involved taking multiple measurements, including of the foot (top left), head (top right and bottom left), and arm span (bottom right).

MILESTONES OF CRIMINAL INVESTIGATION, 1895–1906

✳ INNOVATION

⊕ CASE

⌖ PUBLICATION

‡ INSTITUTION

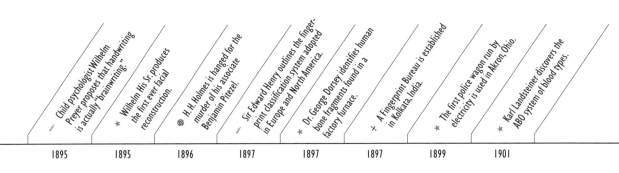

Child psychologist Wilhelm Preyer proposes that handwriting is actually "brainwriting."

Wilhelm His Sr. produces the first ever facial reconstruction.

H.H. Holmes is hanged for the murder of his associate Benjamin Pitezel.

Sir Edward Henry outlines the finger-print classification system adopted in Europe and North America.

Dr. George Dorsey identifies human bone fragments found in a factory furnace.

A Fingerprint Bureau is established in Kolkata, India.

The first police wagon run by electricity is used in Akron, Ohio.

Karl Landsteiner discovers the ABO system of blood types.

| 1895 | 1895 | 1896 | 1897 | 1897 | 1897 | 1899 | 1901 |

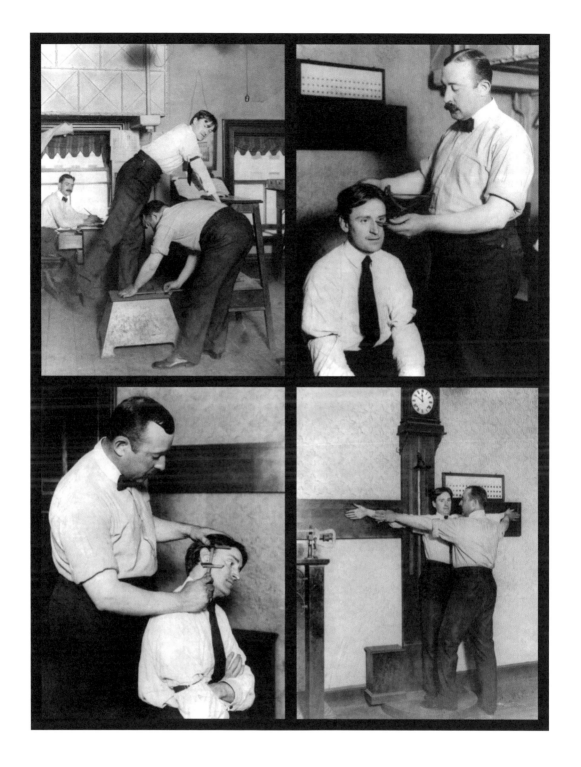

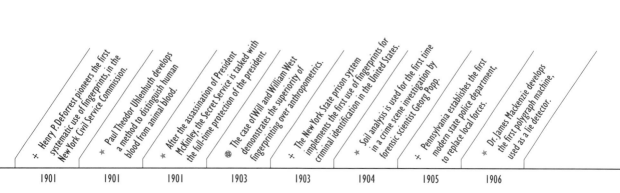

But even as his ideas became mainstream, Bertillon himself was working on the field that would render his facial measurements largely obsolete: fingerprints.

Of course, it had been known for centuries that humans had differing fingerprint patterns, but people were slow to realize just how different they were. In 1823, the Czech scientist Jan Evangelista Purkyně posited that there were nine different fingerprint patterns. Over the course of the following century, researchers became aware that within those pattens were countless minute differences that were nearly unique to the individual. In 1892 Francis Galton, a British statistician, suggested that the likelihood of two people having exactly the same prints was one in sixty-four billion.

ABOVE, LEFT A New York City police officer taking a man's fingerprints in 1917.

ABOVE, CENTER A member of the National Division of Identification and Information, part of the Bureau of Investigation, examining a reproduction of a fingerprint in 1930.

ABOVE, RIGHT Investigators examining files of fingerprints in 1924.

To call Galton—later Sir Francis Galton—a statistician is perhaps to short-change him. Besides his work in statistics, he was noted for his studies in psychology, geology, meteorology, anthropology, and, like so many scientists of his era, eugenics. But his true passion was measuring things, and he put this to use with his study of fingerprints, not only studying them but devising a means of both classifying and analyzing them. Some of his ideas and concepts are still in use today.

The use of fingerprints as evidence remains controversial today, particularly now that DNA can be tested more reliably. However, at that time people interested in the developing science of criminology (and not trying to rival Galton and gain fame for their own theories) were electrified by these new ideas. That fingerprints could be recovered at a crime scene, and make a positive match to a suspect beyond all doubt, was as major an advance as could be imagined at the time.

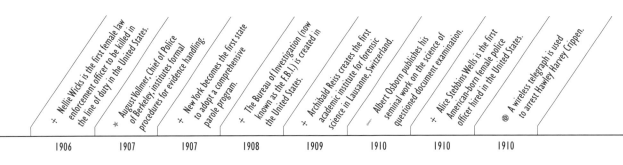

+ Nellie Wicks is the first female law enforcement officer to be killed in the line of duty in the United States.

* August Vollmer, Chief of Police of Berkeley, institutes formal procedures for evidence handling.

+ New York becomes the first state to adopt a comprehensive parole program.

+ The Bureau of Investigation (now known as the F.B.I.) is created in the United States.

+ Archibald Reiss creates the first academic institute for forensic science in Lausanne, Switzerland.

— Albert Osborn publishes his seminal work on the science of questioned document examination.

+ Alice Stebbins Wells is the first American-born female police officer hired in the United States.

⊗ A wireless telegraph is used to arrest Hawley Harvey Crippen.

| 1906 | 1907 | 1907 | 1908 | 1909 | 1910 | 1910 | 1910 |

It was some time before the technique made its way to the United States. The independent American detective Mary E. Holland studied the technique at Scotland Yard, London, and put it to use in the United States, where it helped her to solve cases even if it would not be considered conclusive evidence in court. But when a chauffeur was murdered in an automobile in 1904, the police had Holland examine the prints and bloodstains in the car. The evidence that she found led her to conclude that there must have been a third person on the scene. This did not help solve the crime in the end—it was never solved—but the fact that police took her findings seriously shows that the concept was gaining acceptance.

BELOW, LEFT The F.B.I.'s fingerprint identification card for the notorious gangster Al Capone.

BELOW, RIGHT The F.B.I.'s fingerprint identification card for John Dillinger, a bank robber and associate of Baby Face Nelson.

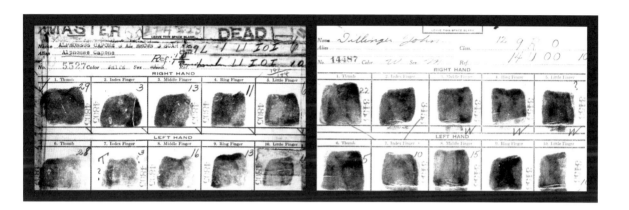

Six years later, a man named Thomas Jennings was arrested for murder in Chicago, and the police matched a fingerprint found near the scene to Jennings's own prints. Holland was among a handful of experts who testified that a match in prints was as good as gold, and Jennings was convicted. A new era in forensics had arrived. Newspapers were shocked; one editorial asked, "Will the criminal of tomorrow be forced to wear gloves as he commits his crimes?" Barely fifteen years had passed since the days when hapless policemen pored over anatomy books, but to investigators, those days must have seemed a lifetime ago. In 1897, successful forensic analysis of bone fragments made the national news for the first time.

In that year, neighbors had noticed that Louisa Luetgert, the wife of a local sausage dealer, had gone missing. Though her husband's factory was closed for repairs and cleaning, strange smoke was seen coming from the chimney around the time she had last been seen. Her husband, Adolph, insisted that his wife was away on a

MILESTONES OF CRIMINAL INVESTIGATION, 1906–15

✳ INNOVATION

⊕ CASE

⊷ PUBLICATION

‡ INSTITUTION

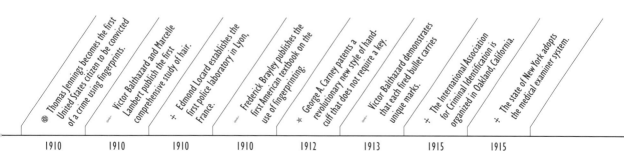

Thomas Jennings becomes the first United States citizen to be convicted of a crime using fingerprints.

Victor Balthazard and Marcelle Lambert publish the first comprehensive study of hair.

Edmond Locard establishes the first police laboratory, in Lyon, France.

Frederick Brayley publishes the first American textbook on the use of fingerprinting.

George A. Carney patents a revolutionary new style of hand-cuff that does not require a key.

Victor Balthazard demonstrates that each fired bullet carries unique marks.

The International Association for Criminal Identification is organized in Oakland, California.

The state of New York adopts the medical examiner system.

| 1910 | 1910 | 1910 | 1910 | 1912 | 1913 | 1915 | 1915 |

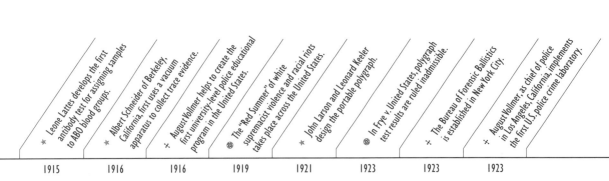

trip, but the police began to investigate the factory. A janitor told them that shortly after Louisa had disappeared he had been asked to stir up a mysterious mixture in one of the sausage curing vats. Though rumours would persist for decades that Louisa had been made into sausages and sold to unsuspecting customers, the police believed that her body had been dissolved in the caustic mixture. On inspecting the vats, a ring was found bearing Louisa's initials, and various fragments of bone were uncovered.

Rather than scrutinizing anatomy books, the police submitted the bone fragments to Dr. George Dorsey, an anthropologist at the Field Columbian Museum, Chicago, who established that in addition to a large piece of thigh bone, the fragments included pieces of human metatarsal, toe, and rib bones, as well as traces of nerves and blood vessels. At the trial he took the stand and asserted to everyone's satisfaction that the bones were human.

Dr. Dorsey and other experts had been working in the days of the Holmes investigation, and if the case had ever come to trial in Chicago, perhaps they would have been called. But by the end of the 19th century expert testimony was far more common, and, given the advances in science, the days when a murderer might walk free because there was not enough of the victim left had come to an end.

In 1913 Victor Balthazard published *Identification of Revolver Projectiles of Plain Lead*, a study that demonstrated that every bullet fired was just as uniquely marked as fingerprints. Using these new ballistic techniques, detectives were often able to trace a bullet back to the gun that fired it. Meanwhile, more and more cities across the United States were switching from untrained coroners to medical examiners to determine the cause of death. To the public, it must have seemed as through the career criminal's days were numbered. How could murderers continue to operate with so many ways for evidence to be traced back to them?

It is difficult not to notice how many of these developments first attracted attention in Chicago. Indeed, it may be that the city's reputation as a "wicked town" is due partly to how often the forensic developments there made national news. It is also because Chicago was a breeding ground for one of the biggest problems that would plague 20th-century policing: corrupt and inefficient local forces.

Being a police officer was hardly a profession in the early 20th century; there was no academy, no civil service exam, and no real formal training process. In 1904, a private investigator hired to look into the activity of the Chicago police force wrote that the men he studied were "Piano movers, bumps, cripples, janitors, ward heelers—anything but policemen." He further noted that

OPPOSITE, TOP Wilmer H. Souder in his laboratory at the National Bureau of Standards in Washington, D.C. in 1935. Souder was a physicist who also worked on forensic science, handwriting analysis and ballistics, notably working on the case of the Lindbergh kidnapping.

OPPOSITE, BOTTOM Calvin Goddard of the Bureau of Forensic Ballistics, New York, examining the inside of a revolver barrel. Goddard was a pioneer in the forensic science of ballistics, and notably worked on the case of the St. Valentine's Day Massacre.

MILESTONES OF CRIMINAL INVESTIGATION, 1915–29

✻ INNOVATION

⊕ CASE

⊶ PUBLICATION

‡ INSTITUTION

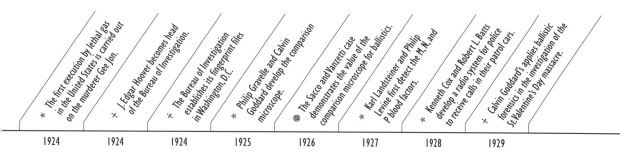

✻ The first execution by lethal gas in the United States is carried out on the murderer Gee Jon.

‡ J. Edgar Hoover becomes head of the Bureau of Investigation.

‡ The Bureau of Investigation establishes its fingerprint files in Washington, D.C.

✻ Philip Gravelle and Calvin Goddard develop the comparison microscope.

⊕ The Sacco and Vanzetti case demonstrates the value of the comparison microscope for ballistics.

✻ Karl Landsteiner and Philip Levine first detect the M, N, and P blood factors.

✻ Kenneth Cox and Robert L. Batts develop a radio system for police to receive calls in their patrol cars.

‡ Calvin Goddard's applies ballistic forensics in the investigation of the St. Valentine's Day massacre.

| 1924 | 1924 | 1924 | 1925 | 1926 | 1927 | 1928 | 1929 |

PHOTOGRAPHER ARTHUR FELLIG, KNOWN AS WEEGEE, ON THE PROCESS OF CAPTURING A CRIME SCENE.

POLICE AT THE SCENE OF A GANG KILLING IN NEW YORK CITY IN 1939, BY CRIME PHOTOGRAPHER WEEGEE.

> "FOR TWO YEARS I WORKED WITHOUT A POLICE CARD…
> WHEN A STORY CAME OVER THE POLICE TELETYPE, I WOULD GO TO IT."

PHOTOGRAPHER WEEGEE REVEALING HOW
HE DISCOVERED CRIME SCENES TO CAPTURE.

A POLICE OFFICER AND A REPORTER AT A MURDER
IN NEW YORK CITY IN 1939, CAPTURED BY WEEGEE.

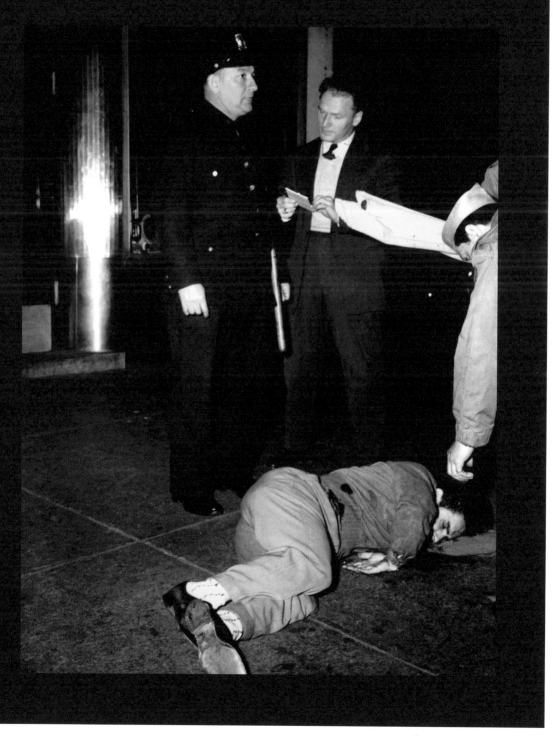

"They have no respect for the law, and depend upon their pull with the alderman to get them out of trouble. Out of all the precincts we have watched, we have found but two patrolmen who did their duty. They sleep when they should be on their rounds. They play the slot machines and drink with anyone who asks them." These revelations would hardly have been surprising to anyone who read the news. Though, then as now, people often made a vocal point of supporting their local officers, believing that this support was a matter of principle, not to necessarily be based on merits.

Though civil service reforms were made to make police more reliable in the first two decades of the 20th century, the launch of Prohibition in 1920 set progress back considerably. The

ABOVE, LEFT Detectives at the crime scene of the murder of the Brooklyn gangster Wild Bill Lovett, discovered in a warehouse in 1923.

ABOVE, CENTER The scene of the murder of the gangster Frankie Yale in 1928. Shots were fired from a moving vehicle, while Yale was driving his Lincoln coupe.

ABOVE, RIGHT A New York bootlegger killed by a rival gang member in 1929.

manufacture, sale, and consumption of alcohol became illegal, but the public appetite for it did not diminish. Indeed, by many metrics, it only increased. Breweries had three options: switch to brewing non-alcoholic beer, shut down altogether, or sell out to criminals. A great many chose the latter. The gangsters and racketeers who took over the nation's liquor services were far more apt to shoot anyone who got in their way than the brewers had been, and it was easier for them to bribe the police. Many officers did not particularly care to enforce Prohibition laws to begin with, and now they had more opportunities for corruption than ever.

When Prohibition ended in the 1930s, policing found itself at an interesting crossroads. The public was fascinated with the new technologies that had emerged, making police and detectives more advanced and efficient than ever. At the same time, they had experienced more than a decade of stories about corruption

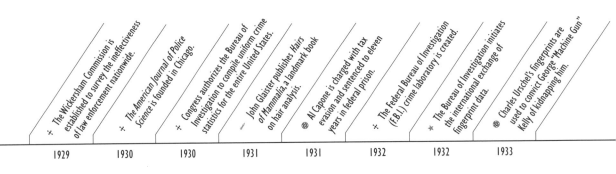

+ The Wickersham Commission is established to survey the ineffectiveness of law enforcement nationwide.

+ The *American Journal of Police Science* is founded in Chicago.

+ Congress authorizes the Bureau of Investigation to compile uniform crime statistics for the entire United States.

John Glaister publishes *Hairs of Mammalia*, a landmark book on hair analysis.

⊛ Al Capone is charged with tax evasion and sentenced to eleven years in federal prison.

+ The Federal Bureau of Investigation (F.B.I.) crime laboratory is created.

* The Bureau of Investigation initiates the international exchange of fingerprint data.

⊛ Charles Urschel's fingerprints are used to convict George "Machine Gun" Kelly of kidnapping him.

| 1929 | 1930 | 1930 | 1931 | 1931 | 1932 | 1932 | 1933 |

within the ranks. After so many of those stories, though, President Hoover had taken action: in 1929, he appointed George Wickersham, a former Attorney General, to form the National Commission on Law Observance and Enforcement, a committee to investigate every aspect of the criminal justice system and make recommendations for improvements. Among its findings were that police were in desperate need of professionalization: for the first time, police officers would be required to take tests and graduate from a police academy before taking on their jobs. It was an improvement, but even to some observers in the 1930s, there were glaring omissions in the report. Some noted that the recommendations seemed to focus entirely on how the police could better protect working-class

BELOW, LEFT Police attend the murder of Dominick Didato. His body was found in front of Sciacca Restaurant on Elizabeth Street, New York, in 1936.

BELOW, CENTER Police at the scene of a murder in Brooklyn in 1939.

BELOW, RIGHT David "the Beetle" Beadle lying dead on the sidewalk in front of the Spot Bar and Grill in Manhattan, where he was murdered in 1939.

white people. Many noted that while the commission detailed many examples of police brutality against African Americans and urged the end of "third degree" methods of interrogation, it did not address the widespread problem of racism within the police, an issue that would continue to plague policing nationwide even as the police became better equipped with the tools to make their investigations more efficient.

The stories in this book take place across this fascinating period in history, when forensic techniques, theories of deduction, and criminological processes were changing so rapidly. Drawn from states across the union between 1865 and 1939, the stories taken as a whole trace the progress of criminology from the lawless days of the Wild West to the modern era. With all the advances made since then, it can seem as though these stories take place in the Dark Ages. And yet, even today, you would have to be awfully naive to believe the old proverb that "murder will out." •

MILESTONES OF CRIMINAL INVESTIGATION, 1929–39

✳ INNOVATION

⊕ CASE

⊷ PUBLICATION

‡ INSTITUTION

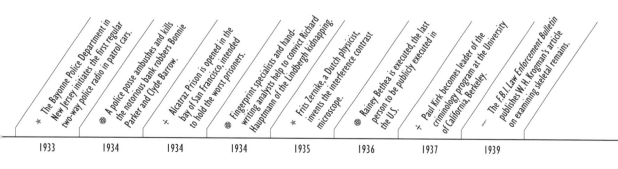

✳ The Bayonne Police Department in New Jersey initiates the first regular two-way police radio in patrol cars.
1933

⊕ A police posse ambushes and kills the notorious bank robbers Bonnie Parker and Clyde Barrow.
1934

‡ Alcatraz Prison is opened in the bay of San Francisco, intended to hold the worst prisoners.
1934

⊕ Fingerprint specialists and handwriting analysts help to convict Richard Hauptmann of the Lindbergh kidnapping.
1934

✳ Frits Zernike, a Dutch physicist, invents the interference contrast microscope.
1935

⊕ Rainey Bethea is executed, the last person to be publicly executed in the U.S.
1936

‡ Paul Kirk becomes leader of the criminology program at the University of California, Berkeley.
1937

⊷ The F.B.I. Law Enforcement Bulletin publishes W. H. Krogman's article on examining skeletal remains.
1939

PART ONE

MASSACHUSETTS

CONNECTICUT | RHODE ISLAND

NEW YORK

NEW JERSEY | PENNSYLVANIA

THE NORTHEAST

JESSE POMEROY | LIZZIE BORDEN
HERBERT HAYDEN | AUGUSTA NACK | LIZZIE HALLIDAY
MARTIN THORN | LEON CZOLGOSZ | ALBERT WILLWORD / CALVIN A. DECKER
GALLEANISTS
RICHARD HAUPTMANN | LUCKY LUCIANO
HENRY HOWARD HOLMES
ELMO NOAKES | HERMAN PETRILLO | PAUL PETRILLO

MA—BOSTON	*March–April 1874*

JESSE POMEROY
✕ Horace Millen ✕ Katie Curran

WEAPON MULTIPLE	TYPOLOGY RANDOM ATTACK	POLICING FOOTPRINTS

**SOUTH BOSTON MARSHES, DORCHESTER BAY
& 327 BROADWAY**

In the summer of 1872, a 10-year-old girl in the south suburbs of Boston went looking for a lost handkerchief. Instead, she found George Pratt, a 7-year-old boy, nearly dead in a boathouse. He had been tied up, stripped, beaten, poked with a pin, slashed with a razor, and left. The brave girl carried George home, where he told the story of an older boy who had lured him into the boathouse.

It was the third such case in recent weeks, and three more would soon follow: young boys lured by an older "boy with a white eye" to a boathouse or a remote stretch of railroad tracks, where the older boy stripped and tortured them, then left them bound and bloody.

"The boy with the white eye" proved to be 12-year-old Jesse Pomeroy, who told reporters he did not know why he had done it. "Every time I did it, I said to myself I would never do it anymore," he said. And yet, he did.

He was sentenced to spend the rest of his youth in a reform school, but he was let out for good behavior at 14. Two months after his release, the body of a 4-year-old boy, Horace Millen, was found in a marsh; he had been mutilated and nearly decapitated. Police immediately suspected Pomeroy; footprints found near the body were traced to him, and when asked if he had killed Horace, Pomeroy replied, "I guess I did."

During the investigation, the body of a 10-year-old girl, Katie Curran, was found concealed under an ash heap in the basement of Pomeroy's mother's dressmaking shop.

Only 15 at the time he was convicted, Pomeroy was the youngest convicted murderer in the history of Massachusetts. Initially sentenced to hang, he had his sentence changed to life in solitary confinement, where he remained for decades, making numerous attempts at escape and suicide. He was moved to the general prison in 1917, and to a hospital for the criminally insane in 1929. He died there three years later at the age of 72. •

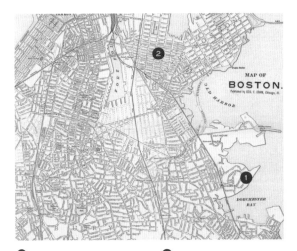

❶ **SOUTH BOSTON MARSHES, DORCHESTER BAY**
The marshes where Horace Millen's mutilated body was found.

❷ **327 WEST BROADWAY, SOUTH BOSTON**
Ruth Pomeroy's dressmaking shop, where Katie Curran's body was found.

ABOVE A contemporary illustration from *Frank Leslie's Illustrated Newspaper* of a shrine created to Horace Millen, where he was found in the marshes of Dorchester Bay.

RIGHT An article from the *New York Journal*, 1897, detailing the multiple escape attempts made by Jesse Pomeroy while in prison.

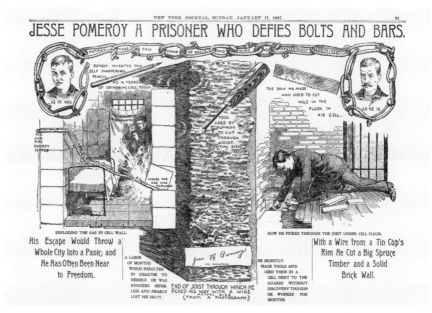

RIGHT A selection of some of the metal files used by Jesse Pomeroy in his escape attempt in 1913, in which he managed to saw through the bars of his cell.

FAR RIGHT Jesse Pomeroy's 1913 escape attempt was thwarted by the prison cat, which saw him in the corridor of the prison and began to mew, alerting a prison guard.

RIGHT Prison bars cut by Jesse Pomeroy in 1913 in one of his attempts to escape from prison. He made at least ten attempts to escape while incarcerated.

LIZZIE BORDEN
✕ Andrew Borden ✕ Abby Borden

WEAPON	TYPOLOGY	POLICING
AXE	DOMESTIC	CRIME SCENE PHOTOGRAPHY

92 SECOND STREET

There is little reason to believe that anyone besides Lizzie Borden was involved in the murder of her father and stepmother. Then again, she was acquitted of the crime, and there are certain points of evidence that have never been totally explained. Either way, the gruesome crime has made Lizzie a part of American folklore.

On August 4, 1892, Bridget "Maggie" Sullivan, the Bordens' live-in maid, let her boss, Andrew Borden, into the house as he had forgotten his key. Finding the door jammed, Maggie swore out loud, and heard the sound of Andrew's daughter, Lizzie, laughing upstairs. What she did not realize was that Lizzie's stepmother, Abby Borden, was upstairs as well, already brutally killed.

Hours later, returning from a shopping trip, Maggie heard Lizzie shouting, "Maggie, come quick! Father's dead. Somebody came in and killed him."

Andrew Borden's body was lying on a couch, still bleeding from nearly a dozen axe wounds across his face. Everything in the room was in its place; there was no sign of struggle or robbery. Abby's body was found in the upstairs bedroom soon thereafter.

Lizzie, dressed in clean clothes, calmly answered questions, though the police failed to interview or examine her thoroughly. She said she had gone out to the barn for a few minutes and came back in to find her father brutally murdered by an unknown assassin who had now fled the premises, leaving no trace behind.

She certainly acted suspiciously. It was known that she had inquired about the purchase of hydrocyanic acid at the town drugstore, and the morning after the murders she was seen burning a dress that she claimed was covered in paint.

But the jury found her innocent, and Lizzie spent nearly thirty-five years living a quiet life thereafter.

Acquitted or not, to this day if you ask people in the United States what Lizzie Borden did, they will likely sing you the playground rhyme about her taking an axe to give her mother forty whacks. •

RIGHT Abby Borden's skull, showing the damage done by the blows from the axe.

FAR RIGHT The hatchet without a handle, found in the barn and suspected to be the murder weapon.

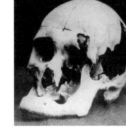

RIGHT A piece of Abby Borden's hair, found near her body in the guest bedroom.

RIGHT The Borden family home in Fall River, Massachusetts. Andrew Borden lived there with his second wife Abby, his two daughters Lizzie and Emma, and their maid Bridget "Maggie" Sullivan.

92 SECOND STREET
The house where Andrew Borden and Abby Borden lived and were found murdered.

THE BORDENS' BARN
The barn where Lizzie Borden claimed to have been at the time of the murders.

90 SECOND STREET
The house where Adelaide B. Churchill lived, who Lizzie Borden fetched after discovering her father, and who testified at the trial.

94 SECOND STREET
The house where Michael and Caroline Kelly lived. Caroline Kelly was one of the last people to see Andrew Borden alive and testified at Lizzie Borden's trial.

DR. SEABURY BOWEN'S HOUSE
Dr. Seabury Bowen was the first to examine the bodies of the victims and testified at the trial.

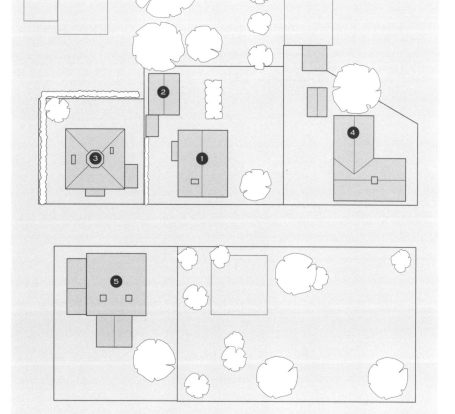

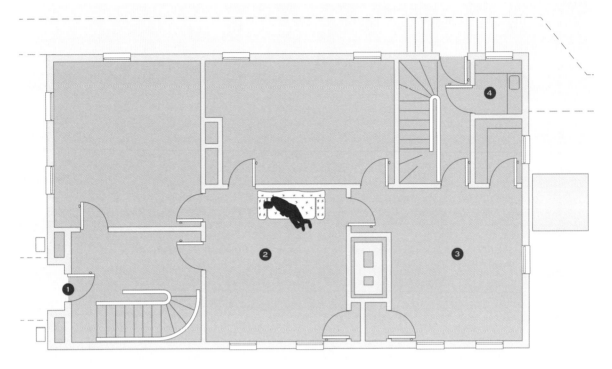

❶ FRONT ENTRY
The entrance to the Bordens' house. On the day of the murders the front door was found jammed when Andrew Borden returned from a morning walk.

❷ SITTING ROOM
The room where Andrew Borden's body was found, lying on a couch and struck ten or eleven times.

❸ KITCHEN
The room where Lizzie Borden was found tearing up and burning a dress the day following the murder.

❹ SINK ROOM
The room used by Bridget "Maggie" Sullivan to wash dishes.

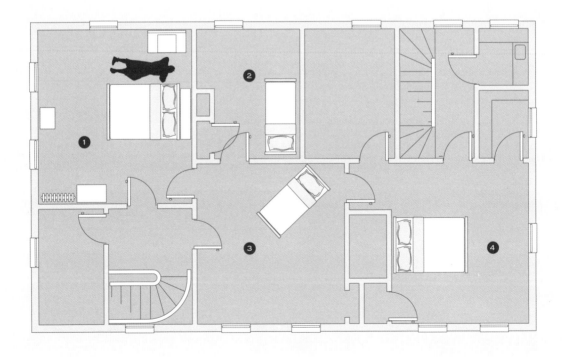

❶ GUEST BEDROOM
The room where Abby Borden's body was found.

❷ BEDROOM
The room where Emma Borden slept.

❸ BEDROOM
The room where Lizzie Borden slept.

❹ MASTER BEDROOM
The room where Andrew and Abby Borden slept.

RIGHT The first of two crime scene photographs showing Abby Borden as the police found her.

RIGHT The second crime scene photograph showing Abby Borden lying dead where she was found in the Bordens' guest bedroom.

RIGHT A crime scene photograph showing Andrew Borden on the couch where he had been sleeping when he was attacked and killed.

RIGHT A second crime scene photograph of Andrew Borden's body on the couch. The wounds sustained from the ten or eleven hits he received from the axe are visible.

HERBERT HAYDEN

✕ Mary Stannard

WEAPON	TYPOLOGY	POLICING
JACKNIFE & ARSENIC	DOMESTIC	TOXICOLOGY

THE WOODS, NEAR A LARGE ROCK

In debt, and with two young children to feed, the Reverend Herbert Hayden took a position in Madison, Connecticut, a town far enough from his home in Rockland that he lived most of each week there, coming back to his family just a day or two per week. When his wife, Rosa, became sick, she needed help with the children, and hired Mary Stannard, a young woman from the farm next door.

When at home, Herbert was seen with Mary frequently, and there were stories of the pair being caught in "passionate moments" in the woods. The affair apparently ended when Stannard took a job elsewhere, but by then she was already pregnant. Herbert arranged to meet her in the woods, where he promised to give her some medicine to take care of the situation. He purchased some arsenic in town before the meeting.

Four hours after the arranged meeting, Mary's father found her body in the woods, beside a large rock and with blood dripping from her neck. She was lying peacefully, as though she had lain down to die and slit her throat. But there was no knife present. Reverend Hayden, it seemed, had attempted to make her death look like a suicide, but had forgotten to leave the weapon in her hand.

The judge, who happened to be a friend of Hayden's, dismissed the case against him at once, but later tests showed that Mary's body contained arsenic, and blood was found on Hayden's knife, and so he was brought to trial again.

The evidence against Reverend Hayden was overwhelming, particularly by the standards of the day, when forensics was still a developing science. But over the course of a thrilling fifteen-week trial, the lawyers' constant questioning of the evidence and the judge's disrespectful treatment of witnesses compared with his respectful treatment of the Reverend meant that the jury could not be convinced. Only one juror was willing to convict a preacher and make a widow of his wife. The sensational trial ended with a mistrial, and the state never took it up again. Hayden worked as a carpenter until his death at age 57. •

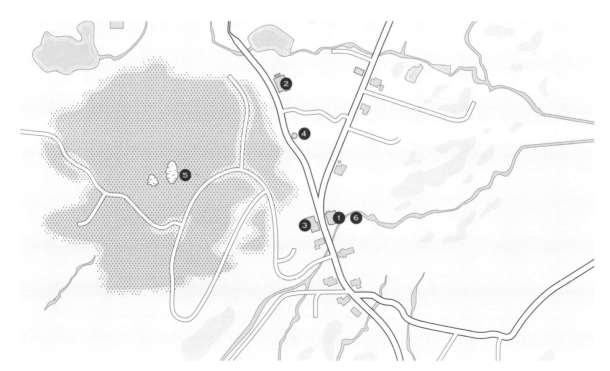

1

THE HAYDEN RESIDENCE
The house where the Revd. Herbert Hayden
lived with his wife Rosa and two children.

2

THE STANNARD RESIDENCE
The house where Mary Stannard lived with
her father, Charles Stannard, and illegitimate
child from a previous relationship, Willie.

3

THE STEVENS RESIDENCE
The house from which witnesses claimed to have
seen the Revd. Herbert Hayden and Mary Stannard
enter his barn together, the day before the murder.

4

THE SPRING
The spring that Mary Stannard went to
for water on the morning of her murder.

5

WHERE THE BODY WAS FOUND
The area of the woods outside Rockland where
Mary Stannard's body was found, lying dead
near a large rock.

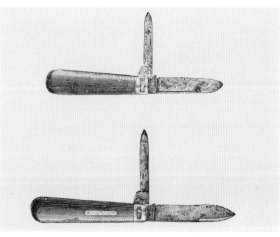

6

THE JACKNIVES
The jacknife belonging to the Revd. Herbert Hayden,
which he hid at his home (above), and a jacknife
found in the woods (below).

UNKNOWN

✕ Danny Walsh

WEAPON UNKNOWN	TYPOLOGY GANG	POLICING —

VICTIM LAST SEEN IN PAWTUXET VILLAGE

By the time the lawless days of Prohibition ended, nearly every major city had its own gang scene, and the criminal underworld had even spread to the small towns of idyllic New England.

When alcohol was first outlawed, Danny Walsh was working as a clerk in a Rhode Island hardware store. But he realized there was a lot of money to be made in the new "alky" trade and he took a job driving booze shipments for gangsters. Soon he was buying his own vehicles, eventually amassing a whole fleet of rum-running crafts that included airplanes and boats.

Walsh made a fortune from his illegal shipments and lived in high style, buying two flashy apartments in Providence and a farm in Charlestown, where he began raising thorough-bred horses. Rhode Island had never bothered to ratify the amendment that outlawed alcohol and it followed that the authorities there were not known to be terribly vigilant.

But law enforcement was often the least of a bootlegger's problems: the real danger was running afoul of other gangsters who wanted you out of the way.

In 1933, the end of Prohibition was in sight, with a new president awaiting inauguration. Having become accustomed to a certain lifestyle, the booze kings were consolidating their power, plotting their next moves. No one was safe. Walsh had never been a notably violent man himself and to some rivals that made him look like an easy target.

Walsh had dinner with several associates on the night of February 2, 1933. He was never seen alive again.

Over the next several years, there were a number of times when authorities believed they were on the verge of finding Walsh's remains. In 1935, officials found an underground "fortress" full of tunnels and subcellars in Warwick, Rhode Island, and announced that when they broke into the cement with pickaxes, they expected to find Walsh's body. They did not. In 2016, a mysterious grave was uncovered in Rhode Island that was initially suspected to be Walsh's. It was not.

Such was the tangled web of the underworld that it is difficult to even guess which gangster had it in for him. It could have been any of dozens. •

LEFT Carl Rettich, another bootlegger operating in Rhode Island, suspected by some of murdering Danny Walsh.

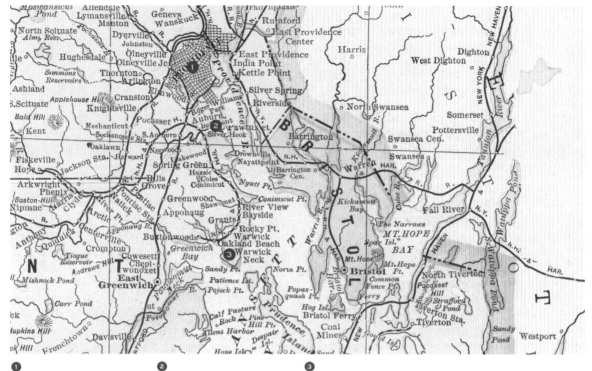

❶
PROVIDENCE
The capital of Rhode Island,
where Danny Walsh
maintained two mansions.

❷
BANK CAFE, POST ROAD,
PAWTUXET VILLAGE
The restaurant where
Danny Walsh was last seen.

❸
KIRBY ROAD, WARWICK NECK
The site of the gangster Carl
Rettich's seaside mansion, which
was investigated by the police.

↑ **ABOVE** Some of the vessels used
for rum running in Danny Walsh's
operation.

↑ **ABOVE** The speedboat *Black Duck*
(third from left), used by Danny
Walsh to smuggle alcohol.

↑ **ABOVE** Investigators searching
Carl Rettich's seaside mansion
on Warwick Neck.

↑ **ABOVE** Police discovered a secret
vault, stolen money, and an arsenal
of weapons, but not Danny Walsh.

↑ **ABOVE** The house was nicknamed
the "crime castle" or "murder
mansion" in the contemporary press.

UNKNOWN
✕ Benjamin Nathan

WEAPON	TYPOLOGY	POLICING
IRON BAR	PROPERTY CRIME	CRIME SCENE INVESTIGATION

12 WEST TWENTY-THIRD STREET, MANHATTAN

Accounts of prominent citizens murdered in America's Gilded Age tend to open by noting that New Yorkers of the day were shocked. But there are so many such stories that you would think the shock would have worn off after a while.

In July 1870, Benjamin Nathan, former vice president of the stock exchange and president of Mount Sinai Hospital, had largely been living in New Jersey, following the old custom of wealthy New Yorkers fleeing the sweltering city for the summer. However he was accustomed to pray for his mother at his synagogue on her *yarzeit*, the anniversary of her death, so he returned to his house on West Twenty-third Street for one night.

That evening brought a terrible storm. The next morning, Nathan's son Washington entered the house and was greeted by the shocking sight of his father's body, badly mutilated and lying in a pool of drying blood. He had been bludgeoned to death. Washington ran out the door, shouting, "Murder!" as he tracked down a policeman.

Investigators assumed that the killer was an ordinary burglar, as a safe had been plundered of jewels. But a lack of wet footprints showed that he must have snuck in before the storm came and concealed himself until night fell, when at some point in the course of robbing the safe, he had been interrupted by Mr. Nathan.

There were signs of a terrific struggle, and a sense that the two had been evenly matched. But the burglar was armed with an iron bar and landed six blows about Nathan's head and body.

Some suspected Washington Nathan, who was known for drinking and reckless living, of the murder, but he had been at a hotel, a bar, and a brothel over the course of the night (though some still find the timeframe impossibly busy). All of the family and household servants were eventually cleared of suspicion and no one was ever brought to trial. The house remains standing, now home to a restaurant and offices, and the case remains a mystery. •

1
12 WEST TWENTY-THIRD STREET
The home of Benjamin Nathan, where he was murdered.

2
ST. JAMES HOTEL, FIFTH AVENUE
The hotel where Washington Nathan had a drink on the night of the murder.

3
DELMONICO'S, 2 SOUTH WILLIAM STREET
The bar where Washington Nathan read the papers on the night of the murder.

4
EAST FOURTEENTH STREET
The brothel where Washington Nathan visited a prostitute on the night of the murder.

ABOVE New York City detectives depicted searching the Nathan property for clues.

ABOVE Washington Nathan was suspected of his father's murder and was hounded by the press.

LIZZIE HALLIDAY
✕ Margaret McQuillan ✕ Sarah McQuillan
✕ Paul Halliday ✕ Nellie Wickes

WEAPON	TYPOLOGY	POLICING
FIREARM & SCISSORS	MENTAL ILLNESS	PROPERTY SEARCH

HALLIDAY FARM, MAMAKATING & MATTEAWAN STATE HOSPITAL FOR THE CRIMINALLY INSANE, BEACON

On the morning of September 26, 1906, Nellie Wickes was going about her job as an attendant at the Matteawan State Hospital for the Criminally Insane. At some point in the morning she stepped into a lavatory. There, a patient named Lizzie Halliday snuck up behind her and knocked her over. She took Wickes's keys, used them to lock the door, then took the pair of scissors that were attached to Wickes's belt and began to attack.

Nellie had recently decided to leave the hospital to train as a nurse. Halliday, unhappy with the change, had threatened to kill Nellie if she left. Halliday often made this kind of threat, so no one had paid her much attention. But now the other attendants heard Nellie scream and rushed to help.

By the time they managed to force their way into the room and overpower Halliday, Nellie had been stabbed more than 200 times. She died two hours later.

Outside of the verbal threats, Lizzie Halliday had been a model prisoner for two years, but before arriving at the hospital, she had killed four people, and possibly more. Born in Ireland around 1859, she had come to New York with her family when she was only a child. As an adult, she had a series of husbands and a series of businesses that burned down after they had been insured.

In 1891, Lizzie's husband Paul vanished and neighbors doubted her story that he was working in another town. When authorities searched her property, they found the bodies of two women who had been shot to death. Both were members of a family Lizzie had known in Philadelphia. Paul's body, badly mutilated, was later found under the floorboards. In jail, Lizzie set fire to her bed and tried to commit suicide in a variety of ways.

Although she was initially convicted and sentenced to the electric chair, a medical commission declared her insane and the governor commuted her sentence to life in Matteawan State Hospital. She died in 1918. •

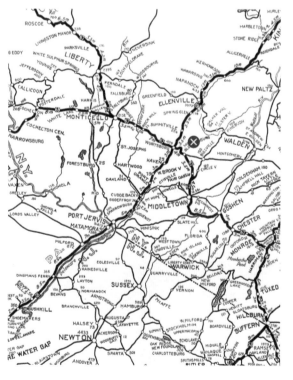

LEFT Lizzie Halliday's shanty. The body of her husband Paul Halliday was found beneath the floorboards.

LEFT The barn on Lizzie Halliday's property, in which the bodies of Margaret and Sarah McQuillan were found.

LEFT Mamakating, Sullivan County, where Lizzie Halliday and Paul Halliday lived, and where the bodies of Margaret McQuillan, Sarah McQuillan, and Paul Halliday were found.

NY—NEW YORK CITY	*June 1897*

AUGUSTA NACK
MARTIN THORN

× William Guldensuppe

WEAPON	TYPOLOGY	POLICING
PISTOL	DOMESTIC	POSTMORTEM IDENTIFICATION

346 SECOND STREET [NOW 55TH STREET], LONG ISLAND

AUGUSTA NACK   MARTIN THORN

The body of William Guldensuppe was found a piece at a time, over a period of days. On June 26, 1897, his headless torso was found in Manhattan's East River. The next day, his lower torso was found in the woods, 8 miles (13 km) north near 176th Street. The legs were found days later near the Brooklyn Naval Yard. The police initially assumed that the body was the remains of a medical cadaver, as tales of them floating ashore piecemeal were not unknown.

But reporters publicized the case tremendously and a reporter for the *World* noted that the fingers on the body resembled the fingers of a man who had given him an alcohol rub. On a hunch, he began to ask massage houses if any of their employees had gone missing. One had, and based on a tell-tale mark, the body was identified as that of Guldensuppe, a masseur who had disappeared days before.

It turned out that Guldensuppe had been living with a midwife named Augusta Nack; she claimed not to know where William was and insisted that she did not care. A barber, Martin Thorn, admitted that he had been having an affair with Nack, which the two carried on while Guldensuppe was at work. Guldensuppe had once caught them in the act and, according to Thorn, beaten Thorn so badly that he required hospitalization.

After that, the couple learned to be more discreet and Thorn vowed to get revenge. He purchased a pistol, lured Guldensuppe to a house in Woodside, and shot him in the back of the head. He and Nack then threw him into the bathtub, decapitated him, and scattered the parts around New York City. The head was covered in plaster of Paris and thrown into the river, where it sank.

Or that was how Thorn told the story when he was first arrested. Later, he said that Nack had already killed Guldensuppe when he arrived and he had only helped with disposing of the body. In the end, both were found guilty of murder. Nack was sentenced to fifteen years in prison, and Thorn was executed at Sing Sing in 1898. •

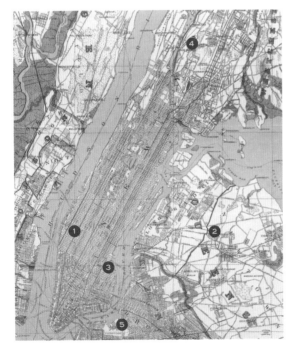

①
439 NINTH AVENUE
The house where Augusta Nack lived with William Guldensuppe.

②
346 SECOND STREET
The house in which Martin Thorn and Augusta Nack killed William Guldensuppe.

③
PIER, EAST ELEVENTH STREET
The pier where William Guldensuppe's upper torso was found.

④
176TH STREET
The woods where William Guldensuppe's lower torso was found.

⑤
BROOKLYN NAVAL YARD, FLUSHING AVENUE
The yard where William Guldensuppe's legs were found.

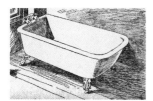

THE BATH IN WHICH WILLIAM
GULDENSUPPE WAS DISMEMBERED.

HOW AUGUSTA NACK FIRED THE SHOT,
ACCORDING TO MARTIN THORN.

THE BLOODSTAINED KNIFE FOUND
IN AUGUSTA NACK'S APARTMENT.

THE BLOODSTAINED SAW FOUND
IN AUGUSTA NACK'S APARTMENT.

**WHERE MARTIN THORN
STOOD**
The place Martin Thorn stood
to shoot William Guldensuppe
in the back of the head.

**WHERE WILLIAM
GULDENSUPPE STOOD**
The place where William
Guldensuppe was standing
when he was shot.

THE BATHTUB
The bathtub in which
Augusta Nack and Martin
Thorn dismembered William
Guldensuppe's body.

BLOODSTAINS
The place in the bathroom
where bloodstains were
found by investigators.

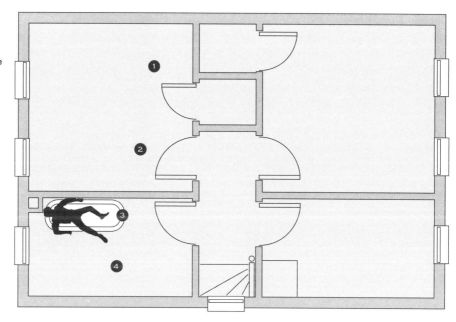

① BOYS SWIMMING IN THE
EAST RIVER DISCOVER
A TORSO.

② THE LOWER PART OF
THE TORSO IS DISCOVERED
IN THE WOODS.

③ THE REMAINS ARE
IDENTIFIED AS BEING
WILLIAM GULDENSUPPE.

④ AUGUSTA NACK IS ARRESTED
WHILE PREPARING TO
LEAVE FOR EUROPE.

⑤ LEGS ARE DISCOVERED
AT BROOKLYN NAVAL YARD.

⑥ AUGUSTA NACK IS
POSITIVELY IDENTIFIED.

⑦ A SURREY RENTED BY
AUGUSTA NACK AND MARTIN
THORN IS IDENTIFIED.

⑧ IT IS DISCOVERED
THAT MARTIN THORN
IS STILL IN NEW YORK.

⑨ MARTIN THORN
IS ARRESTED.

⑩ THE POLICE LOCATE
THE SCENE OF THE CRIME
AND FIND BLOODSTAINS.

⑪ MARTIN THORN'S
CONFESSION IS GIVEN TO
THE POLICE BY A FRIEND.

⑫ MARTIN THORN IS FOUND
GUILTY OF MURDER.

LEON CZOLGOSZ

✕ William McKinley

WEAPON	TYPOLOGY	POLICING
PISTOL	ASSASSINATION	PSYCHIATRY

TEMPLE OF MUSIC, PAN-AMERICAN EXPOSITION

In the autumn of 1901, it had been just over twenty years since a president was assassinated in the United States. Concerns for the president's safety had even relaxed so far that President William McKinley could be advertised as an attraction at the Pan-American Exposition in Buffalo, where he planned to spend the morning of September 6 greeting well-wishers in the exposition's Temple of Music.

Among those who attended that day was Leon Czolgosz, a Michigan-born laborer. Always a loner, never known to have any friends or romantic interests, as a teenager he had taken an interest in socialism. When in 1900 King Umberto of Italy was shot to death by an anarchist, Czolgosz was galvanized. The local socialists he had met were not nearly as radical as all that, but he began to study anarchy, decided that the structure of government was the root of all problems, and plotted to take matters into his own hands.

As Czolgosz traveled around the midwest, other anarchists took notice of him, but his social awkwardness was too much even for them. When he asked numerous organizations for help committing acts of violence against society, they assumed that he was a spy doing a bad job of setting them up.

So he traveled to Buffalo, where President McKinley was scheduled to appear. He dutifully waited in line to greet the president, and when McKinley stretched out his hand to greet the 18-year-old, Czolgosz pulled out his .32 caliber pistol and shot twice. Remarkably, only one of the point-blank shots did any damage, the first ricocheting off a button on McKinley's coat but the second lodging in the president's stomach. As a crowd began attacking Czolgosz, McKinley was even heard to say, "Go easy on him, boys."

The wound proved fatal; an infection developed and McKinley died eight days later. Though the jury who convicted Czolgosz believed that he was almost certainly insane, the unrepentant assassin was put to death in the electric chair only forty-five days later. •

ABOVE The Temple of Music at the Pan-American Exposition in Buffalo, where William McKinley was shot.

ABOVE An artist's impression of the moment at which President McKinley was shot by Leon Czolgosz, while meeting crowds at the Pan-American Exposition.

AN AERIAL VIEW OF THE PAN-AMERICAN
EXPOSITION IN BUFFALO.

THE TEMPLE OF MUSIC BUILDING
AT THE EXPOSITION.

THE PISTOL USED BY LEON CZOLGOSZ
TO ASSASSINATE THE PRESIDENT.

THE AMBULANCE USED TO TRANSPORT
PRESIDENT McKINLEY TO HOSPITAL.

↑ **ABOVE, TOP** The exact
location where William
McKinley was shot.

↑ **ABOVE, BOTTOM** William
McKinley at the Pan-
American Exposition.

↑ **ABOVE** Leon Czolgosz behind bars. While incarcerated
he refused to interact with the lawyers sent to defend
him, or the psychiatrist sent to examine him.

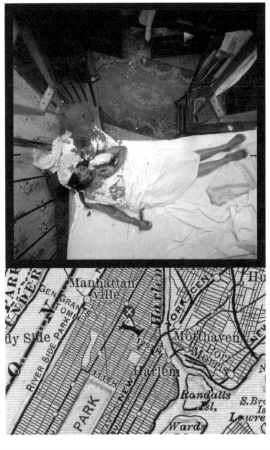

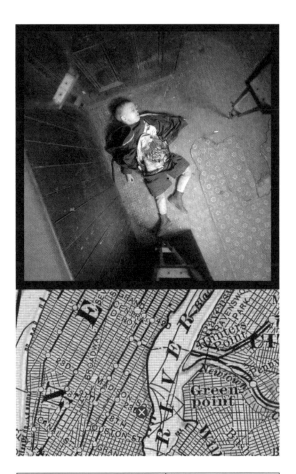

NY—NEW YORK CITY	*April 14, 1914*

ALBERT WILLWORD

✕ Alberta Thomas

WEAPON	TYPOLOGY	POLICING
PISTOL	DOMESTIC	CRIME SCENE PHOTOGRAPHY
69 WEST 136TH STREET, HARLEM		

NY—NEW YORK CITY	*May 3, 1915*

UNKNOWN

✕ Charles Murray

WEAPON	TYPOLOGY	POLICING
KNIFE	RANDOM ATTACK	CRIME SCENE PHOTOGRAPHY
270 FIRST AVENUE, MANHATTAN		

Alberta Thomas had become suspicious that her boyfriend of a year, Albert Willword, was attracted to another woman, and finally decided to confront him about it. He responded by drawing a gun and firing four times. Of the four shots, two struck Alberta, one in the breast and the other in the neck. Willword threw the gun under his bed, jumped out of the second-story window, and ran into the New York night, clad only in his underwear. However, he broke his ankle in the fall and was quickly caught. •

In 1915, the New York papers began to speculate that a "Jack the Ripper" style killer was operating on the East Side. In March, a 5-year-old girl named Lenore Cohn was found killed in a tenement hallway and her mother reportedly received a letter from the killer boasting of the crime. Two months later, 4-year-old Charles Murray was slashed to death in his home. His mother also received a letter, promising further killings. The police believed that the crimes were committed by the same killer, but no suspect was found and the mystery was never solved. •

↑ **ABOVE** The crime scene photograph of Alberta Thomas in her Harlem apartment taken by the New York Police Department.

↑ **ABOVE** The crime scene photograph of Charles Murray taken by the New York Police Department. The bird's-eye view was achieved by placing the camera on stilts.

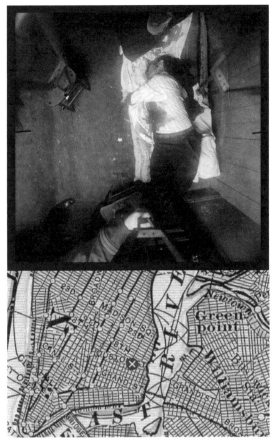

NY—NEW YORK CITY	*September 9, 1915*

UNKNOWN
✕ Giuseppe Letto

WEAPON	TYPOLOGY	POLICING
KNIFE	GANG	CRIME SCENE PHOTOGRAPHY
203 FORSYTH STREET, BOWERY		

NY—NEW YORK CITY	*October 13, 1915*

CALVIN A. DECKER
✕ Marion Hart

WEAPON	TYPOLOGY	POLICING
SHOTGUN	DOMESTIC	CRIME SCENE PHOTOGRAPHY
1098 OLD STONE ROAD, BULL'S HEAD, STATEN ISLAND		

In the 1910s, before organized crime had crystalized into its modern form among the Prohibition gangs, people spoke of the "Black Hand," a shadowy criminal organization operating among Italian neighborhoods. Whenever there was a crime wave, it was claimed that the Black Hand was active. After a period of relative calm, in the fall of 1915 Giuseppe Letto was murdered at Joseph Raffo's grocery store near Houston Street, reigniting fears among locals that the Black Hand had returned. •

Though it is often said that the wheels of justice turn slowly, occasionally they seem to have moved too fast. Such may have been the case when Marion Hart, a 39-year-old woman, was killed with a shotgun in a one-room shack on the western shore of Staten Island. Her roommate (and possibly lover), Calvin A. Decker, was acquitted of second degree murder just thirteen days later. Some suggest that he was never investigated carefully enough and was most likely guilty. •

↑ **ABOVE** The crime scene photograph of Giuseppe Letto taken by the New York Police Department. The men taking the photograph are visible in the bottom left corner.

↑ **ABOVE** The crime scene photograph of Marion Hart in her Staten Island home taken by the New York Police Department.

GALLEANISTS
× 40

WEAPON	TYPOLOGY	POLICING
BOMB	BOMBING	BOMB RECONSTRUCTION

23 WALL STREET, MANHATTAN

OPPOSITE Following the blast large crowds gathered on Wall Street and police officers rushed to the scene. Within one minute, the New York Stock Exchange suspended trading in order to prevent panic.

While fear of a terrorist attack may be experienced in even the most remote and unremarkable towns, the biggest targets will always be the busiest places. In 1920, the deadliest attack in New York City history, up to that time, occurred at one of the busiest intersections in the Financial District, outside the J. P. Morgan bank on Wall Street.

At noon on September 16, as lunchtime crowds gathered outside the stock exchange, a horse-drawn carriage pulled up at 23 Wall Street. It probably did not look very different from the other delivery wagons that filled the narrow old streets, but this one was loaded with a 100 lb (45 kg) of dynamite and 500 lb (230 kg) of cast-iron sash window weights. The driver left the carriage in the road and a timed detonator set off the dynamite, obliterating the carriage and sending the sash weights flying in every direction.

There were hundreds of injuries, including 143 serious wounds, and 40 fatalities. Though it was presumed that the city's financial titans would have been the target for such an attack, most of the fatalities were just young workers—clerks, stenographers, and other lower-level employees.

Trading was suspended on the floor of the stock exchange within a minute and rescue efforts had to be made before any investigations even began. Though fliers from an Italian anarchist, or Galleanist, group taking credit for the explosion were posted in the area, there was no way to tell who was responsible. Though some believed it may have been an act of war by a hostile foreign nation, when days passed and no follow-up arrived, it was apparent that it was the work of an independent group. The New York Police Department managed to reconstruct the bomb, but as all of the parts were widely available it did little to further the investigation. The government's Bureau of Investigation, whose general intelligence division was run by 25-year-old J. Edgar Hoover, investigated the case for years without ever finding a solid enough lead to bring about any indictments, and the origin of the bombing remains a mystery. •

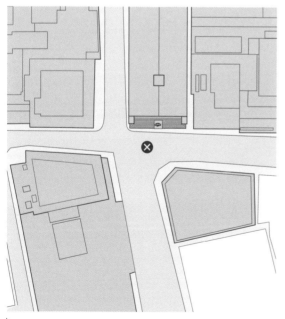

ABOVE The bomb detonated on the corner of Wall Street and Nassau Street, opposite the headquarters of J. P. Morgan & Co.

LEFT The explosion was caused by 100 lb (45 kg) of dynamite concealed within a horse-drawn wagon with 500 lb (230 kg) of iron window weights, as seen here.

LEFT Chemists analyzing the elements of the bomb, as part of investigations into the bombing. The N.Y.P.D. was able to reconstruct the bomb and its fuse mechanism.

LEFT Florean Zelenska (left) with a police officer (right). Zelenska was a suspect in the bombing but was subsequently cleared.

BELOW The explosion caused extensive destruction
to the nearby buildings. The damage was cleared away
overnight, allowing Wall Street to return to business
the following day, but removing physical evidence
that today would be crucial to police investigations.

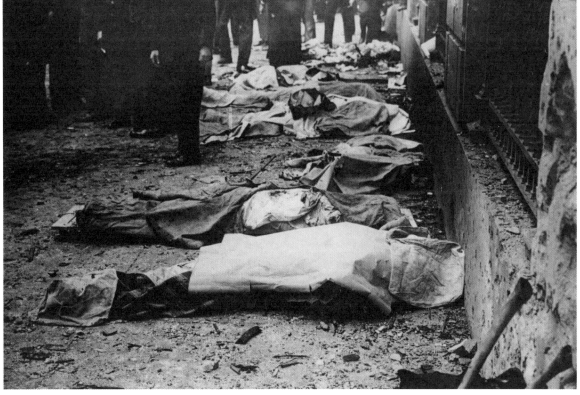

UNKNOWN

✕ Arnold Rothstein

WEAPON	TYPOLOGY	POLICING
REVOLVER	GANG	—

PARK CENTRAL HOTEL, SEVENTH AVENUE, MANHATTAN

Gangland kingpins do not have a long life expectancy. While the law caught up with relatively few major gangsters in the lawless 1920s, the gangsters caught up with each other often enough.

Arnold "The Brain" Rothstein was fairly old for a gangster when he died aged 46. By then, stories of his exploits had grown to the status of legend, and it is difficult to separate fact from fiction. Some say he had been involved in fixing the 1919 World Series, though there is strong evidence both for and against the claim.

What is indisputable is that he played a major role in taking organized crime—which became far more lucrative during Prohibition than it had ever been before—and making it into a proper business. There had been gangs before—safecrackers, counterfeiters, hold-up men, and the like—but they had never run their organizations in the manner of a business empire. Nor had they made the sort of money that a business empire could.

By 1928 Rothstein's bootlegging and drugs business meant that he was known as "the king of Broadway's night life." In the October of that year, he lost over $300,000—millions in modern money—in a high stakes poker game that lasted for three days. Claiming that the game had been rigged (which, by most accounts, it was), he refused to pay up.

A few days later, Rothstein met with associates in Room 349 of the Park Central Hotel in Manhattan. Telling them he would not pay off the lost bet, he assumed that he could bully them into accepting. "That," wrote the *New York Daily News*, "was another bet that Rothstein lost."

One of the creditors present lost his temper, pulled a gun and shot Rothstein. He died in a hospital two days later. Though many theories circulate as to who, exactly, pulled the trigger, the truth may never be known. When asked who had shot him, Rothstein put a finger to his lips and smiled, honoring gangland's code of silence to the end. •

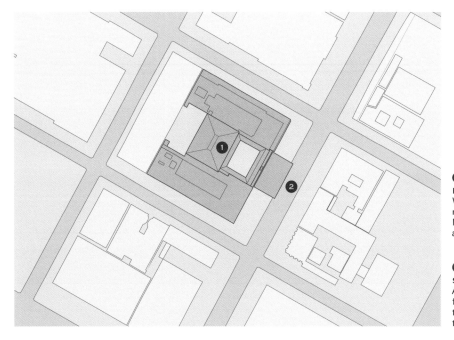

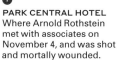

PARK CENTRAL HOTEL
Where Arnold Rothstein met with associates on November 4, and was shot and mortally wounded.

SEVENTH AVENUE
A .38-caliber revolver was found on the street below the Park Hotel following the shooting.

RIGHT Arnold Rothstein, credited with revolutionizing the world of organized crime, running his empire like a corporation, and realizing the business opportunity presented by Prohibition.

FAR RIGHT The Park Central Hotel in Manhattan, where Arnold Rothstein was shot during a meeting with some associates.

RIGHT Arnold Rothstein's body being removed from Polyclinic Hospital in New York City on its way to the morgue for a final autopsy.

RIGHT Arnold Rothstein's filing cabinet, supposed to contain details of his criminal dealings, being carried into the district attorney's office.

CHARLES LUCKY LUCIANO

✕ Giuseppe "Joe the Boss" Masseria

WEAPON	TYPOLOGY	POLICING
PISTOL	GANG	—

NUOVA VILLA TAMMARO, 2715 WEST FIFTEENTH STREET, CONEY ISLAND

Although many Prohibition-era gangs tried to get along with each other, fights were inevitable, and sometimes those fights grew into wars. The Castellammarese War of 1930–31 in New York City was one such deadly rivalry.

Born in Sicily in 1882, Giuseppe "Joe" Masseria came to the United States in 1902 and spent much of the 1910s in prison for burglaries. He was released just as Prohibition was revolutionizing the criminal underworld and quickly rose to leader of the Morello gang, surviving numerous assassination attempts over the course of the 1920s. In one attempt, two bullets shot through his straw hat, but failed to kill him, or even knock the hat off his head. Some whispered that he was bulletproof.

As head of the Morello family, Masseria began demanding payments and tributes from other crime families for protection. By 1930, a conflict with the gang led by Salvatore Maranzano had escalated into a full-scale war (nicknamed the Castellammarese War for Maranzano's Sicilian hometown) that claimed dozens of lives.

Masseria brought in Charles "Lucky" Luciano as a lieutenant. Luciano had been in the Five Points Gang, which had given Al Capone his start around the same time, and had been mentored by Arnold "The Brain" Rothstein. He was a good man to have in one's organization, but Masseria miscalculated his loyalty. After meeting with Maranzano, Lucky arranged to have Masseria killed on Maranzano's behalf.

Luciano had Masseria meet him at a restaurant in Coney Island. While Masseria played cards with a few other men, two men walked into the restaurant and shot Masseria five times. The *New York Daily News* reported that his body was found with an ace of spades clutched in his hand.

The murder ended the war and left Luciano free to restructure organized crime in New York with the establishment of The Commission, the governing body of the American Mafia, which is known to have lasted until the 1980s and by some accounts still existed in the 21st century. •

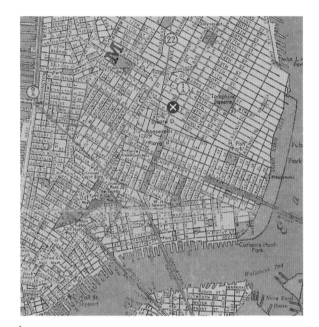

ABOVE The location of Joe Masseria's apartment at 80 Second Avenue, where an attempt was made on his life on August 9, 1922. He survived unscathed, though with two holes in his straw hat.

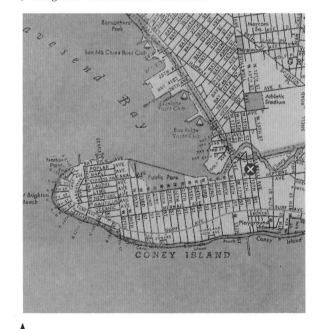

ABOVE The location of the restaurant Nuova Villa Tammaro on Coney Island, where Joe Masseria was shot on April 15, 1931.

↑ **ABOVE, TOP** Nuova Villa Tammaro restaurant in Coney Island.

ABOVE, BOTTOM Joe Masseria was killed while playing cards, though it is likely the ace of spades was added after his death, for dramatic effect.

↑ **ABOVE** Charles "Lucky" Luciano was questioned by the police, but ultimately no one was convicted for Joe Masseria's murder.

BELOW The gunmen alleged to have been hired to kill Joe Masseria. All were influential players in New York's gangland. ▼

☐ ALBERT ANASTASIA ☐

☐ VITO GENOVESE ☐

☐ BUGSY SIEGEL ☐

☐ JOE ADONIS ☐

☐ CIRO TERRANOVA ☐

CHARLES "LUCKY" LUCIANO,
NEAR THE END OF HIS LIFE.

CHARLES "LUCKY" LUCIANO (THIRD LEFT) WITH
HIS ASSOCIATES IN SICILY, 1948.

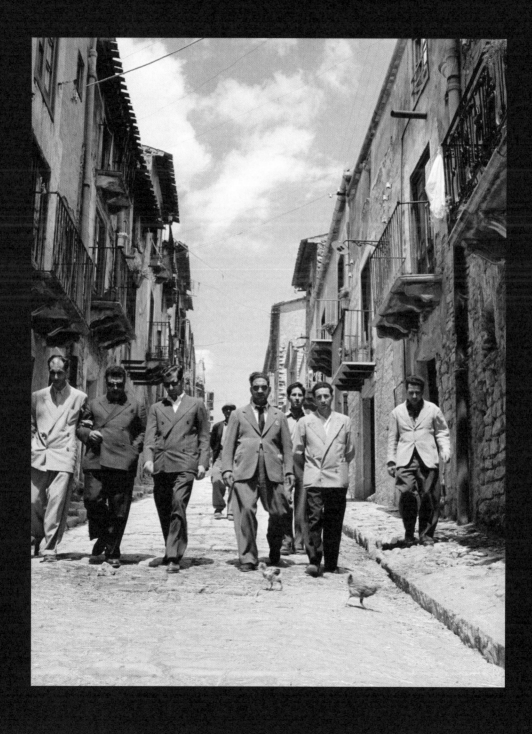

RICHARD HAUPTMANN

✕ Charles Augustus Lindbergh Jr.

WEAPON	TYPOLOGY	POLICING
THERMOS BOTTLE	KIDNAPPING	MARKED BILLS

WOODS NEAR MOUNT ROSE

It is impossible to overstate the international excitement created by Charles Lindbergh landing his airplane in Paris in 1927. News of his solo transatlantic flight electrified society; church bells rang and people danced in the streets with joy. It was the dawning of a new age of travel, one in which the world was markedly smaller than it had been only hours before. Charles Lindbergh, previously brushed off as a low-level daredevil and airmail pilot whose attempt to cross the ocean was likely to end with him at the bottom of the Atlantic, became the most famous man on the planet, showered with awards from governments around the world.

Never comfortable in the spotlight, Lindbergh married his financial advisor in 1929 and the next year the couple welcomed their first child, Charles Jr.

BELOW Richard Hauptmann in police custody following his arrest on the charge of passing one of the Lindbergh ransom bills.

However, in 1932, the Lindberghs' nurse noticed that the baby wasn't with his mother, as she had thought he was. Charles ran to his son's room, where, in place of the child, he found a ransom note demanding $50,000 for the child's return.

The news hit the papers immediately and Charles began talks with law enforcement officers, all of whom assumed that the kidnapping was the work of high-powered figures in the underworld, looking for new lines of income now that the end of Prohibition seemed on the horizon. Al Capone offered to use his connections to find the child, if only they would let him out of prison for a couple of weeks. The police questioned one household servant so harshly that she committed suicide, even though her alibi was later confirmed.

Eventually, through an intermediary, Lindbergh made a ransom payment. But the child was not returned and on May 12, two months after the kidnapping, the toddler's body was found in the woods, badly decomposed, his skull crushed from a heavy blow, likely from a dented thermos bottle found nearby.

Clues were slow in coming, but the investigators had one ace up their sleeve: the serial numbers of the bills used to pay the ransom had been recorded. These bills were old-fashioned "gold certificates" and the newly inaugurated President Roosevelt ordered all such bills to be exchanged for new ones. Whoever had the ransom money was going to have to do something with it.

In 1934, a Manhattan bank teller received one of the ransom bills and it was traced to a Bronx man named Richard Hauptmann. Investigators stormed Hauptmann's home and found many more ransom bills, as well as a bit of wood that proved to be from the ladder used to sneak into the Lindbergh home.

The investigation was sloppy and Hauptmann was brutally beaten by police, leaving room for modern investigators to question whether he was simply a patsy in a larger conspiracy, or guilty at all. But the court believed he was the killer and he was executed in the electric chair in 1936. •

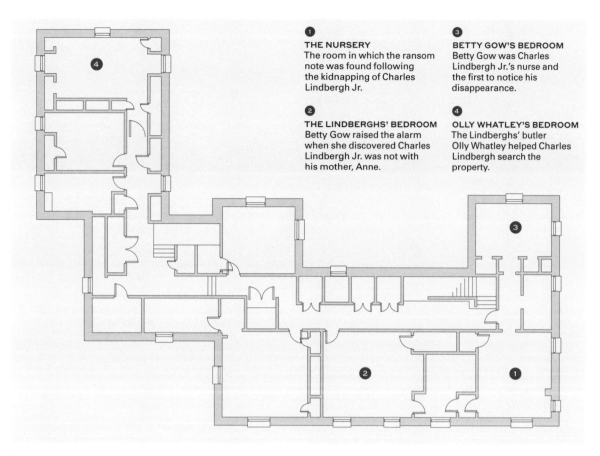

1 THE NURSERY
The room in which the ransom note was found following the kidnapping of Charles Lindbergh Jr.

2 THE LINDBERGHS' BEDROOM
Betty Gow raised the alarm when she discovered Charles Lindbergh Jr. was not with his mother, Anne.

3 BETTY GOW'S BEDROOM
Betty Gow was Charles Lindbergh Jr.'s nurse and the first to notice his disappearance.

4 OLLY WHATLEY'S BEDROOM
The Lindberghs' butler Olly Whatley helped Charles Lindbergh search the property.

BELOW, TOP Police photographs of the ladder discovered outside the baby's bedroom.

BELOW, BOTTOM Hauptmann's attic, showing the missing wood used to construct the ladder.

BELOW, TOP Hauptmann's handwriting compared with the ransom notes (left), and one of the notes (right).

BELOW, BOTTOM Charles Lindbergh Jr.'s thumb guard, found on the road outside the Lindbergh home.

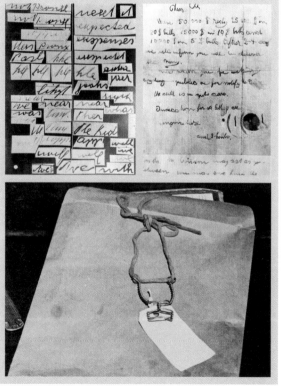

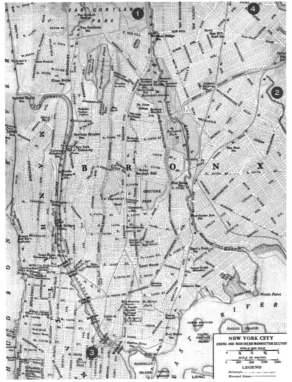

① **WOODLAWN CEMETERY,**
NEAR 233RD STREET
AND JEROME AVENUE
On March 12, the Lindberghs'
intermediary John Condon
met a "John" here.

② **ST RAYMOND'S CEMETERY**
On April 2, John Condon,
with Charles Lindbergh
nearby, paid the ransom
of $50,000 to "John."

③ **GASOLINE STATION, 127TH**
STREET AND LEXINGTON
AVENUE
The gasoline station where
Richard Hauptmann spent
the bill on September 15,
then identified by a bank teller.

④ **1279 EAST 222ND STREET**
Richard Hauptmann's home,
where he was arrested on
September 19.

① **HOPEWELL, MERCER COUNTY**
Where the Lindberghs lived.
It was here that Charles
Lindbergh Jr. was kidnapped
from his nursery.

② **MOUNT ROSE, MERCER COUNTY**
Charles Lindbergh Jr.'s body
was found in the woods near
Mount Rose.

RIGHT, TOP The crowds gathered outside Richard Hauptmann's trial, held in Flemington, New Jersey.

RIGHT, CENTER Richard Hauptmann appearing in court. The trial was highly publicized and closely followed across the country.

RIGHT, BOTTOM Richard Hauptmann being escorted to prison. He was found guilty and sentenced to death.

OPPOSITE, LEFT The closet in Richard Hauptmann's home in which he placed the bills used to pay the ransom.

OPPOSITE, CENTER Police searching Richard Hauptmann's home.

OPPOSITE, RIGHT The remains of Charles Lindbergh Jr.

OPPOSITE, LEFT Reporters examine Richard Hauptmann's license plate.

OPPOSITE, CENTER Investigators digging in Richard Hauptmann's garage.

OPPOSITE, RIGHT One of the ransom notes issued to the Lindberghs, used by handwriting analysts.

BELOW Richard Hauptmann behind bars, on which a contemporary artist has superimposed illustrations of the various pieces of evidence against him, including handwriting analysis of his notes, the ladder found to be made from wood in his attic, his sudden wealth after the kidnapping, and a map of Hopewell found in the trunk of his car.

ABOVE, TOP An artist's impression
of Richard Hauptmann, caught in the web
of evidence presented by the prosecution,
including the ladder, the ransom notes,
and the gold certificates.

ABOVE, BOTTOM A composite photograph
created for the press by the artist John
Wolters to depict the electrocution of
Richard Hauptmann, as cameras are
not permitted at executions.

HENRY HOWARD HOLMES

✕ Benjamin Pitezel + 3

WEAPON	TYPOLOGY	POLICING
CHLOROFORM & POISON	PROPERTY CRIME	PINKERTON DETECTIVES

1316 CALLOWHILL STREET, PHILADELPHIA & 241 JULIAN AVENUE, IRVINGTON, INDIANAPOLIS &16 ST VINCENT STREET, TORONTO, CANADA

In September, 1894, H. H. Holmes surprised his friend Benjamin Pitezel by murdering him in Philadelphia. This contradicted the plan the accomplices had concocted the previous year, which was to fake Pitezel's death, substitute a cadaver for his body, then cash in the $10,000 insurance policy they had taken out on his life.

It is possible that Holmes did initially plan to fake Pitezel's death, but at some point decided it would be better to really kill him. It would not have been the first time; three of his girlfriends had vanished from Chicago over the previous three years, along with a couple of their family members. He had been conducting affairs with them despite having a wife in the Chicago suburbs, another in his native New Hampshire, and a third who had accompanied him to Philadelphia.

In Philadelphia, Holmes went to the Callowhill Street house Pitezel had rented and most likely got him drinking until he passed out. He then killed Pitezel by pouring chloroform down his throat, afterwards burning his face to make it appear that he had accidentally blown himself up while lighting his pipe too close to explosive chemicals.

The body was buried in a pauper's field and Holmes informed the insurance company that the man buried as "B. F. Perry" was really Benjamin Pitezel. He traveled to Philadelphia to make an identification when the body was exhumed, casually using a knife to cut a wart used as an identifying mark from the neck of the putrid body.

The decomposed corpse was covered, except for the teeth, when Pitezel's teenage daughter, Alice, identified the body as her father's. As Holmes was still claiming privately that Pitezel was still alive, as per their original plan, this made Alice dangerous to him—she knew too much. Assuring Pitezel's widow that her husband was still alive, Holmes managed to manipulate her into placing three of the Pitezel children in his custody, who he then traveled with across the United States. He killed Alice and her sister Nellie in Toronto and buried them in a shallow grave in the cellar of a rented property. Though he later claimed to have gassed them, the house did not have gas connections; he more likely poisoned them. By the time they were found, they were too decomposed for a cause of death to be determined.

By the time he killed the girls, Holmes had already killed their brother, Howard—again, likely with poison—on the outskirts of Indianapolis. Holmes was afraid that, like his sisters, Howard knew too much.

By November, the insurance company suspected they had been duped. Detectives from the Pinkerton National Detective Agency tracked Holmes to Boston, where he was arrested. Following the arrest Holmes became a media sensation, even though he was only suspected of insurance fraud, not murder. A few people in Chicago remembered a story from 1893 revealing Holmes had been hiding stolen furniture in secret rooms in a building on the South Side, but suggestions to investigate it were initially ignored.

In the summer of 1895, detectives found the bodies of the girls, and then of Howard, whom Holmes had attempted to cremate in a stove. As it was clear that Holmes had murdered the children, it stood to reason that he had murdered Pitezel as well. Now, police began to excavate his Chicago building. Spurred on by the hunt, reporters dubbed the building "Holmes Castle" and published lurid reports that it was filled with secret chambers, rigged with various killing devices. The *World*, a New York paper, published a largely fanciful diagram and suggested that Holmes had used the house as a hotel and preyed on visitors during the recent World's Fair.

Most of the stories turned out to be phony, but Holmes reveled in the attention. He was convicted and hanged for the murder of Benjamin Pitezel, but confessed to twenty-six more. He was lying about most of them; some of his "victims" were not even really dead, and his story of burning Pitezel alive was certainly not what really happened. Over the decades, though, the tale has grown taller and taller, and it is now common to see hundreds, or even thousands, of murders attributed to him. •

HOWARD PITEZEL

ETTA "ALICE" PITEZEL

ROSA NELL "NELLIE" PITEZEL

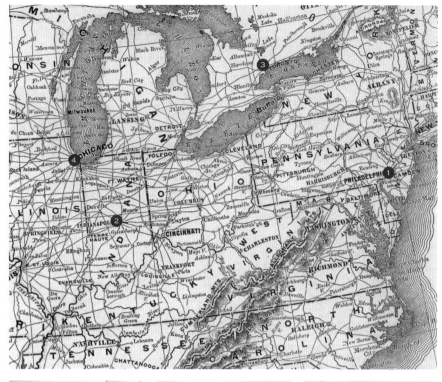

1 1316 CALLOWHILL
STREET, PHILADELPHIA
The house in which
H. H. Holmes murdered
Benjamin Pitezel.

2 241 JULIAN AVENUE,
IRVINGTON, INDIANAPOLIS
The house in which
H. H. Holmes murdered
Howard Pitezel.

3 16 ST. VINCENT STREET,
TORONTO, ON, CANADA
The house in which
H. H. Holmes murdered
Alice and Nellie Pitezel.

4 "HOLMES CASTLE,"
ENGLEWOOD, CHICAGO
The building in which H. H.
Holmes claimed to have
killed multiple guests.

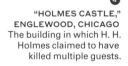

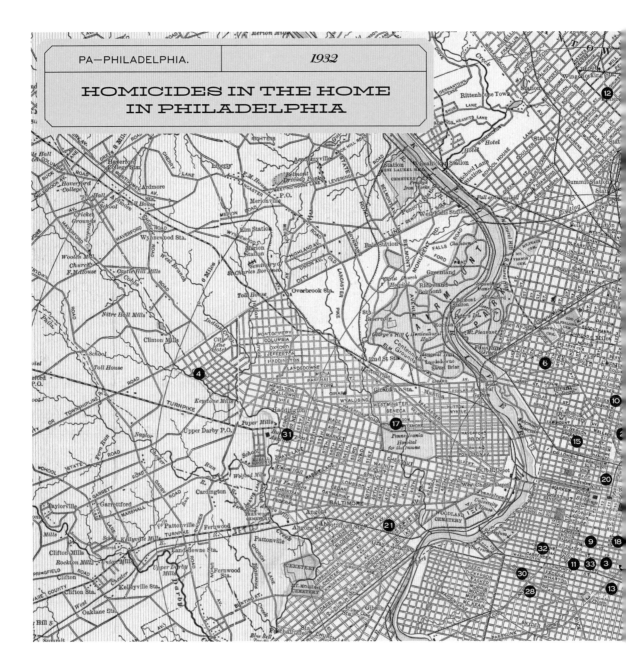

PA—PHILADELPHIA.   *1932*

HOMICIDES IN THE HOME
IN PHILADELPHIA

1 1932
2542 HOWARD STREET
JOHN WEBB
✕ JOS. A. HENDRICK

2 1932
726 NORTH THIRTEENTH
STREET
JOHN FLOURNOY
✕ JOHN WHITEFIELD

3 1932 514 SOUTH
TWELFTH STREET
JAMES GROOMS
✕ ANDREW BECKETT

4 1932
4521 HAVERFORD AVENUE
WILLIAM TAYLOR
✕ JENNIE McCARTHY
HILL

5 1932
2313 NORTH CAMAC STREET
MOSES HESTER
✕ ADDIE McCLIMON

6 1932
2609 WEST OXFORD STREET
ROBERT ROLAND
LILLY
✕ ANNA LILLY

7 1932
519 RISING SUN AVENUE
ANTHONY
POMANTE JR.
✕ ANTHONY POMANTE SR.

8 1932
1343 DELHI STREET
CHARLES
ANDERSON
✕ CLARENCE SCOTT

9 1932
1332 LOMBARD STREET
GEORGE GRANDSON
✕ CHARLES ALENCANDU

10 1932
1240 BURNS STREET
JOHN MARSHALL,
ALICE MARSHALL
✕ RICHARD BURNS

11 1932
1611 FITZWATER STREET
JAMES MILLER
✕ FRED JOHNSON

12 1932
5021 GERMANTOWN
AVENUE
FELIX MAZZES
✕ GATANO DONOFRIO

13 1932
1023 MONTROSE STREET
FRANK MAGLIOCCO
✕ GABRIELLA CANTONE

14 1932
2851 NORTH FIFTH STREET
ONOFRIO V. SPANO
✕ ANGELINA F. SPANO

15 1932
1939 MOUNT VERNON STREET
ROBERT E. PUGH
✕ HARRY K. LOTZ

16 1932
1623 NORTH TENTH STREET
JOSEPH GARNET
✕ GEORGE WANE

17 1932
889 JUNE STREET

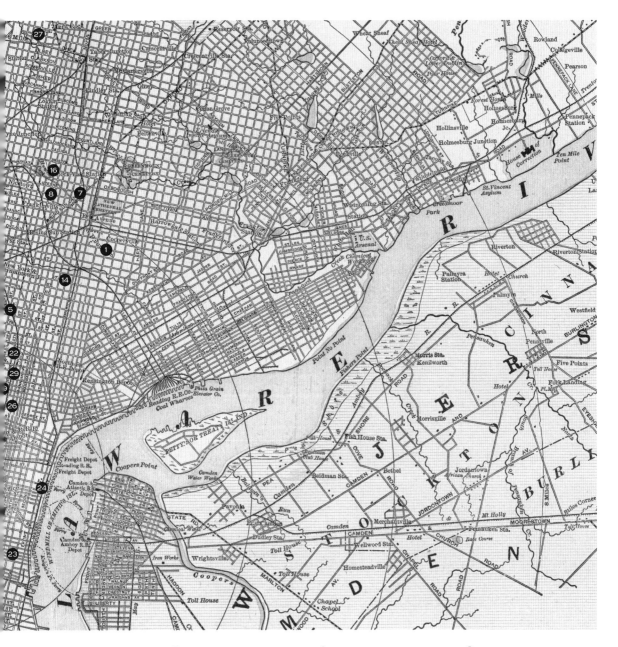

DOUGLAS COLEMAN
✕ FLETCHER FRENCH

18 1932
415 SOUTH ELEVENTH STREET
ELLIS H. FISCHER
✕ ALBERTA FISCHER

19 1932
1263 NORTH JESSUP STREET
JOSHUA MATTHEWS
✕ CHARLES OWENS

20 1932
2210 WOOD STREET
ARTHUR JONES
✕ AUGUSTUS CLARK

21 1932
608 WEST FORTY-SIXTH STREET
MARY ARMSTRONG
✕ JESSE J. ARMSTRONG

22 1932
1747 NORTH ELEVENTH
STREET
ALICE KING
✕ VIOLA KITCHEN

23 1932
535 DELANCEY STREET
OPHELIA SUTTON
✕ JOHN SUTTON

24 1932
316 NORTH AMERICAN
STREET
JOHN SAUNDERS
✕ RUTH SAUNDERS

25 1932
906 LOMBARD STREET
JAMES JONES,
CHARLES HARPEN
✕ FRANK CLARK

26 1932
926 NORTH HUTCHINSON
STREET
ESTELLA SUMMERS
✕ SAMUEL FELTON

27 1932
5634 SYDENHAM STREET
CLARENCE J.
HOWELL
✕ ELLEN E. REEVES

28 1932
1438 SOUTH TWENTIETH
STREET
ALONZO L. MARTIN
✕ IRVIN HAWLEY

29 1932
1023 OXFORD STREET
ELIZABETH DELFI
✕ FRANCK CHANCEY

30 1932
1115 SOUTH TWENTY-
THIRD STREET
LEWIS BANKS
✕ GERTRUDE BANKS

31 1932
3729 MARKET STREET
WILLIAM JACKSON
✕ EDWARD GLENN

32 1932
2121 RODMAN STREET
GEORGE HEBRON
✕ HENRY MONROE

33 1932
615 CLARION STREET
ESTELLA COLEMAN
✕ CALEB COOPER

ELMO NOAKES

✕ Norma Sedgewick ✕ Dewilla Noakes
✕ Cordelia Noakes ✕ Winifred Pierce

WEAPON	TYPOLOGY	POLICING
SUFFOCATION & GUN	DOMESTIC	FORENSICS

PINE GROVE FURNACE & RAILROAD STATION NEAR DUNCANSVILLE

ELMO NOAKES   NORMA SEDGEWICK

CORDELIA NOAKES   DEWILLA NOAKES

In the early morning of November 24, two men wandered into the forest of South Mountain, searching for firewood. Instead, under a blanket, they found the dead bodies of three young girls, lying together neatly arranged.

Police rushed to the scene and began to formulate theories. Forensic analysis by Dr. Milton Eddy showed that the girls were sisters, and that they had not eaten for some time before their death, caused by suffocation.

The next morning, a man and a woman were found dead from gunshot wounds in a car 100 miles (161 km) away. They were 32-year-old Elmo Noakes and his 18-year-old niece, Winifred Pierce. More tests revealed that Elmo was the father of two of the dead girls found in the wood. His wife, the mother of all three of the girls, had died two years earlier.

Exactly what was going through Elmo's mind when he decided to kill his daughters, then his niece, and finally himself, can never truly be known. There has been much speculation that he was in a romantic relationship with Winifred and that they were fleeing from their disapproving extended family. But even if this were true, why did it end so violently, less than two weeks after

Elmo had left home with Winifred and the girls in his new blue sedan?

Some have speculated, based on a mark on daughter Norma's head, that it might have been a ritualistic murder, but the mark was almost certainly a wound, not an occult symbol. It is more commonly suggested that Noakes, unable to find a job, killed the girls because he could not bear to see them starve to death. Others suggest that they accidentally died from breathing car exhaust fumes, then Noakes hid the bodies and killed Winifred and himself in distress.

The truth will never be known. In the 1960s, a blue sign was installed stating "On this spot were found three babes in the woods, Nov. 24, 1934." •

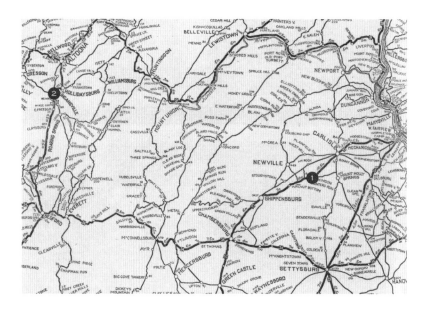

PINE GROVE FURNACE
Norma Sedgewick and Dewilla and Cordelia Noakes were found dead under a blanket in Pine Grove Furnace Park. The cause of their death was determined to be "suffocation by external means."

RAILROAD STATION NEAR DUNCANSVILLE
The station where Winifred Pierce and Elmo Noakes's bodies were found. Winifred was shot through the heart, and then in the head. Elmo was killed by a single gunshot wound to his head.

RIGHT The bodies of Norma Sedgewick and Dewilla and Cordelia Noakes, or the "babes in the woods," who were discovered in Pine Grove Furnace.

RIGHT State Trooper Carl Hartman examining some of the dresses that were found near the bodies of the girls.

RIGHT The death masks of the murdered girls, made by the police in order to aid in the search for the girls' identities after they had been buried.

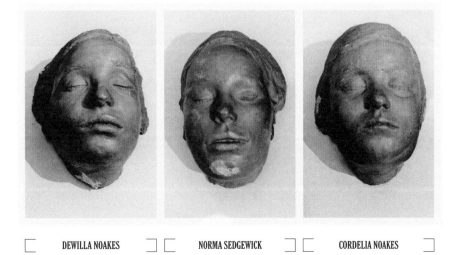

DEWILLA NOAKES   NORMA SEDGEWICK   CORDELIA NOAKES

PA—PHILADELPHIA	October 27, 1938

HERMAN PETRILLO
PAUL PETRILLO
✕ Ferdinando Alfonsi

WEAPON	TYPOLOGY	POLICING
POISON	CONTRACT	DOUBLE AGENT

NATIONAL STOMACH HOSPITAL, NORTH FIFTEENTH STREET

HERMAN PETRILLO | PAUL PETRILLO

The Depression era led many people to seek creative, and not entirely legal, ways to make a living. Bootleg alcohol made plenty of people rich in the 1920s, but even the kingpins of that era, if not dead or in jail, had trouble finding new ways to make money when Prohibition ended. Tricks from the late 19th century, such as torching buildings for insurance money, came back into vogue.

In Philadelphia, Herman Petrillo moved from insurance fraud to counterfeiting. His cousin Paul sold cheap insurance policies, with himself as a beneficiary, to people he knew were about to die. Lower-tier policies did not require a medical exam, which opened up plenty of avenues for fraud.

Eventually, the two cousins teamed up to form what came to be known as the Philadelphia Poison Ring. They would pair widows with new husbands, arrange life insurance policies, and then, strangely enough, the new husbands would come to "accidental" deaths.

In 1938, the cousins made a deal with George Meyer, whose upholstery business was in dire straits: he would arrange for the death of a man named Ferdinando Alfonsi, and for his trouble he would be given $3,000 from a mix of insurance payouts and counterfeit cash. At one point it was suggested that he make it look as though Alfonsi had died in a car accident.

Meyer was, in reality, a double agent working for the law and did not carry out the killing, but Alfonsi died of arsenic poisoning anyway, apparently taken care of by someone else. His death was enough for the agents Meyer worked with to bring Herman Petrillo in for questioning. To their astonishment, he confessed not only to the murder of Alfonsi, but to dozens of others, most of whom had been killed with arsenic. The Petrillo cousins were sent to the electric chair seven months apart in 1940. More than a dozen other "ring" members were given long prison terms. •

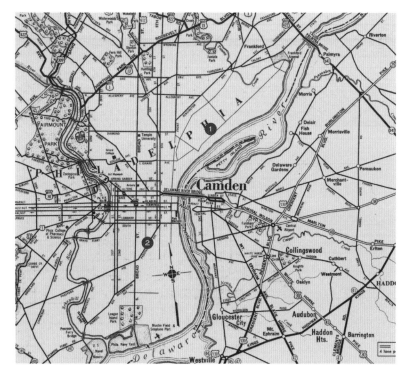

 2515 EAST ANN STREET
The house where Ferdinando Alfonsi lived. He was found there by detectives, gravely ill from arsenic poisoning, and taken to the National Stomach Hospital, where he died.

 EAST PASSYUNK AVENUE
The tailor shop owned by Paul Petrillo, "Paul Petrillo, Custom Tailor to the Classy Dressers." The cousins' insurance scam was run from the back of the shop.

NO. 175384 — GRACE GIOVANNETTI

NO. 175432 — JOSEPHINE ROMUALDO

NO. 175304 — GAETANO CICCINOTI

NO. 175422 — —

NO. 175300 — —

NO. 175299 — DORA SHERMAN

NO. 171989 — CARINA FAVATO

NO. 175303 — —

MUGSHOTS OF CONSPIRATORS IN THE PHILADELPHIA POISON RING

NO. 175164 — —

NO. 175425 — CHRISTINE CERRONE

NO. 175162 — —

NO. 175301 — —

NO. 75329 — —

NO. 175429 — JOSEPH SWARTZ

NO. 175427 — ANNA ARENA

NO. 175420 — CESARE VALENTI

NO. 175426 — MILLIE GIACOBBE

NO. 175302 — MORRIS BOLBER

NO. 175298 — SAMUEL SORTINO

NO. 175261 — STELLA ALFONSI

PART TWO

OHIO **INDIANA** **ILLINOIS**

MINNESOTA **IOWA**

MISSOURI

NEBRASKA **KANSAS**

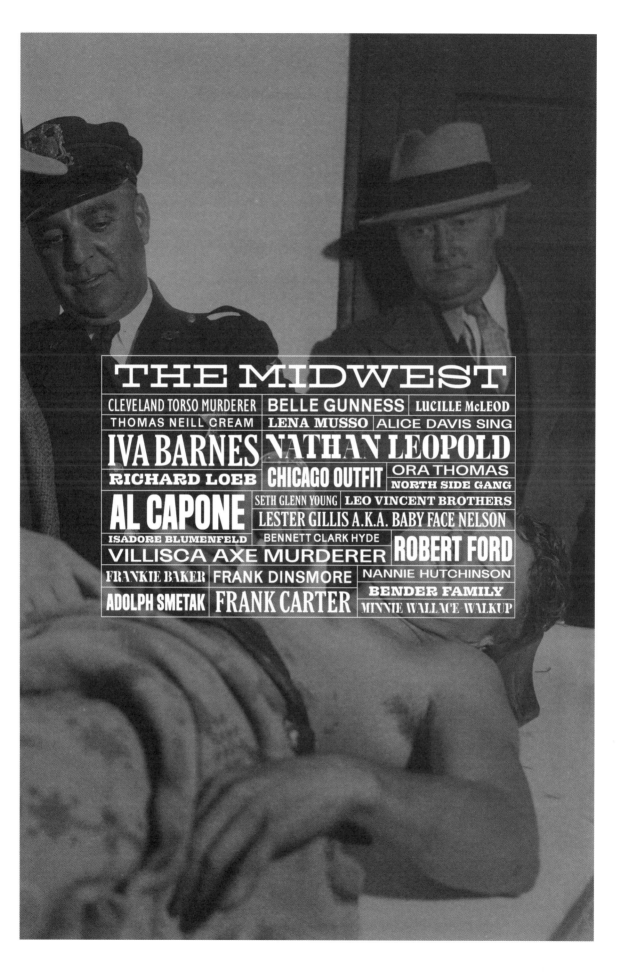

THE MIDWEST

CLEVELAND TORSO MURDERER · BELLE GUNNESS · Lucille McLEOD
THOMAS NEILL CREAM · LENA MUSSO · ALICE DAVIS SING
IVA BARNES **NATHAN LEOPOLD**
RICHARD LOEB **CHICAGO OUTFIT** ORA THOMAS · NORTH SIDE GANG
AL CAPONE SETH GLENN YOUNG · LEO VINCENT BROTHERS
LESTER GILLIS A.K.A. BABY FACE NELSON
ISADORE BLUMENFELD · BENNETT CLARK HYDE
VILLISCA AXE MURDERER **ROBERT FORD**
FRANKIE BAKER · FRANK DINSMORE · NANNIE HUTCHINSON
ADOLPH SMETAK · FRANK CARTER · BENDER FAMILY
MINNIE WALLACE-WALKUP

CLEVELAND TORSO MURDERER

×12–20

WEAPON	TYPOLOGY	POLICING
SHARP OBJECT	RANDOM ATTACK	POLYGRAPH

KINGSBURY RUN

In the early 1930s the United States fell into a deep economic recession. Millions were out of work, and many of these jobless men and women became drifters, hopping freight trains and riding the rails from city to city, looking for work and a place to stay warm. Rail yards and empty lots everywhere became "hobo jungles." The old courthouse in Chicago became a homeless shelter, nicknamed the Hotel Hoover after the president that so many blamed for the economic downturn.

Although Cleveland was considered an up-and-coming city in those days, in the area known as Kingsbury Run a "hobo jungle" appeared just east of a neighborhood of brothels and gambling dens known as the Roaring Third. These two areas were filled with people on the run, people wanting to disappear. It was, in short, a criminal's paradise.

In September, 1935, two teenagers discovered a corpse in the area of Kingsbury Run known as "Jackass Hill." The victim was a white male, nude except for socks and decapitated, emasculated, drained of blood, and covered with a chemical

preservative. Fingerprints identified the victim as Edward Andrassy and the coroner determined that the man had still been alive when he was decapitated. The chemical preservative linked the crime to a woman's body, mutilated and treated with the same chemical, that had washed up on the shores of Lake Erie a year before.

Cleveland, it seemed, had a serial killer.

Over the next few years, there would be eleven more murders attributed to the same killer—all found decapitated and dismembered. Only a couple of the victims were ever identified and in some cases the heads were never found. A death mask was created of one victim, but none of the hundred thousand people who viewed the mask at the Great Lakes Exposition in 1936, where it was put on display, could connect it to a missing person they recognized.

Most serial killers have a clear preference for their type of victim, but the "torso murderer" killed both men and women. Most victims were white, but not all. It seemed that victims were instead chosen because they lived in Cleveland's seediest districts. They were the kind of people nobody would think to look for.

In 1939, the police arrested a man named Frank Dolezal. They were able to torture a confession out of him, but he died in prison—supposedly a suicide, though some suspected foul play—before he could stand trial. Few researchers now believe that Dolezal was the killer.

Elliot Ness, at the time famous for his work battling gangs in Chicago, was put on the case by Mayor Burton. Ness conducted a raid of the Kingsbury Run area, evicting hundreds of squatters and even going so far as to burn down some of the shanty buildings. He believed that the killer was a man named Dr. Francis Sweeney, who had worked in field amputations during World War I. Sweeney failed primitive polygraph tests, but when he had himself confined to a hospital, Ness believed there was little chance of a conviction and gave up. Sweeney would send Ness threatening letters from the hospital for over a decade, and died in a veterans' hospital in 1964. •

ABOVE Investigators searching in the vegetation beneath a bridge between Kinsman Road and East 65 Street, Kingsbury Run.

ABOVE The body of Edward Andrassy where it was discovered in Jackass Hill. The body had been both decapitated and emasculated.

RIGHT Police officers searching for bodies in Kingsbury Run.

FAR RIGHT Edward Andrassy, the first victim of the Torso Murderer to be discovered, but likely the second to be killed.

RIGHT Police officers searching for bodies. Andrassy was discovered in the Jackass Hill area of Kingsbury Run (near East 49th Street and Praha Avenue).

FAR RIGHT The head of Edward Andrassy. The heads of many of the killer's other victims were not recovered.

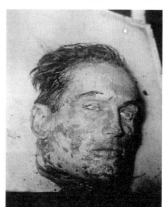

①

EDWARD ANDRASSY
Discovered September 23, 1935,
in Jackass Hill.

②

JOHN DOE I
Discovered September 23, 1935,
in Jackass Hill.

③

FLORENCE GENEVIEVE POLILLO
Discovered January 26, 1936,
at 2315 and 2325 East
Twentieth Street.

④

JOHN DOE II
Discovered June 5, 1936,
at East Fifty-Fifth Street

⑤

JOHN DOE III
Discovered July 22, 1936,
in Big Creek.

⑥

JOHN DOE IV
Discovered September 10, 1936,
at East Thirty-Seventh Street.

⑦

JANE DOE I
Discovered February 23, 1937,
at East 156th Street.

⑧

JANE DOE II
Discovered June 6, 1937,
at Lorain Carnegie Bridge.

⑨

JOHN DOE V
Discovered July 6, 1937, in
the Cuyahoga River, near West
Third Street and Clinton Road.

⑩

JANE DOE III
Her foot discovered April 8, 1938,
on Superior Avenue.

⑪

JANE DOE IV
Discovered August 16, 1938,
at Lakeshore Dump, East
Ninth Street.

⑫

JOHN DOE VI
Discovered August 16, 1938,
at Lakeshore dump, East
Ninth Street.

OPPOSITE, ABOVE Police officers
searching for bodies in Kingsbury Run.

OPPOSITE, BELOW Officials removing
the trunk of a woman from Lake Erie
in a burlap bag, in 1938.

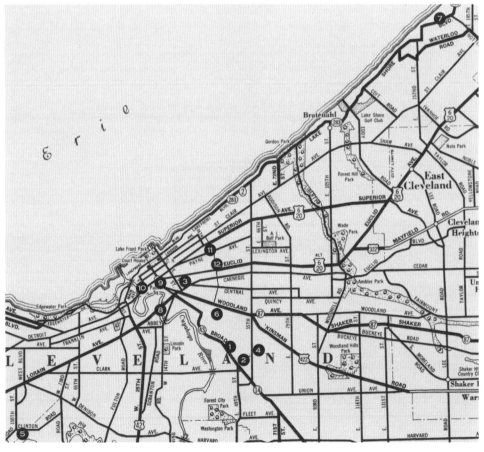

OHIO

Investigators examining human remains left by the Torso Murderer.

Workmen removing shacks beneath the Superior Avenue viaduct.

Detectives searching for evidence at a dump in Kingsbury Run.

Investigators searching for human remains.

Investigators searching inside a sewer in Kingsbury Run.

Near to Superior Avenue, and described as "Torso Man's Cave."

Homeless people in Kingsbury Run washing in a stream.

A collection of the shanty houses found in Kingsbury Run.

Investigators searching in water for evidence or remains.

Inhabitants of Kingsbury Run, near to where one of the victims was found.

Investigators James Hogan and Don Barrett handling evidence.

Kingsbury Run during a police raid of the area searching for the killer.

Fire Warden Patrick Barrett (right) examining a shack in Kingsbury Run.

A trunk of blankets found under a bridge near Kinsman Street.

The remains of one of the victims of the Torso Murderer.

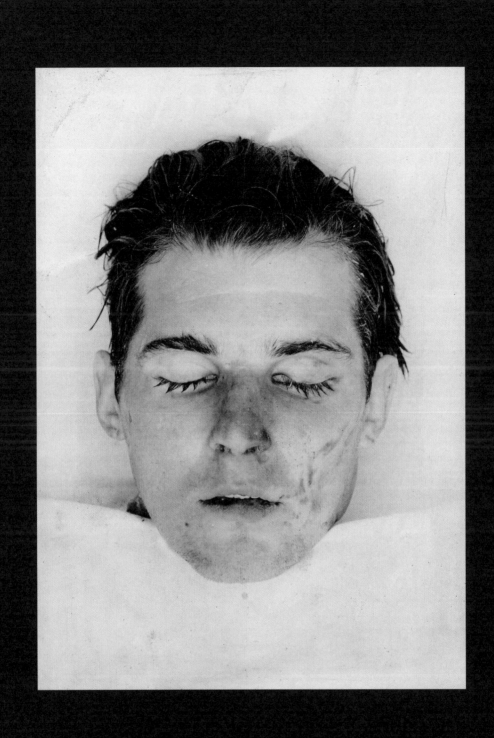

ABOVE The decapitated head of the victim found on June 5, 1936. Notes on the reverse of the photo record that he had several tattoos. His identity was never discovered.

IN—LA PORTE	*1884–1908*

BELLE GUNNESS
×40

WEAPON	TYPOLOGY	POLICING
VARIOUS	PROPERTY CRIME	POSTMORTEM IDENTIFICATION

GUNNESS FARM, MACLUNG ROAD

Although there are rumors that Belle Gunness started committing murders in her native Norway, so far as it is known her career began, like so many others, in Chicago.

Setting up in a neighborhood just a few blocks north of Thomas Neill Cream's office (see page 76), Belle and her husband initially ran a candy store. However, the insurance money collected when the store was destroyed by fire, combined with the life insurance money from her husband's death, allowed Belle to leave Chicago and purchase a farm in La Porte, Indiana.

In 1908, a fire wrecked the farm, killing Belle and three children. When investigators started to sort through the rubble, they began to find bodies. At least a dozen, and perhaps as many as four dozen, were discovered dismembered and buried near the pig pen and around the lake.

In short order, the farm became a carnival, as hundreds of people from neighboring towns arrived to watch the bodies being uncovered. From recovered letters, it seemed that Belle had been placing advertisements in newspapers, posing as a wealthy widow in search of a husband. When rich men responded, she would lure them to the farm and kill them. One of her recovered letters contained the particularly ominous phrase: "Come prepared to stay forever."

As the bodies were removed, stories spread in Chicago of children who had been seen in Belle's care during her time in the city, but who had eventually disappeared. Stories also circulated that Belle had not died in the fire—a headless body found in the smoldering rubble had been identified as hers, but the head had not been found. Newspapers made crude mock-ups of how Belle might look in any number of disguises and a nationwide manhunt ensued until some teeth identified as Belle's were located on the grounds.

But mysteries remain. How many people Belle might have killed can only be speculated, and who set the fire, and why, remains unclear. In the early 21st century her body was exhumed from a suburban Chicago cemetery to see if it was really her. Results were inconclusive. •

GUNNESS FARM.

South View Gunness Farm

THE GUNNESS CHILDREN'S PONY
WONDER COOK PHOTO CO.

West View Gunness Farm.

① 1894
✕ MADS SORENSEN
POISONED WITH STRYCHNINE

② 1902
✕ PETER GUNNESS
BLUDGEONED WITH MEAT GRINDER

③ 1908
✕ LUCY SORENSEN
BURNED IN FARMHOUSE

④ 1908
✕ MYRTLE SORENSEN
BURNED IN FARMHOUSE

⑤ 1908
✕ PHILIP GUNNESS
BURNED IN FARMHOUSE

⑥ 1906
✕ JENNIE OLSEN
BLUDGEONED

⑦ 1908
✕ ANDREW HELGELIEN
BLUDGEONED & DISMEMBERED

⑧ 1908 (DISCOVERED)
✕ OLE B. BUDSBERG
BLUDGEONED & DISMEMBERED

⑨ 1908 (DISCOVERED)
✕ HENRY GURHOLDT
BLUDGEONED & DISMEMBERED

⑩ 1908 (DISCOVERED)
✕ JOHN MOE
BLUDGEONED & DISMEMBERED

⑪ 1908 (DISCOVERED)
✕ THOMAS LINDBOE
BLUDGEONED & DISMEMBERED

⑫ 1908 (DISCOVERED)
✕ OLAF SVENHERUD
BLUDGEONED & DISMEMBERED

⑬ 1908 (DISCOVERED)
✕ OLAF LINDBLOOM
BLUDGEONED & DISMEMBERED

⑭ — ㊵
BODY PARTS UNEARTHED EQUATING TO A POSSIBLE 27 FURTHER VICTIMS

Human remains found buried in the grounds of Gunness Farm.

A crate of bones and body parts uncovered by investigators at the farm.

Rings found in the ruins of the farm. One was marked "S. B. May 28, 1907."

Bridgework identified as belonging to Belle Gunness.

The remains of Andrew Helgelien, one of Belle Gunness's victims.

The skull of one of Belle's unidentified victims, found on the farm.

An assortment of bones and body parts uncovered by investigators.

The decapitated head of one of Belle's many victims.

Investigators searching the basement of the farmhouse.

Shovels used in excavations, placed in the farmhouse cellar.

Investigators searching for bodies near the lake on the farm.

An investigator standing in the remains of the farmhouse.

A former miner was hired to build a sluice in order to sift through the debris.

The area of the farm where nine bodies were found buried.

A crowd of onlookers observing the investigation of the farm.

The makeshift morgue for victims, surrounded by onlookers.

Spectators standing at the ruins of Belle Gunness's house.

The area of the farm where ten bodies were found during investigations.

The area of the farm where four bodies were found buried.

An investigator making notes while he searches the farm.

Bodies found in the burned-down farmhouse.

Bodies and body parts found in the pig pen.

Bodies and body parts found in the grounds.

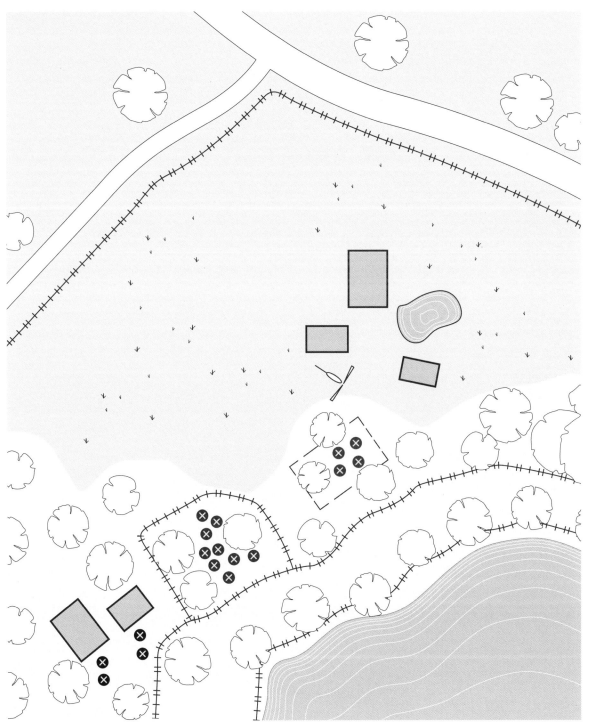

THOMAS NEILL CREAM

✕ Alice Montgomery ✕ Daniel Stott

WEAPON	TYPOLOGY	POLICING
STRYCHNINE	DOMESTIC	TOXICOLOGY

SHELDON HOUSE, WEST MADISON AND LOOMIS STREETS & GARDEN PRAIRIE, BOONE COUNTY

Sheldon House was a small boarding house in what is now Chicago's West Loop area, near the intersection of Madison and Loomis streets. On a spring afternoon in 1881, a room was rented to woman named Alice Montgomery. She declined to give her name, saying she would only be staying the night. After being shown to her room, she requested a glass and a teaspoon, and asked to be directed to the "ladies' private closet."

Minutes later, another guest saw her staggering from the water closet in what appeared to be terrible pain. She collapsed to the floor writhing in agony and a doctor who arrived on the scene determined that she had attempted suicide by ingesting strychnine. She died half an hour later.

An inquest determined that her death was not exactly suicide—she had undergone an illegal abortion before arriving at Sheldon House. The medicine she had taken was presumably supposed to be a painkiller, but had been laced with too much strychnine.

It is something of a mystery that no one at the time noted that Sheldon House was barely a block away from the offices of Dr. Thomas Neill Cream, a physician who had been acquitted of murder only months before, after a patient died at his hands during an abortion. Adding poison to painkillers would become a favored method of murder for him in later years, but in Chicago his crimes had not yet formed a pattern.

Shortly after Alice died, Cream was arrested for poisoning his girlfriend's husband in Garden Prairie, Illinois. The husband, Daniel Stott, has a tombstone that still reads "Poisoned by his wife and Dr. Cream."

While in jail, Cream allegedly admitted to the murder of Alice Montgomery, though little note was taken of it at the time. On his release from Joliet prison he returned to his native U.K. There, he was arrested for poisoning other young women with strychnine and was hanged in London in 1892. •

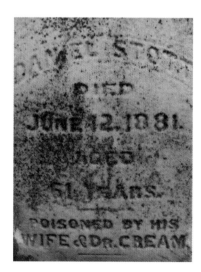

ABOVE Daniel Stott's gravestone, with the inscription "poisoned by his wife & Dr. Cream." Stott died after taking a medicine prescribed to him by Thomas Neill Cream.

❶ 434 WEST MADISON STREET [NOW 1255] The location of Thomas Neill Cream's Chicago office, where he practiced as a doctor.

❷ SHELDON HOUSE, WEST MADISON AND LOOMIS STREETS The boarding house where Alice Montgomery died on April 9, 1881, following an illegal abortion.

❸ BUCK AND RAYNER'S PHARMACY, STATE AND MADISON STREETS The chemist where Julia Stott purchased the medicine for her husband, which Thomas Neill Cream fatally altered.

RIGHT The McGill
University graduating
class in medicine, 1876.
Thomas Neill Cream
attended the university
in Montreal, Canada, before
undertaking post-graduate
training at St. Thomas's
Hospital in London, U.K.
In this photograph he is in
the cluster of men seated at
the front, second from the
left and wearing a striped tie.

RIGHT Thomas Neill
Cream's pocket medicine
case, now in the possession
of the Metropolitan Police
in London, U.K., following
his arrest there in June 1892.

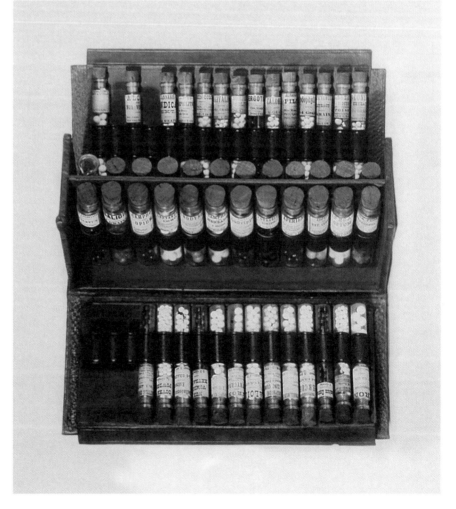

IL—CHICAGO	1906

LUCILLE McLEOD
✕ William Nieman

WEAPON PISTOL	TYPOLOGY DOMESTIC	POLICING —

EMPIRE HOTEL, 345 WABASH AVENUE

IL—CHICAGO	1912

LENA MUSSO
✕ Peter Noto

WEAPON PISTOL	TYPOLOGY DOMESTIC	POLICING —

1027 LARRABEE STREET

Not many accused murderers are able to continue with their normal lives while under the shadow of their trial, but in 1906, on the evening before her trial was to begin, Lucille Mcleod married F. H. Menhard. She had been indicted for the murder of William Nieman, who had been shot in the Empire Hotel. Lucille was shot in the same room herself but survived—authorities suspected a failed murder-suicide. The trial was heavily focused on Lucille's character, with the defense depicting Nieman as her guileful seducer and the prosecution emphasizing Lucille's past as a chorus girl. The jury returned a not-guilty verdict. •

Lena married Peter Musso at the age of 16 and lived with him in the part of Chicago known as "Little Hell." Later, papers would describe her smiling pleasantly as she told reporters how and where she had shot and killed Peter. She explained that she had committed the murder in self defense, saying, "If I had not killed my husband, he would have killed me. He said he was going to shoot me... then changed his mind because somebody might hear the shot." Lena was found innocent, one of the many women protected by a trend, referred to at the time as the "new unwritten law," which exonerated the majority of wives who killed their husbands. •

↑ **ABOVE** Accused murderer Lucille Mcleod photographed at the police station.

↑ **ABOVE** Lena Musso photographed with her daughter Catherine.

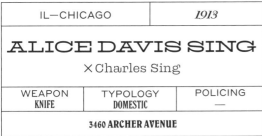

IL—CHICAGO	1913

ALICE DAVIS SING

✕ Charles Sing

WEAPON	TYPOLOGY	POLICING
KNIFE	DOMESTIC	—

3460 ARCHER AVENUE

IL—CHICAGO	1916

IVA BARNES

✕ James Barnes

WEAPON	TYPOLOGY	POLICING
KNIFE	DOMESTIC	—

WASHINGTON PARK

In the 1910s, when the first Chinese restaurants opened in Chicago, rumors spread that the owners were luring young white girls into the restaurants, and then into "white slavery," using hypnotic music and cigarettes. When Alice Davis, a missionary, killed her Chinese-American husband Charles Sing, some therefore believed that it must have been done in self defense. The police, on the other hand, believed that she had murdered him for planning a trip to China without her. However, the evidence against her was slight and she was eventually acquitted. •

James Barnes was walking with his wife, Iva, in Washington Park when he was shot. Iva said he had accidentally shot himself, while trying to shoot her, but the police believed that she was the shooter. Iva had recently been traveling around the Chicago area collecting evidence that James had been seeing other girls, and a divorce suit was pending. She put on a tearful courtroom scene and a reporter described her as "a crumpled figure in a sable garb of woe." Like most of the husband-killers of this period, she was found innocent. •

↑ **ABOVE** The missionary and accused murderer Alice Davis Sing, photographed by the police.

↑ **ABOVE** Iva Barnes, wearing mourning dress and photographed by police.

RICHARD LOEB
NATHAN LEOPOLD

× Bobby Franks

WEAPON	TYPOLOGY	POLICING
CHISEL	THRILL KILL	FORENSICS

EAST FIFTIETH STREET, BETWEEN SOUTH ELLIS AVENUE AND SOUTH GREENWOOD AVENUE

RICHARD LOEB   NATHAN LEOPOLD

In the 1920s the murder of Bobby Franks by Richard Loeb and Nathan Leopold was referred to as "The Crime of the Century." Franks, a 14-year-old boy, had been picked up by Leopold and Loeb, two older neighbors, who were driving through the neighborhood and told Franks that they wanted to ask his opinion about a tennis racket. Once Franks was in the car, one of the two young men—probably Loeb—drove a chisel into the boy's head. His body was left in a railroad culvert near Wolf Lake on the southern outskirts of the city.

The crime was solved in a matter of days. A rented car was traced back to the boys, a ransom note was traced to a typewriter that had been stolen from Loeb's old fraternity house, and an unusual pair of glasses, discovered near the corpse, were found to belong to Leopold. The two men confessed within days and only the brilliant

arguments of lawyer Clarence Darrow saved them from the gallows. Instead, they were sentenced to terms of life plus ninety-nine years in prison.

The case still resonates today because there has never been a truly satisfying explanation for why Leopold and Loeb did what they did.

They were exceptionally clever young men, both from well-to-do South Side homes. Leopold had studied fifteen languages and spoke five fluently, and had already made a name for himself as an ornithologist. Only 19 years old, he had completed an undergraduate degree at the University of Chicago.

Loeb, for his part, had graduated from the University of Michigan aged 17, the youngest person ever to earn a degree there. The son of a Sears Roebuck executive, it is generally believed that the idea to commit a murder originated with Loeb. Often, when there are two murderers, one seems to be the mastermind behind the crime and the other seems to be under their spell.

But exactly what was motivating the two is hard to pin down. At various times it has been suggested that the two believed that they were Nietzschean "supermen" and that normal laws did not apply to them. At other times it seemed that Loeb believed that the greatest intellectual thrill would be to commit "the perfect crime." There was strong evidence that Leopold was in love with Loeb and willing to do almost anything in exchange for sexual attention. A few newspapers at the time suggested that they were simply products of the "Jazz Age," ever-cynical and searching for the next fleeting thrill. Murder, then, was just a way to pass the time. None of these are totally satisfying explanations.

Loeb was eventually murdered himself in prison and Leopold worked to restore his own reputation, even allowing himself to be injected with malaria as part of a study towards a vaccine. He was released in 1958 and lived the last years of his life in Puerto Rico, where he kept a framed picture of Loeb by his bed. When he visited Loeb's family plot at Rosehill Cemetery, he would have walked right past the Franks mausoleum. •

ABOVE Nathan Leopold and Richard Loeb during their trial. Loeb's family hired Clarence Darrow, a renowned criminal defense lawyer, to lead the defense team.

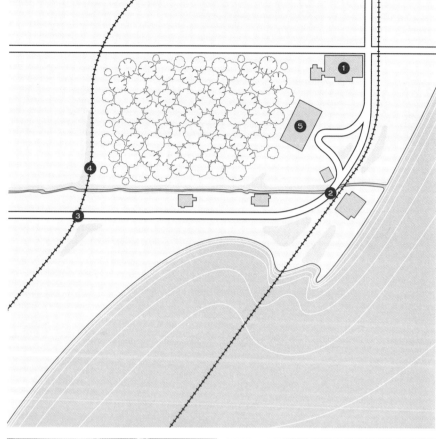

1

FIREWORKS FACTORY
The night before the crime, the driver of a gray car asked the factory watchman for directions.

2

SHED
On the night of the crime, and several before, a gray car was seen by the watchman parked here.

3

CULVERT
Bobby Franks's body was discovered in a culvert along the Pennsylvania Railroad tracks.

4

BESIDE RAILWAY TRACKS
Leopold and Loeb removed Bobby Franks's clothes after the murder. One of his stockings was found here.

5

VACANT BUNKHOUSE
During investigations, a window of the bunkhouse was found open, as though it had been entered.

RIGHT, ABOVE Scenes from the search for evidence, following the discovery of Bobby Franks's body the day after his murder. Richard Loeb joined the search himself.

RIGHT, BELOW The culvert in which Bobby Franks's body was eventually found.

Dear Sir:

    As you no doubt know by this time your son has been kidnapped. Allow us to assure you that he is at present well and safe. You need fear no physical harm for him provided you live up carefully to the following instructions, and such others as you will receive by future communications. Should you however, disobey any of our instructions even slightly, his death will be the penalty.

    1. For obvious reasons make absolutely no attempt to communicate with either the police authorities, or any private agency. Should you already have communicated with the police, allow them to continue their investigations, but do not mention this letter.

    2. Secure before noon today ten thousand dollars, ($10,000.00). This money must be composed entirely of OLD BILLS of the following denominations;
        $2,000.00 in twenty dollar bills
        $8,000.00 in fifty dollar bills
The money must be old. Any attempt to include new or marked bills will render the entire venture futile.

LEFT The ransom note delivered to Bobby Franks's family. The killers decided to pretend the murder was a kidnapping in order to obfuscate the precise nature of their crime and their motive. The typewriter used to type the note was eventually recovered from Jackson Park Lagoon and used as evidence.

OPPOSITE The police found a pair of eyeglasses near the body. Although common in prescription and frame, they were fitted with an unusual hinge purchased by only three customers in Chicago, one of whom was Nathan Leopold.

OPPOSITE, LEFT The ashes of the blanket that Nathan Leopold and Richard Loeb used to move the body, and subsequently burned.

OPPOSITE, RIGHT A duplicate of the car used on the night of the murder, a Willys-Knight automobile. The car was rented by Nathan Leopold from the Rent-A-Car Company, Chicago, using a false name.

OPPOSITE, LEFT A stocking that was found stuffed in Bobby Franks's mouth, and the glasses found near the scene of the crime.

OPPOSITE, RIGHT Assistant State's Attorney Milton Smith (left) and Assistant State's Attorney Joseph Savage (right) examining the evidence.

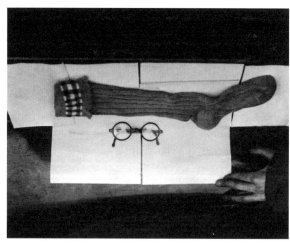

IL—HERRIN		*January 24, 1925*

SETH GLENN YOUNG
✕ Ora Thomas
ORA THOMAS
✕ Seth Glenn Young

WEAPON FIREARM	TYPOLOGY POLITICAL	POLICING —

EUROPEAN HOTEL, WEST MONROE STREET

SETH GLENN YOUNG

Corrupt public officials in 1920s Illinois were so common as to be a cliché, and the problem extended far beyond just Chicago. The towns in the southern part of the state were smaller and more sparsely populated, but every bit as dangerous and crooked as the city. And the federal agents enforcing Prohibition laws were not necessarily any less corrupt than the dirty cops who were ignoring them.

Seth Glenn Young was a fine example of the darker side of the feds. Assigned to track down bootleggers in East Saint Louis, he was fired after only a few months on the job for shooting a bootlegger dead (he claimed self defense), helping himself to the cash he confiscated, and taking his mistress on official business. Like too many law enforcement officers, he believed that his position put him above the law.

After he was fired by the feds, the the local Ku Klux Klan put him in charge of cleaning up illegal liquor in Williamson County, where he gleefully launched violent raids on anyone who made their own wine. Eventually, Young arrested the mayor and sheriff and declared himself the de facto head of the town.

In January, 1935, Young heard that Ora Thomas, an anti-Klan deputy whom he considered a mortal enemy, had returned to Williamson County. The previous August, Ora had been involved in an intense gunfight between Klan and anti-Klan forces that left six men dead; as part of a post-battle truce, both Thomas and Young had agreed to leave town. Young returned first, and when Thomas returned as well, the two began "gunning" for each other.

Young led a delegation of his followers to Thomas's hotel and a firefight broke out near a cigar store. By the time the dust settled, Young and Thomas had shot each other dead.

The mayor declared that with both leaders dead, the troubles in Williamson County would be over. They were not, and shoot-outs continued there between the two rival factions for years. •

▲ **ABOVE** Seth Glenn Young armed and equipped for one of the raiding operations that he carried out on behalf of the Ku Klux Klan.

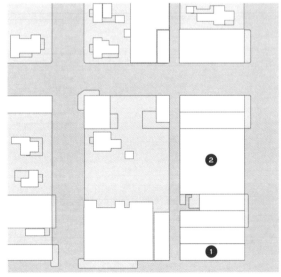

①
THE EUROPEAN HOTEL, WEST MONROE STREET
Where the shootout occured between Young and Thomas.

②
SMITH'S GARAGE IN HERRIN
The garage was a Klan headquarters, and was where six men were killed in 1934.

↑ **ABOVE** The City Hall in Herrin, from which Seth Glenn Young directed his raids across the county.

↑ **ABOVE** The cigar shop attached to the European Hotel, where the shootout occured.

RIGHT A photograph of Smith's Garage in Herrin, known as a Klan headquarters, and where a shoot-out occurred in August, 1934, in which six men were killed.

SMITH'S GARAGE-HERRIN, ILL. IN FRONT OF WHICH THE 6 MEN WERE KILLED.

ONE OF THE SEVERAL BATTLE SCENES

RIGHT A photograph of Smith's Garage, inscribed with the words: "The death car—at the exact spot where six men were shot down. We were fortunate to see this car, as it was replevined on the day we took "shots of Bloody Herrin."

HT THE DEATH CAR-AT THE EXACT SPOT WHERE 6 MEN WERE SHOT DOWN. WE WERE FORTUNATE TO SEE THIS CAR, AS IT WAS REPLEVINED ON THE DAY WE TOOK "SHOTS OF BLOODY HERRIN

THE REPLEVINED DEATH CAR - HERRIN ILL.

UNKNOWN, ATTRIB. AL CAPONE

× William McSwiggin

WEAPON	TYPOLOGY	POLICING
FIREARM	GANG	RAIDS

5615 WEST ROOSEVELT ROAD

At the age of 26, William McSwiggin was a rising star in the Chicago legal profession. An assistant state's attorney, he was considered to have a spotless reputation in a city where that quality was a rarity for public officials.

While by 1926 the city's gangland was largely run by Al Capone on the South Side and Bugs Moran on the North, there were countless other, smaller gangs whose loyalty was known to change from day to day. The Genna Brothers of Little Italy worked for Capone, but it may have been Capone who had some of them killed. The West Side O'Donnell gang had nominally worked for Capone, but must have run afoul of him at some point.

In April, 1926, a couple members of the O'Donnell gang were standing outside of the Pony Inn in suburban Cicero when a car pulled up and emptied dozens of rounds of machine gun fire out of the window. Two gangsters, Tom Duffy and Jim Doherty, were killed along with their companion – William McSwiggin.

The city was shocked. What had the upstanding young lawyer been doing at a speakeasy with two gangsters? Some simply assumed that he liked an illicit beer as much as anyone else and happened to be in the wrong place at the wrong time. Others insisted that he must have been doing undercover research. Others claimed that the members of the O'Donnell gang were old childhood friends of McSwiggin and that they had remained friends.

The most logical explanation for the shooting was that someone was sent to kill the gangsters, and McSwiggin, whatever he was doing with them, was just unlucky to be present. Capone was accused not just of ordering the killing, but of actually being the trigger man, and was jailed for a few days before being freed for a lack of evidence. "I liked the kid," Capone insisted when asked about McSwiggin.

The killing led to a series of police raids of typical Capone haunts. They never managed to solve the McSwiggin murder, but one of the raids did uncover a ledger that would become key in Capone's prosecution for tax evasion five years later. •

1

WHERE WILLIAM McSWIGGIN STOOD
The spot outside Madigan and Wendell's Saloon on West Roosevelt Road, where William McSwiggin was shot.

2

KLONDIKE O'DONNELL'S CAR
The position of the car belonging to gangster Klondike O'Donnell, in which McSwiggin arrived at the saloon.

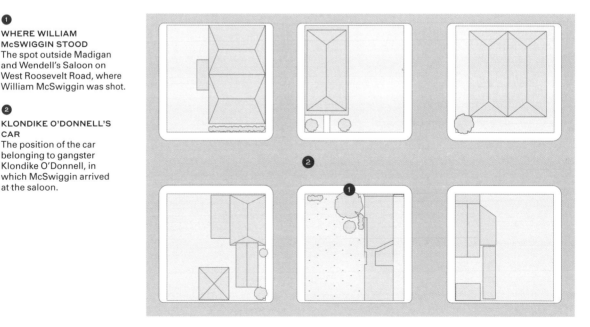

ABOVE, TOP Klondike O'Donnell's Lincoln automobile being examined by the police (left). The car window was broken during the shooting. Hundreds of people lining the streets for the funeral of William McSwiggin (right).

ABOVE, BOTTOM Captain John Stege of the Chicago Police beside the Lincoln automobile in which William McSwiggin arrived at the saloon, and which Klondike and Myles O'Donnell used to transport McSwiggin's bullet-ridden body away from the crime scene.

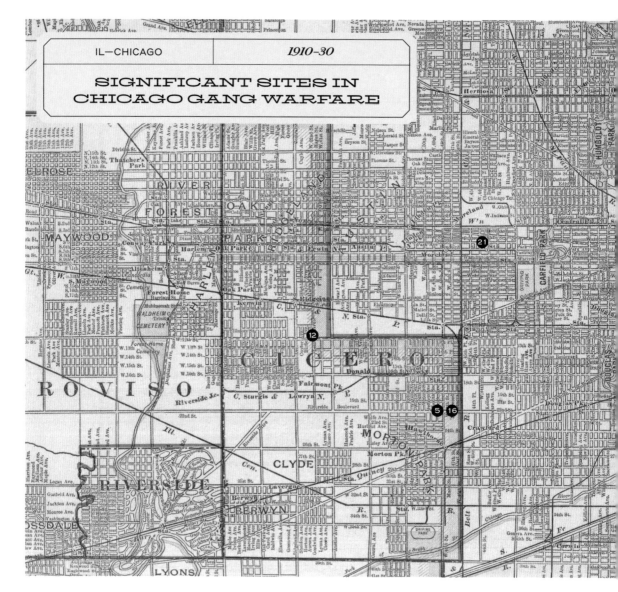

SIGNIFICANT SITES IN CHICAGO GANG WARFARE

❶ January 1, 1910–March 26, 1911
DEATH CORNER, MILTON AVENUE
[NOW NORTH CLEVELAND AVENUE]
AND WEST OAK STREET
SHOTGUN MAN
✕ FIFTEEN ITALIAN IMMIGRANTS

❷ 1916–21
DEAD MAN'S TREE, 725 LOOMIS
STREET
Where the names of victims were carved
during the war between Johnny "De Pow"
Powers and Anthony d'Andrea

❸ 1920
COLOSIMO'S CAFE, 2126 SOUTH
WABASH AVENUE
ATTRIB. FRANKIE YALE
(Masseria Crime Family)
✕ BIG JIM COLOSIMO (Chicago Outfit)

❹ February 1924
THE FOUR DEUCES, 2222 SOUTH
WABASH AVENUE
DEAN OBANION (North Side Gang)
✕ JOHN DUFFY (North Side Gang)

❺ April 1924
CICERO AVENUE AND TWENTY-SECOND
STREET
PHILLIP J. McGLYNN (Police)
✕ FRANK CAPONE (Chicago Outfit)

❻ May 1924
HEINE JACOBS'S SALOON, 2300
SOUTH WABASH AVENUE
AL CAPONE (Chicago Outfit)
✕ JOE HOWARD

❼ May 1924
SIEBEN BREWERY, 1466 NORTH
LARRABEE STREET
The brewery that was set to be
raided by police and sold by Dean O'Banion
(North Side Gang) to John Torrio (Chicago
Outfit) in a double cross

❽ November 1924
SCHOFIELD'S FLOWER SHOP, 738
NORTH STATE STREET
FRANKIE YALE (Masseria Crime
Family)
✕ DEAN O'BANION (North Side Gang)

❾ May 1925
HUDSON AVENUE, MENOMONEE STREET
AND OGDEN AVENUE
HYMIE WEISS, BUGS
MORAN, VINCENT DRUCCI
(North Side Gang)
✕ ANGELO GENNA (Genna Brothers)

❿ July 1925
GRAND AVENUE AND CURTIS STREET.
ATTRIB. BUGS MORAN,
VINCENT DRUCCI (North Side Gang)
✕ ANTONIO GENNA (Genna Brothers)

⓫ November 1925
BARBERSHOP ON ROOSEVELT ROAD
VINCENT DRUCCI,
JIM DOHERTY (North Side Gang)
✕ SAMUZZO AMATUNA

⓬ April 1926
5615 WEST ROOSEVELT ROAD
ATTRIB. AL CAPONE
(Chicago Outfit)
✕ WILLIAM McSWIGGIN (Assistant
State Attorney)

13 August 1926
NINTH STREET AND MICHIGAN AVENUE
LOUIS BARKO (Chicago Outfit)
Unsuccessful attempt on Vincent Drucci
and Hymie Weiss (North Side Gang)

14 October 1926
HOTEL SHERMAN, CLARK STREET
AND RANDOLPH STREET
Peace meeting between Chicago Outfit
and North Side Gang chaired by Al Capone
(Chicago Outfit) and mediated by Big Bill
Thompson, former mayor

15 October 1926
SUPERIOR STREET
TWO HITMEN (Chicago Outfit)
✕ HYMIE WEISS (North Side Gang)
✕ PADDY MURRAY (North Side Gang)

16 November 1926
THE HAWTHORNE HOTEL, TWENTY-
SECOND STREET AND CICERO AVENUE
Headquarters of Al Capone (Chicago Outfit),
machine-gunned by North Side Gang
cavalcade

17 March 1928
800 SOUTH OAKLEY BOULEVARD
HITMEN (Attrib. Chicago Outfit)
✕ DIAMOND JOE ESPOSITO (Politician,
affiliated to Genna Brothers)

18 September 1928
INTERSECTION OF MADISON
STREET AND DEARBORN STREET
HITMEN (Attrib. North Side Gang
and Joe Aiello)
✕ TONY LOMBARDO (Ally to Al Capone)
✕ JOSEPH FERRARA (Bodyguard)

19 February 1929
LINCOLN PARK
FOUR HITMEN (Chicago Outfit)
✕ SEVEN MEMBERS OF NORTH SIDE
GANG

20 June 1930
UNDERPASS, ILLINOIS CENTRAL
RANDOLPH STREET STATION
LEO VINCENT BROTHERS
✕ ALFRED "JAKE" LINGLE (Journalist,
affiliated with Chicago Outfit)

21 October 1930
205 KOLMAR AVENUE
TWO HITMEN (Chicago Outfit)
✕ JOE AIELLO (Ally to North Side Gang)

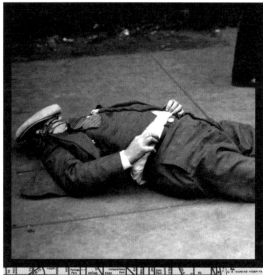

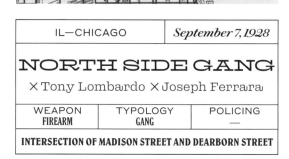

IL—CHICAGO	*October 11, 1926*

CHICAGO OUTFIT

✕ Hymie Weiss

WEAPON FIREARM	TYPOLOGY GANG	POLICING —

NORTH STATE STREET

IL—CHICAGO	*September 7, 1928*

NORTH SIDE GANG

✕ Tony Lombardo ✕ Joseph Ferrara

WEAPON FIREARM	TYPOLOGY GANG	POLICING —

INTERSECTION OF MADISON STREET AND DEARBORN STREET

After the death of Dean O'Banion, several members of the North Side Gang took revenge by working together to attack John Torrio, O'Banion's chief rival. Among those involved in the attack was Hymie Weiss. Shortly afterwards, the South Siders took their revenge: Weiss, accompanied by four of his men (Sam Pellar, Paddy Murray, William W. O'Brien and Benjamin Jacobs), was shot by a sniper as he walked past Holy Name Cathedral, across the street from O'Banion's flower shop. A false-but-popular urban legend claims that a bullet hole is still visible in the church. •

In the outskirts of Chicago, nearly every small town has stories of how 1920s mobsters used to dump bodies in their town. It may be true in a few cases, but usually gangsters liked bodies to fall where people would see them. It sent a message. But no killing was more public than that of Tony Lombardo. Soon after he became head of the Union Siciliana, he was shot dead during rush hour at the intersection of Madison Street and Dearborn Street. His bodyguard Joseph Ferrara was also killed, although bodyguard Joe Lolordo survived. •

ABOVE The body of Hymie Weiss on North State Street, where he was killed by members of Capone's Chicago Outfit.

ABOVE The body of Tony Lombardo at the intersection of Madison and Dearborn Streets, one of Chicago's busiest intersections.

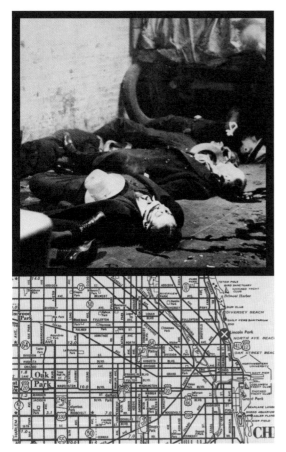

IL—CHICAGO	*February 14, 1929*
CHICAGO OUTFIT ×7	

WEAPON	TYPOLOGY	POLICING
FIREARM	GANG	—

LINCOLN PARK

IL—CHICAGO	*June 1930*
LEO VINCENT BROTHERS × Alfred "Jake" Lingle	

WEAPON	TYPOLOGY	POLICING
FIREARM	GANG	—

UNDERPASS LEADING TO THE ILLINOIS CENTRAL RANDOLPH STREET STATION

By 1929, Bugs Moran was the only serious rival to Al Capone. On Valentine's Day, 1929, five of Moran's men, plus two others, were lined up against a garage wall by men dressed as police officers. They had come into the garage as though it was a routine liquor raid. But the "cops" were really gangsters in disguise. They shot all seven men dead and then drove away in a stolen police car. Moran himself was not present, having left his Parkway Hotel apartment late. Approaching the warehouse from a side street, he saw the police car and immediately turned around. Theories abound, but the shooters have never been identified. •

The city went into mourning when Alfred "Jake" Lingle, a reporter for the *Chicago Tribune*, was shot dead in the underpass to the railway station underneath Michigan Avenue. It was assumed that he had been murdered by gangsters who were angry about his investigations into their activities. It was not until some time later that it was revealed that Lingle had been involved with the Capone gang himself, and that his murder was probably due to his underworld activities, rather than his reporting. Leo Vincent Brothers, who worked for Al Capone's Chicago Outfit, was convicted of the killing. •

ABOVE The bodies of Bugs Moran's men where they were killed in a Lincoln Park garage. The massacre is one of the most infamous incidents of Chicago's gang wars.

ABOVE The scene of Alfred "Jake" Lingle's murder. There were plenty of witnesses and the police offered a $25,000 reward for any information leading to the killer.

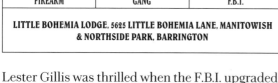

WI—MANITOWISH IL—BARRINGTON	*April 20 & November 27, 1934*

LESTER GILLIS
A.K.A. BABY FACE NELSON

✕ W. Carter Baum ✕ Ed Hollis
✕ Samuel Cowley

WEAPON	TYPOLOGY	POLICING
FIREARM	GANG	F.B.I.

LITTLE BOHEMIA LODGE, 5625 LITTLE BOHEMIA LANE, MANITOWISH & NORTHSIDE PARK, BARRINGTON

Lester Gillis was thrilled when the F.B.I. upgraded him to "Public Enemy Number One." Known in the papers (but not to his face) as Baby Face Nelson, Gillis reportedly boasted that with his new status, he would rob a bank every day.

Gillis was first arrested at the age of 12, for accidentally shooting a playmate in the jaw with a pistol he had found. By his mid-teens, with arrests for car theft already under his belt, he was leading neighborhood gangs in the suburbs of Chicago. Although too young to take part in the bootlegging game, by 1930 Gillis was making huge hauls from robbing banks. In 1933 he and his gang stole over $30,000 from a bank in Brainerd, Minnesota, gleefully spraying bullets from his submachine gun through the town as he fled in a getaway car.

His gang helped to orchestrate fellow robber John Dillinger's escape from prison in Indiana in early 1934, and Gillis eventually met up with Dillinger at a resort in Wisconsin. When the F.B.I. raided the lodge, Gillis shot and killed agent W. Carter Baum, stole an F.B.I. car, and made another escape. When the gang managed to regroup, Gillis returned to robbing banks, now in company with Dillinger himself.

In July of that year, Dillinger was gunned down by the F.B.I. outside of a Chicago theater and Gillis took his place as the agency's biggest target. Though he bragged that he would keep robbing banks, he is not known to have been involved in any robberies after Dillinger's death; he spent the next few months on the run with his wife, hiding out in auto camps across the country.

In November, while driving a stolen car, Gillis caught sight of federal agents on the road near Barrington, Illinois. A 70-mile-per-hour car chase ensued, followed by a shootout in which agents Ed Hollis and Samuel Cowley were killed. Gillis was hit several times, but made it to a safehouse, where he died of his wounds. His blanket-wrapped body was found dumped in a cemetery the following day. •

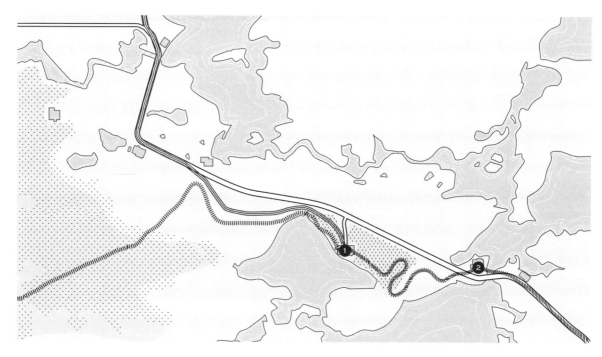

W. CARTER BAUM

ED HOLLIS

SAMUEL COWLEY

❶

LITTLE BOHEMIA LODGE, LITTLE STAR LAKE
The lodge where Baby Face Nelson, John Dillinger, Tommy Carroll, and several of their associates were ambushed by F.B.I. agents.

❷

THE HOME OF ALVIN KOERNER, SPIDER LAKE
Nelson stopped here, apparently dissatisfied with the speed of his getaway car. When the F.B.I. agents caught up with him, agent W. Carter Baum was killed and the F.B.I. car commandeered by Nelson.

 NELSON'S GETAWAY ROUTE

 DILLINGER'S GETAWAY ROUTE

⚌ CARROLL'S GETAWAY ROUTE

BELOW, TOP The entrance to the Little Bohemia resort.

BELOW, CENTER The lodge at Little Bohemia.

BELOW, BOTTOM The car of the F.B.I. agents.

ABOVE Various shots of the resort at Little Bohemia. Gillis and his associates, including his wife Helen, had arrived at the lodge for a weekend of rest, before they were ambushed by F.B.I. agents, tipped off by the resort owner's wife.

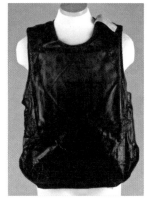

542742

DIVISION OF INVESTIGATION
U. S. DEPARTMENT OF JUSTICE
WASHINGTON, D. C.

Fingerprint Classification

18 5 Ra 16

19 Wa

WANTED

LESTER M. GILLIS, with aliases GEORGE NELSON, BABY FACE NELSON,

ALEX GILLIS, LESTER GILES; "BIG GEORGE" NELSON, "JIMMIE".

MURDER

DESCRIPTION

Age, 25 years
Height, 5 feet 4⅞ inches
Weight, 133 pounds
Build, medium
Eyes, yellow and grey slate
Hair, light chestnut
Complexion, light
Occupation, oiler

RELATIVES:

Mrs. Mary Gillis, mother,
5516 South Marshfield St.,
Chicago, Ill.
Mrs. Helen Gillis, alias
Mrs. Helen Nelson, wife,
148 North Mayfield,
Chicago, Ill.
Mrs. Juliette Fitzsimmons, sister
5516 South Marshfield St.,
Chicago, Ill.

PHOTOGRAPH TAKEN JULY 17, 1931.

George Nelson

CRIMINAL RECORD

As George Nelson, #5437, arrested
Police Department, Chicago,
Illinois, January 15, 1931;
charge, robbery; sentence,
1 year to life;
As George Nelson, #5437, received
State Penitentiary, Joliet,
Illinois, July 17, 1931; crime,
robbery; sentence, 1 year to
life; escaped February 17, 1932.✓

Lester M. Gillis is wanted for the murder of W. Carter Baum, Special Agent, Division of Investigation, U. S. Department of Justice, near Rhinelander, Wisconsin, on April 23, 1934.

Law enforcement agencies kindly transmit any additional information or criminal record to the nearest office of the Division of Investigation, U. S. Department of Justice.

If apprehended, please notify the Director, Division of Investigation, U. S. Department of Justice, Washington, D. C., or the Special Agent in Charge of the office of Division of Investigation listed on the back thereof which is nearest your city.

(over)

Issued by: J. EDGAR HOOVER, DIRECTOR.

ABOVE, TOP LEFT Baby Face Nelson's mugshot, taken in 1931 when he was arrested for a bank robbery in Chicago.

ABOVE, TOP RIGHT The bullet-proof vest worn by Baby Face Nelson, recovered by the F.B.I. following the shootout in Barrington.

ABOVE, BOTTOM Baby Face Nelson's Identification Order, classing him as "WANTED" and including his mugshot, fingerprints, physical description, relatives, and criminal record. The order was issued by J. Edgar Hoover, the first Director of the F.B.I.

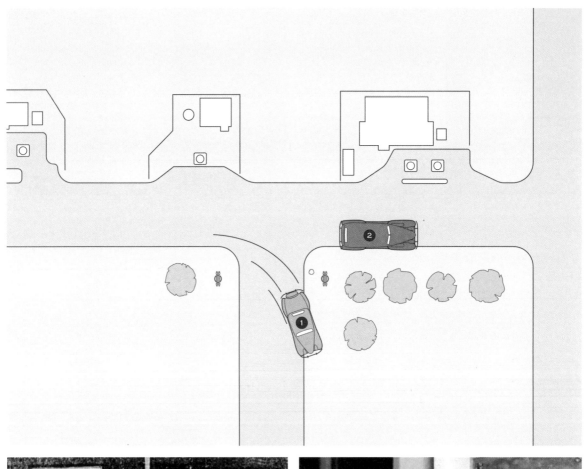

①
NELSON'S CAR
The position of Baby Face
Nelson's car—which suddenly
turned off the highway—during
the Battle of Barrington. Nelson
fired from behind his car.

②
THE AGENTS' CAR
The position of the F.B.I.
agents' car during the Battle
of Barrington, on the Northwest
Highway. They fired from
behind the telegraph pole.

ABOVE J. Edgar Hoover observing the list of
F.B.I. agents killed in the line of duty, including
three killed by Baby Face Nelson.

OPPOSITE, TOP Baby Face Nelson's body in
the morgue and, surrounded by police officers,
following the Battle of Barrington.

OPPOSITE, BOTTOM A crowd gathering outside
the Sadowski funeral home, prior to the funeral of
Baby Face Nelson. He is buried in River Grove, Illinois.

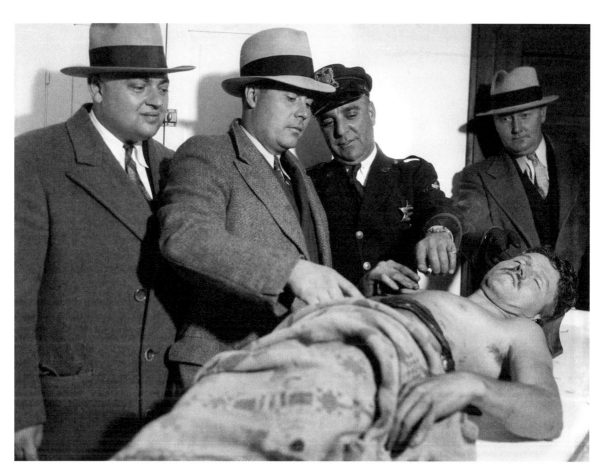

"BANKS ARE AN ALMOST IRRESISTIBLE ATTRACTION FOR
THAT ELEMENT OF OUR SOCIETY WHICH SEEKS UNEARNED MONEY."

| J. EDGAR HOOVER, DIRECTOR OF THE F.B.I., ON BANK ROBBERIES. | WANTED POSTER FOR LESTER GILLIS, A.K.A. BABY FACE NELSON, ISSUED BY THE F.B.I. |

WANTED

LESTER M. GILLIS,

aliases GEORGE NELSON, "BABY FACE" NELSON, ALEX GILLIS, LESTER GILES,

"BIG GEORGE" NELSON, "JIMMIE", "JIMMY" WILLIAMS .

On June 23, 1934, HOMER S. CUMMINGS, Attorney General of the United States, under the au-
thority vested in him by an Act of Congress approved June 6, 1934, offered a reward of

$5,000.00

for the capture of Lester M. Gillis or a reward of

$2,500.00

for information leading to the arrest of Lester M. Gillis.

DESCRIPTION

Age, 25 years; Height, 5 feet 4-3/4 inches; Weight,
133 pounds; Build, medium; Eyes, yellow and grey
slate; Hair, light chestnut; Complexion, light; Occupation, oiler.

All claims to any of the aforesaid rewards and all questions and disputes that may arise
as among claimants to the foregoing rewards shall be passed upon by the Attorney General and
his decisions shall be final and conclusive. The right is reserved to divide and allocate
portions of any of said rewards as between several claimants. No part of the aforesaid rewards shall be paid to any official or employee of the Department of Justice.

If you are in possession of any information concerning the whereabouts of Lester M. Gillis,
communicate immediately by telephone or telegraph collect to the nearest office of the Division of Investigation, United States Department of Justice, the local offices of which are set
forth on the reverse side of this notice.

The apprehension of Lester M. Gillis is sought in connection with the murder of Special
Agent W. C. Baum of the Division of Investigation near Rhinelander, Wisconsin on April 23,
1934.

JOHN EDGAR HOOVER, DIRECTOR,
DIVISION OF INVESTIGATION,
UNITED STATES DEPARTMENT OF JUSTICE,
WASHINGTON, D. C.

June 25, 1934

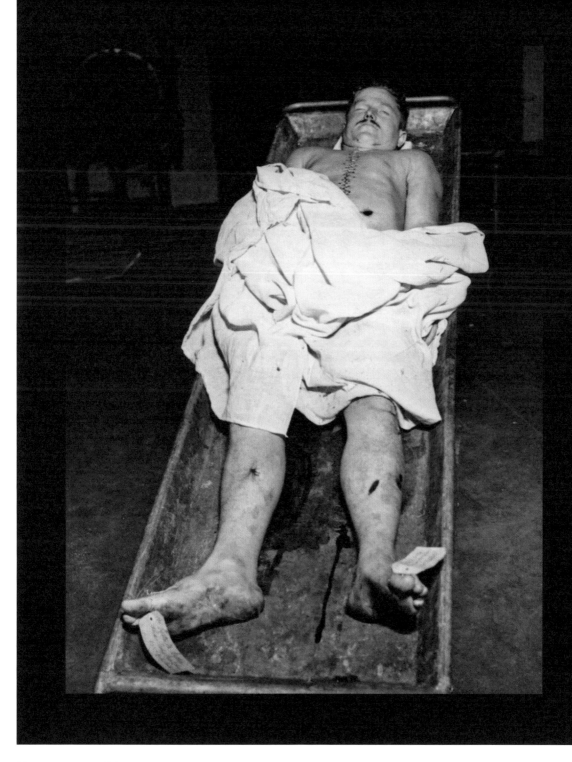

> "WE ARE A FACT-GATHERING ORGANIZATION ONLY.
> WE DON'T CLEAR ANYBODY. WE DON'T CONDEMN ANYBODY."

 J. EDGAR HOOVER, DIRECTOR OF THE F.B.I., ON THE AGENCY'S PURPOSE.

BABY FACE NELSON IN THE MORGUE, AFTER HE WAS FATALLY SHOT BY F.B.I. AGENTS AT THE BATTLE OF BARRINGTON. ▼

MN—MINNEAPOLIS		*December 9, 1935*
ISADORE BLUMENFELD ✕ Walter William Liggett		
WEAPON SUBMACHINE GUN	TYPOLOGY POLITICAL	POLICING POLICE LINE-UP
1825 SECOND AVENUE SOUTH		

Exposing corruption has always been dangerous work—the people being exposed, naturally, have a lot to lose and are likely already working with a loose sense of morals and ethics. Reporters who investigate crooked figures know that they are taking their lives into their hands when they go to work.

Walter William Liggett was not shy about making enemies; throughout the 1920s he wrote a series of articles detailing the corruption that was flourishing in large cities under Prohibition. He testified on the issue in Congress in 1930 and was nominated for a Pulitzer Prize in 1931 for his articles. He even wrote an unflattering book about President Hoover, whom he had known for a decade, during the 1932 election. Hoover—and Prohibition—went on to lose in a landslide.

After the election, Liggett began working to make the Farmer-Labor Party a viable third party in American politics, but ended up writing articles exposing corruption within the fledgling party. This ruffled plenty of the wrong feathers, including those of Isadore "Kid Cann" Blumenfeld, an organized crime figure who, Liggett reported, was working with several high-ranking party members, including the Minnesota governor Floyd B. Olson.

Throughout 1935, Blumenfeld and his associates did their best to convince Liggett to keep quiet, including attempted bribery, beating him up, and even having him arrested on trumped up kidnapping charges. But Liggett only increased his attacks on Governor Olson. When threats of lawsuits did not work any better than the physical violence had, Blumenfeld allegedly suggested that there were other ways to keep Liggett from talking.

In December, 1935, Liggett was returning from the grocery store with his wife and daughter. As he stepped out of his car, groceries in hand, a car drove up the street, shooting bullets out of the window from a Thompson submachine gun. Liggett died on the spot.

His widow and three other witnesses identified Blumenfeld as the killer, but he was acquitted in a trial widely assumed to have been rigged. Blumenfeld outlived most gangsters of his era, dying of natural causes in 1981. •

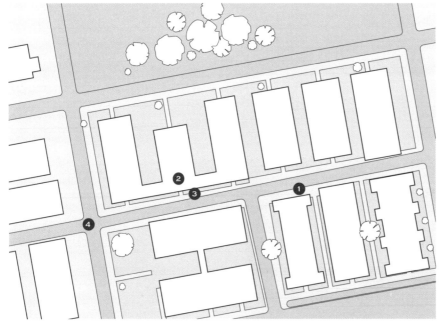

①
DOORWAY WHERE WESLEY ANDERSON WAS STANDING
The doorway in which one witness was standing during the shooting.

②
LIGGETT APARTMENT
Where Walter William Liggett lived with his wife and daughter.

③
SITE OF THE SHOOTING
The position where Walter William Liggett exited his car and was shot on December 9, 1935.

④
WHERE THE CAR TURNED
Witnesses to the crime were unsure whether the car of the shooter turned right or left following the shooting.

ABOVE The scene of the murder of Walter William Liggett, lying covered on the street, attended by his wife, witnesses, and police.

BELOW An illustration from the *Minneapolis Star*, showing the shooter's car, Walter William Liggett, and the direction of the bullet.

BELOW The trial of Isadore Blumenfeld, also known as "Kid Cann," who was charged with the murder of Walter William Liggett, before being acquitted.

IA—VILLISCA	*June 10, 1912*

UNKNOWN
✕ Moore family (6 members)
✕ Ina Stillinger ✕ Lena Stillinger

WEAPON	TYPOLOGY	POLICING
AXE	RANDOM ATTACK	POSTMORTEM

508 EAST SECOND STREET

JOSIAH MOORE

SARAH MOORE

Villisca is a small town in southwest Iowa. In 1910 the population stood at just over 2,000. By the standards of the time, it would have been a fairly large town for the vicinity, and Josiah Moore's hardware store was not the only one in town; his old boss, F. F. Jones, was still running one of his own. But it was the sort of community where people would notice if you were not following your usual daily routine.

On June 10, 1912, Josiah, his wife, and their four children attended children's day services at a local Presbyterian church and came home around 10 o'clock, along with Ina and Lena Stillinger, two friends of 10-year-old Mary Moore. After Josiah closed the door, no one saw the eight alive again.

The next day a neighbor became concerned when no one came outside to do the morning chores. When no one answered the door, Josiah's brother, Ross Moore, was brought in to use his copy of the key to enter the house. Inside, he found a scene of horror that was unimaginable anywhere, let alone in quiet Villisca. All six of the Moores and both of the Stillinger girls had been bludgeoned to death with an axe. Josiah seemed to have been the main target; his face was hacked to bits and his eyes were missing.

Two cigarettes found in the attic indicated that the killer had been hiding there until the house occupants were asleep. Investigators were able to determine that the killer had murdered most of his victims without waking them, and then returned to the master bedroom to inflict further blows on Josiah and his wife's already-dead bodies.

Several suspects, including Josiah's old boss F. F. Jones, were suggested over the following weeks, and the Reverend George Kelly, a traveling minister with a reputation for being "peculiar," was brought to trial twice, resulting in one hung jury and one acquittal. Some investigators connected the crime to William Mansfield, who had been accused of similar axe murders across the country. But the murders remain a mystery. •

FIRST FLOOR

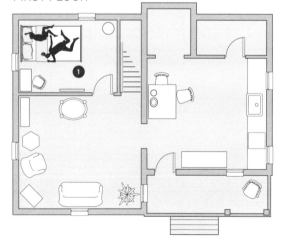

SECOND FLOOR

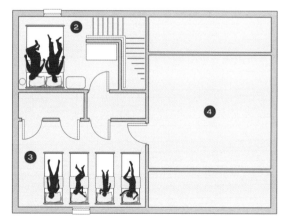

❶ GUEST BEDROOM
The room in which Ina and Lena Stillinger were murdered.

❷ MASTER BEDROOM
The room in which Josiah and Sarah Moore were murdered.

❸ CHILDREN'S BEDROOM
The room in which Herman, Mary, Arthur, and Paul Moore were murdered.

❹ ATTIC
The room in which the murderer hid, waiting for his victims to fall asleep.

BENNETT CLARK HYDE

X Thomas Swope

WEAPON	TYPOLOGY	POLICING
POISON	PROPERTY CRIME	TOXICOLOGY

406 SOUTH PLEASANT STREET, INDEPENDENCE

Thomas Swope was not your average millionaire. Though he had a law degree, he realized that there was more money in real estate and mining. After purchasing a huge amount of land in Kansas, he amassed a fortune and started calling himself "colonel," even though he had never seen military service. A lifelong bachelor, he moved into his brother's mansion and took public transportation to his Kansas City office building.

When he reached his early eighties, he began to occupy himself with the long-overdue task of arranging his estate. He was also treated by his niece's husband, Dr. Bennett Clark Hyde.

Hyde was a gentleman of questionable demeanor. He was so hated by the Swope family that Frances Swope had married him in secret, even though she knew at least one other woman was suing him on breach of promise charges. Despite this, when the will was drawn up, Frances and Dr. Hyde stood to be well provided for.

In 1909, Swope became violently ill at the Hydes' home and asked the doctor for some medicine to calm his ailing stomach. But the pills he took only made things worse. He began to convulse, even as his legs began to stiffen. In what was nearly his last breath, he reportedly said, "I wish I had not taken that medicine. I wish I were dead." Moments later, he passed away.

Dr. Hyde gave the cause of death as "apoplexy," which in those days was often used as shorthand for any sudden death. Only days before, Hyde had given the same verdict as a cause of death of James Moss Hunton, a cousin of Thomas, who had taken medicine from the doctor as well.

Frances's mother told the police she was suspicious of Dr. Hyde, and an investigation showed that Swope's remains contained strychnine. It seemed clear that the doctor had been intending to kill not just Swope, but every other relative who stood to take up a share of the inheritance, leaving a larger portion for himself.

Though taken to trial repeatedly, Dr. Hyde managed to escape on technicalities. Frances divorced him in 1920. •

↑ **ABOVE** The house belonging to Thomas Swope's brother Logan. Thomas moved to the residence in later life and died there in 1909.

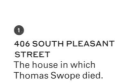

① 406 SOUTH PLEASANT STREET
The house in which Thomas Swope died.

② SWOPE PARK
A park built on land donated to the city by Thomas Swope in 1896.

MO—ST. JOSEPH	*April 3, 1882*

ROBERT FORD
✕ Jesse James

WEAPON	TYPOLOGY	POLICING
PISTOL	**REWARD**	**REWARD**

1318 LAFAYETTE STREET

Jesse James is remembered as a noble Wild West outlaw, memorialized in folk songs as a robber with "a hand and a heart and a brain." It is difficult to think of another historical figure for whom the folk songs are so far from the reality.

In reality, Frank and his brother Jesse were widely understood in their time to be Confederate terrorists who did not surrender when Robert E. Lee did. During the war, the two brothers, lifelong enslavers, joined Quantrill's Raiders, a band of guerrilla fighters who would ride into a town, kill anyone they did not think was sufficiently pro-slavery, and then ride out of town dragging the scalps of their victims behind their horses. In their later careers as the heads of a gang of train robbers, their targets were often rail companies associated with the Union cause.

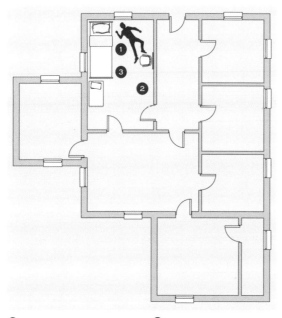

❶ JESSE JAMES
The place where Jesse James stood, dusting a picture.

❷ ROBERT FORD
The place where Robert Ford stood to shoot James from behind.

❸ CHARLEY FORD
The place where Charley Ford stood, his own revolver ready.

In 1881, Jesse and Frank wanted to retire to quieter lives, following more than a decade outside the law. After one last robbery of the Glendale train, Jesse moved his family to St. Joseph, Missouri, and attempted to settle down under the name Thomas Howard. The only old comrades he felt he could trust were two brothers, Charles and Robert Ford. Robert had been a great admirer of Jesse as a teenager and had worked his way into the outlaw's inner circle by the time he was 20. He lived with the James family in St. Joseph, sharing meals with them nightly.

But in early 1882, Robert met with Governor Crittenden, who had promised in his inaugural address that the James brothers would be captured. In trouble with the law himself, Ford was offered a full pardon and a $10,000 reward if he could assassinate Jesse. With pressure building, Ford decided to do the deed.

As word spread that a former associate was giving confessions to the authorities, Jesse was growing increasingly paranoid. After breakfast on the morning of April 3, Jesse brought Robert and his brother into the living room to discuss the recent betrayals. Noticing that a picture on the wall was dusty, Jesse turned around to clean it. In that moment, Robert drew his pistol and shot Jesse dead while his back was turned.

The Ford brothers immediately informed the governor, but were arrested and sentenced to hang later that day. They were granted a pardon hours later, but never managed to claim their reward.

As the Wild West faded into memory and legend, and the late Jesse became a figure of myth, Robert went into history as "the coward Robert Ford." He earned a living for a time re-enacting the killing of Jesse in dime museums and traveling stage shows, then opened a string of saloons across Colorado. In 1892, a man named Edward O'Kelley walked into one of Ford's saloons and shot Robert in the back, killing him just as he had killed Jesse a decade before. O'Kelley's motives have never been clear, but his gravestone identifies him as the "Man Who Killed the Man Who Killed Jesse James." •

RIGHT A studio portrait from *c.* 1870 of the infamous James-Younger Gang. Standing are Cole Younger (left) and Jesse James (right) and seated are Bob Younger (left) and Frank James (right).

RIGHT The revolver used by Robert Ford to kill Jesse James. James was shot in the back of the head while dusting a picture.

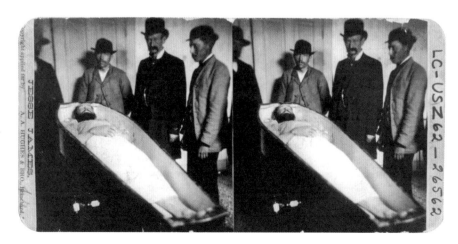

RIGHT Jesse James in his coffin. Following his death crowds pressed into the little house in St. Joseph to see the dead bandit. The house has been preserved, though it is now in a different location in St. Joseph.

"JESSE JAMES...HAS A FACE AS SMOOTH AND INNOCENT
AS THE FACE OF A SCHOOL GIRL."

JESSE JAMES, AS DESCRIBED BY HIS CONTEMPORARY
AND ADMIRER MAJOR JOHN NEWMAN EDWARDS.

FRANK (LEFT) AND JESSE (RIGHT) JAMES,
PHOTOGRAPHED IN AROUND 1865.

6 THE ROBBERY AT GALLATIN

7 THE ROBBERY AT CORYDON

8 THE ROBBERY AT COLUMBIA

9 THE ROBBERY AT KANSAS CITY

10 THE ROBBERY AT ST. GENEVIEVE

11 THE ROBBERY AT ADAIR

12 THE ROBBERY AT HOT SPRINGS

13 THE ROBBERY AT GADS HILL

14 THE ROBBERY AT CLAY COUNTY

15 THE ROBBERY AT AUSTIN

17 THE ROBBERY AT HUNTINGTON

19 THE ROBBERY AT NORTHFIELD

23 THE ROBBERY AT WINSTON

24 THE ROBBERY AT BLUE CUT

25 JAMES'S HOME IN ST. JOSEPH

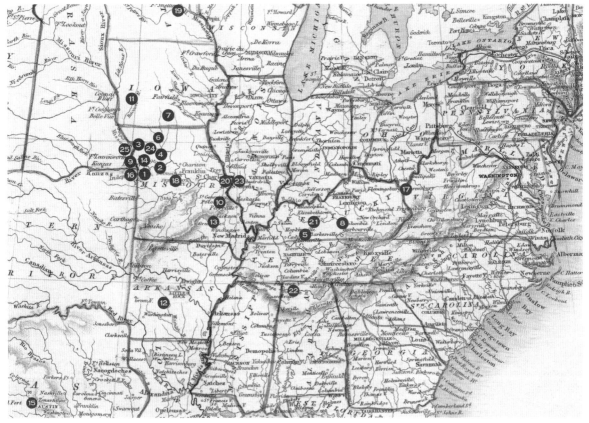

**❶ FEBRUARY 13, 1866,
LIBERTY, MO**
Clay County Savings
bank robbed of $62,000.

**❷ OCTOBER 30, 1866,
LEXINGTON, MO**
Alexander Mitchell and Co.
bank robbed of $2,000.

**❸ MARCH 2, 1867,
SAVANNAH, MO**
Judge John McClain
banking house robbed.

**❹ MAY 22, 1867,
RICHMOND, MO**
Hughes and Watson
bank robbed of $4,000.

**❺ MARCH 20, 1868,
RUSSELLVILLE, KY**
Nimrod Long Banking Co.
robbed of $14,000.

**❻ DECEMBER 7, 1869,
GALLATIN, MO**
Davies County Savings
bank robbed of $700.

**❼ JUNE 3, 1871,
CORYDON, IO**
Ocobock Brothers' bank
robbed of $6,000.

**❽ APRIL 29, 1872,
COLUMBIA, KY**
Bank of Columbia robbed of
$6,000 and the cashier killed.

**❾ SEPTEMBER 26, 1872,
KANSAS CITY, MO**
Kansas City Exposition ticket
office robbed of $8,000.

**❿ MAY 27, 1873,
ST. GENEVIEVE, MO**
St. Genevieve Savings
bank robbed of $4,100.

⓫ JULY 21, 1873, ADAIR, IO
Chicago, Rock Island, and
Pacific Railroad train robbed of
$3,000 and the engineer killed.

**⓬ JANUARY 15, 1874,
HOT SPRINGS, AR**
A stagecoach robbed
of $3,000.

**⓭ JANUARY 31, 1874, GADS HILL,
MO** St. Louis Iron Mountain
and Southern Railroad train
robbed of $12,000.

**⓮ MARCH 10, 1874
CLAY COUNTY, MO**
Pinkerton agent Joseph
Whicher shot three times.

**⓯ APRIL, 1874,
AUSTIN, TX**
A stagecoach robbed
of $3,000.

**⓰ DECEMBER 8, 1874,
MUNCIE, KA**
Kansas Pacific Railroad
train robbed of $55,000.

**⓱ SEPTEMBER 5, 1875,
HUNTINGDON, WV**
Huntington bank robbed of
between $10,000 and $20,000.

**⓲ JULY 7, 1876, ROCKEY CUT,
NEAR OTTERVILLE, MO**
Missouri-Pacific Railroad
train robbed of $15,000.

**⓳ SEPTEMBER 7, 1876,
NORTHFIELD, MN**
A failed attempt to to rob
the First National bank.

**⓴ OCTOBER 8, 1879,
GLENDALE, MO**
Chicago, Alton and St. Louis
train robbed of $10,000.

**㉑ SEPTEMBER 3, 1880,
MAMMOTH CAVE, KY**
A stagecoach robbed
of $1,800.

**㉒ MARCH 11, 1881,
MUSCLE SHOALS, AL**
A bank paymaster
robbed of $5,200.

㉓ JULY 15, 1881, WINSTON, MO
Chicago, Rock Island, and
Pacific Railroad train
robbed of $2,000.

**㉔ SEPTEMBER 7, 1881,
BLUE CUT, GLENDALE, MO**
Chicago, Alton and St. Louis
train robbed of $3,000.

**㉕ APRIL 3, 1882,
ST. JOSEPH, MO**
Jesse James killed by
Robert Ford in his own home.

MO—ST. LOUIS	*October 16, 1899*

FRANKIE BAKER
✕ Allen Britt

WEAPON	TYPOLOGY	POLICING
PISTOL	DOMESTIC	—

212 TARGEE STREET

The legend of "Frankie and Johnny" has frustrated folklorists for years. By the mid-20th century, the song of Johnny, who was Frankie's man "but he done her wrong," was a standard in folk song concerts and there was endless speculation about whether a real murder had inspired the tune. It seems to have originated with an 1899 murder in St. Louis, though the victim's name was Allen Britt, not Johnny. Perhaps "Johnny" simply sounded better in a tune. But some early versions of the tune were known as "Frankie and Albert," and before they came into print, perhaps the singers had been saying "Frankie and Al Britt."

Frankie Baker was a young woman living in a rooming house on Targee Street in St. Louis. She shared the place with her boyfriend—in some accounts her pimp—whose name was Allen Britt. Britt worked as a ragtime piano player in the many clubs around Targee Street. Baker seems to have been in love with Britt, even though she was in her mid-twenties and he was only 17. One night, after going to see him play piano in the Phoenix Hotel, she caught him in the company of a woman closer to his own age named Alice Pryor. The two commenced a loud argument in the street outside the hotel that ended with Frankie going home alone. But at 3 a.m. that night, Britt entered Baker's apartment to continue the fight. Britt had brought along a knife and when he brandished it in front of her, Frankie took a Harrington & Richardson .38 pistol that she kept under her pillow and shot him. He died in the hospital three days later; the *Post-Dispatch* reflected that "Allen Britt's brief experience in the art of love cost him his life."

Though the courts ruled that Frankie had killed Allen Britt in self defense, early versions of the song were being performed around St. Louis before Britt's body was cold, with Alice Pryor's name changed to Alice Pry, which was a lot easier to rhyme. People reportedly began singing it whenever they saw Frankie in the street. She attempted to move to Omaha, but the song had already spread there by the time she arrived. She was never able to escape the tune.

Ironically, though, she could never prove that the song was about her, despite occasional attempts to do so in court. Movies based on the song were released during her lifetime; 1935's *She Done Him Wrong* with Mae West and Cary Grant, and 1936 *Frankie and Johnnie* with Helen Morgan. Her attempts to sue brought in witnesses who testified that they had first heard the song in the streets and clubs of St. Louis only days after Britt's death. One woman even testified that she had seen Allen Britt waltzing with Alice Pryor at the Lone Star Club shortly before the shooting, and that she had heard the "ballet" only a week after Britt's death. But Frankie lost both cases.

Frankie Baker died in an Oregon institution in 1952, at the age of 75. By then Targee Street had been reduced to an alley behind an auditorium, but the song survived. •

ABOVE 212 Targee Street, St. Louis, where Frankie Baker killed Allen Britt in a domestic argument that became immortalized in the popular folk song "Frankie and Johnny."

I'LL TELL YOU THE STORY OF FRANKIE AND JOHNNY WHO LOVED THEIR LIFE AWAY

FRANKIE AND JOHNNY WERE LOVERS OHO MY GOD HOW THEY LOVED

FRANKIE WORKED DOWN IN A CRIB-HOUSE

SHE GAVE ALL HER MONEY TO JOHNNY WHO SPENT IT ON PARLORHOUSE WHORES

GAVE HER JOHNNY A HUNDRED DOLLARS TO BUY A NEW SUIT OF CLOTHES

OH MY GOD—SAID FRANKIE— DON'T MY JOHNNY LOOK CUTE?

FRANKIE WENT UP TO OGDEN SHE WENT ON THE MORNING TRAIN

SHE SAID TO THE BIG FAT BAR TENDER HAS MY LOVIN' JOHNNY BEEN HERE?

THEN UP SPOKE THE BIG FAT BARTENDER

SHE AIMED AND SHOT AT THE CEILING AND SHOT A HOLE IN THE FLOOR

IN HER YELLOW KIMONA WAS A BLUE BARRELED FORTY-FOUR GUN

STAND BACK ALL YOU PIMPS AND CHIPPIES OR I'LL BLOW YOU ALL TO HELL

THERE ON A BED WAS HER JOHNNY A LOVIN' UP NELLY BLYE

AND THE GUN WENT ROOT-I-TOOT-TOOT

TURN ME OVER TO THE RIGHT SIDE SO THE BULLET WON'T HURT ME SO!

O LORD HAVE MERCY ON ME I WISH I COULD TAKE HIS PLACE

ABOVE Woodcuts taken from *The Saga of Frankie and Johnny*, illustrated by John Held Jr., first published in 1930. Allen Britt appears as Johnny, and Alice Pryor as Nellie Blye.

NE—ODESSA		*1899*

FRANK DINSMORE

✕ Lillian Dinsmore ✕ Fred Laue

WEAPON	TYPOLOGY	POLICING
FIREARM	DOMESTIC	—
ODESSA, BUFFALO COUNTY		

NE—BOSTWICK		*1903*

NANNIE HUTCHINSON

✕ Eli Feasel

WEAPON	TYPOLOGY	POLICING
KNIFE	DOMESTIC	FOOTPRINTS
FEASEL'S FARM, SOUTHWEST OF BOSTWICK		

The dapper Frank Dinsmore called a doctor on a December night in 1899, claiming that he had heard gunshots and now his wife and roommate were dead. The police came to believe that Dinsmore had shot them himself and then attempted to make the crime scene appear like a murder-suicide. He was sentenced to hang, but as most of the evidence was circumstantial, his sentence was later commuted to life in prison. Twenty years after the killing, he was freed by Governor McKelvey. •

When neighbors stopped seeing Eli Feasel around his farm, his housekeeper, Nannie Hutchinson, told everyone that he had gone to Kansas City. Eventually, however, the neighbors became suspicious enough to investigate, and Hutchinson and her adult son, Charles, were arrested. They could not be held long, though—there was no evidence that a crime had been committed at all. But months later, investigators found hair, a whiskey bottle, and a human hand on Feasel's farm, and footprints matching Hutchinson's shoes. This time Nannie and her son were arrested and convicted. •

↑ **ABOVE** The Nebraska State Penitentiary mugshot of Frank Dinsmore.

↑ **ABOVE** The Nebraska State Penitentiary mugshot of Nannie Hutchinson.

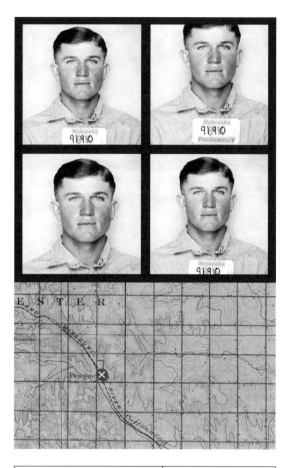

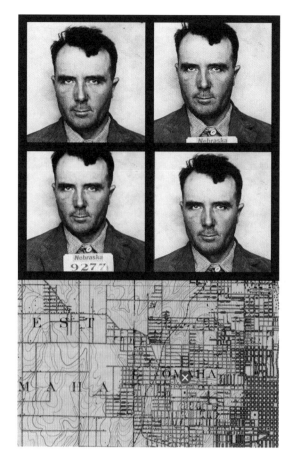

NE—PRAGUE		*1925*
ADOLPH SMETAK		
✕ John Smetak		
WEAPON	TYPOLOGY	POLICING
HAMMER	DOMESTIC	—
SMETAK'S FARM, PRAGUE		

NE—OMAHA		*1927*
FRANK CARTER		
✕ 2		
WEAPON	TYPOLOGY	POLICING
PISTOL	RANDOM ATTACK	—
OMAHA, DOUGLAS COUNTY		

Nebraska murder tales often begin with neighbors wondering why a man has not been seen around his farm. When John Smetak vanished in the summer of 1925, his son, Adolph, told people that John had gone to visit relatives. However, Adolph later confessed to having killed his father with a hammer during one of their many fights. John had been known as a violent brute and it may have been self defense, but Adolph spent fifteen years in prison for the crime. •

Although only convicted of two killings, Frank Carter tried to take the credit for more than forty. A laborer in Omaha who had done time for killing cattle, Carter committed his first known murder, of a mechanic, in 1926 using a pistol. When two other shootings followed, residents were told to stay away from their windows after dark. However, the killings continued during the day, bringing life in Omaha to a standstill until Carter was captured several weeks later. He cheerfully confessed and was executed in the electric chair in 1927. •

ABOVE The Nebraska State Penitentiary mugshot of Adolph Smetak.

ABOVE The Nebraska State Penitentiary mugshot of Frank Carter.

BENDER FAMILY
× 20 +

WEAPON	TYPOLOGY	POLICING
KNIFE & HAMMER	PROPERTY CRIME	MANHUNT

THE BENDER FARM, NORTHEAST OF CHERRYVILLE

The Bender family settled in Labette County, Kansas, in the years after the Civil War. To this day, very little is known about them. John and Elvira did not speak English, or at least pretended not to, and are presumed to have been immigrants, but no one is certain what country they came from. Some say that their adult children, John Jr. and Kate, were not their children at all, but a married couple only posing as siblings. But these are perhaps the least of the mysteries. We may also only speculate over what led the family to kill.

The Benders set up an inn, general store, and farm in the early 1870s. John Jr. and Kate, who spoke English with no accent, did most of the communicating, and Kate, who claimed to be a medium, hosted seances. A few years after they arrived, there were stories told of travelers coming to their small corner of Kansas and not returning home.

In March, 1873, Dr. William York went to Kansas to locate a neighbor who had gone missing the year before. After William went missing too, his brother came to town to take up the search, and he and the neighbors began to suspect that the Bender family had something to do with the disappearances. Realizing they were under suspicion, the Benders fled the area.

No one noticed that they were gone until a passing traveler saw that their cattle had not been eating. A posse was formed to investigate the empty building and Dr. York's body was found in a shallow grave on the property. Eventually, more than a dozen bodies were found on the farm, their throats slit and their heads bashed in. In all, the Benders were suspected of at least twenty murders. Presumably the motivation was robbery, but it is impossible to know.

A large posse formed to find them, allegedly including Charles Ingalls, who would become immortalized as "Pa" in his daughter's *Little House on the Prairie* books. For years reports circulated that some captured outlaw or con artist may have been one of the Benders, but so far as is known, they were never truly found. •

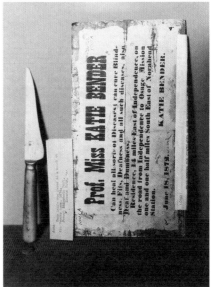

ABOVE, TOP The hammers belonging to the Bender family, with which they were believed to have killed their victims from behind.

ABOVE, BOTTOM The knife belonging to Kate Bender, and an advertisement for her skills as a medium and her ability to "heal all sorts of diseases."

JOHN BENDER SR.

ELVIRA BENDER

JOHN BENDER JR.

KATE BENDER

RIGHT Two views of the Bender cabin, captured after the Benders had fled the area.

RIGHT The Bender cabin, surrounded by spectators who had come to observe the search for bodies.

RIGHT Investigators digging a hole alongside the Bender cabin, during the search of the property for the remains of their victims.

Photographed by Julius Plooty
nnendence Kas. May. 9th 1873

McCarty's Grave;

Browns Grave

Grimmey's Grave

Jenks Grave

Old Well. Sconces Grave.

Loncher and
Little girls grave.

South West View

G. K. Gamble
Photographer
Parsons. Kan.

RIGHT Map showing where the Benders' victims were found.

1 JOHN GEARY

2 W. F. McCROTTY

3 JOHN NEWTON LONGCOR AND HIS BABY GIRL

4 JOHNNY BOYLE

5 BEN BROWN

6 HARRY McKENZIE

7 DR. YORK

8 FIVE UNIDENTIFIED BODIES FOUND IN DRUM CREEK

9 TWO UNIDENTIFIED BODIES FOUND IN THE PRAIRIE

10 TWO UNIDENTIFIED BODIES AND ASSORTED BODY PARTS ALSO FOUND IN THE ORCHARD

RIGHT Floorplan of the Bender cabin.

Where John Bender Sr. stood behind a canvas sheet to strike his victims.

Where visitors to the cabin sat before being killed from behind.

OPPOSITE, TOP
Investigators and spectators standing with the bodies found on the Bender farm, either in coffins or covered.

OPPOSITE, BOTTOM
The Bender farm, with the cabin in the background, with handwritten text indicating where the bodies of several of the Benders' victims were buried.

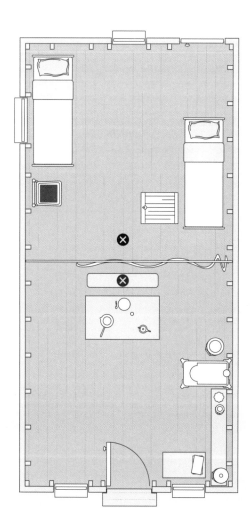

MINNIE WALLACE-WALKUP

✕ James Walkup

WEAPON	TYPOLOGY	POLICING
POISON	PROPERTY CRIME	TOXICOLOGY

EMPORIA, LYON COUNTY

Minnie Wallace, a girl from New Orleans, was only 16 when she married James Walkup, the mayor of Emporia, Kansas. Walkup had officially visited New Orleans for the World's Industrial and Cotton Centennial Exposition, but his appetite for sex workers was well documented. Minnie was the daughter of the couple who kept the boarding house where he stayed; the night after he met her he declared that he wanted to marry her. After months of bargaining, Minnie agreed. The two were married and Minnie followed him to Emporia.

After only a few months of marriage, Minnie began visiting drugstores. One of them turned down her request to purchase strychnine because she would not reveal why she wanted it, but another merely had her write her purpose in their "poison book" and did not check to see that she had left the space blank. When Walkup recovered from a malady that suggested strychnine poisoning, Minnie purchased some arsenic. When he took sick again, he told his doctors that Minnie should be arrested. When he passed away, authorities took her into custody.

It came out in court that over the years Walkup had been using several different poisons to treat various sexually transmitted diseases. Despite strong evidence against her, this was enough to give the jury, reluctant to send a teenage girl to the gallows, an excuse to find Minnie innocent.

Minnie then moved to Chicago, where she married a wealthy man named John Ketchum. Like Walkup, he was decades older than Minnie.

After moving into the fine home Minnie had purchased with money inherited from Walkup, Ketchum died less than two weeks after modifying his will to make Minnie his sole heir. Despite suspicion, the cause of death was given as alcoholism and Minnie inherited his fortune despite the objections of his family, who were not even aware of the marriage until after Ketchum's death.

To those suspicious of her habit of marrying older men, she reportedly said, "Their knowledge of life fascinates me. A man must know how to woo a woman to win me—and young men have not the experience."

Minnie was eventually brought to court for unpaid attorney's fees, but during the trial (which was settled out of court) she met De Lancy Louderback, another wealthy man, at one of the city's fashionable hotels. The two never married, but were certainly attached, and he was so in love with her that he built her a fine house on the Northwest Side. It was said to be rigged with any number of devices to allow him to spy on Minnie and to keep any other man from visiting her without his knowledge. But she never moved in—instead, she moved to London, where she sent back word that she had married. Days later, Louderback died of cyanide poisoning. The reading of his will revealed that a fourth of his estate had been left to Minnie, though word had it that he had already given most of it to her.

Minnie, never convicted of any murder, lived a quiet life until her death in 1957. •

JAMES WALKUP

JOHN KETCHUM

DE LANCY LOUDERBACK

NEW ORLEANS
Minnie was born in New Orleans.

EMPORIA
Minnie moved to Emporia with James Walkup.

CHICAGO
Minnie met John Ketchum and De Lancy Louderback in Chicago.

ABOVE An article on Minnie Wallace-Walkup from the *Washington Times*, 1918, detailing her various marriages and the home De Lancy Louderback was alleged to have built her.

BELOW The home built for Minnie Wallace-Walkup by De Lancy Louderback in Ravenswood, Chicago. Some claimed that it had a curious "house within a house" design. Minnie never moved in.

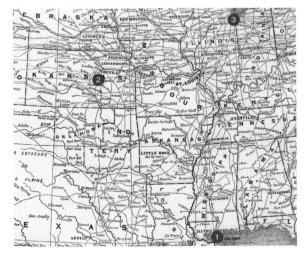

PART THREE

WASHINGTON, D.C. KENTUCKY

WEST VIRGINIA

VIRGINIA GEORGIA FLORIDA

ARKANSAS LOUISIANA

OKLAHOMA TEXAS

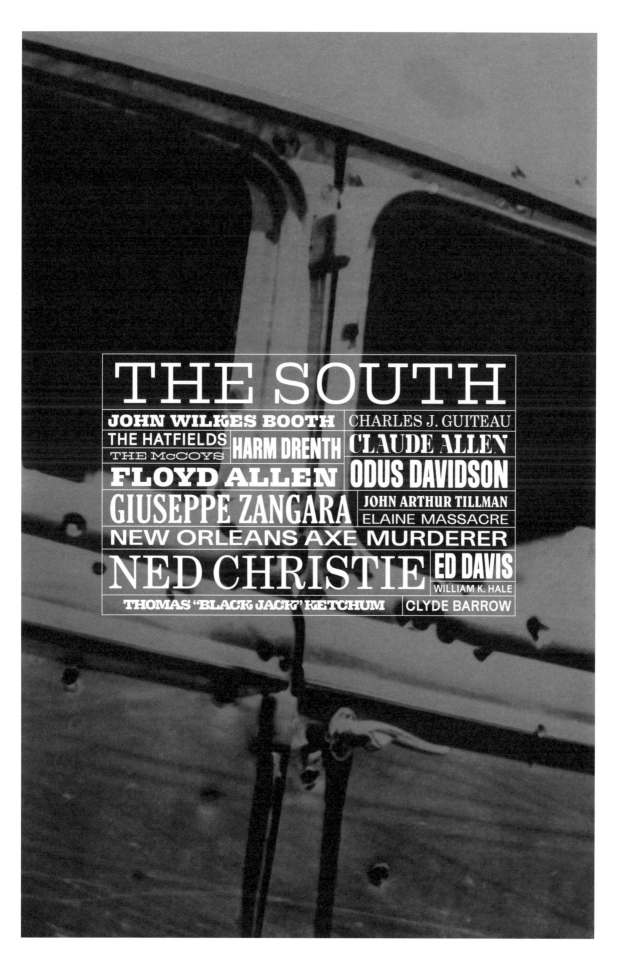

THE SOUTH

JOHN WILKES BOOTH   CHARLES J. GUITEAU
THE HATFIELDS   **HARM DRENTH**   **CLAUDE ALLEN**
THE McCOYS
FLOYD ALLEN   **ODUS DAVIDSON**
GIUSEPPE ZANGARA   JOHN ARTHUR TILLMAN
ELAINE MASSACRE
NEW ORLEANS AXE MURDERER
NED CHRISTIE   **ED DAVIS**
WILLIAM K. HALE
THOMAS "BLACK JACK" KETCHUM   CLYDE BARROW

WASHINGTON, D.C.	*April 14, 1865*	

JOHN WILKES BOOTH

✕ Abraham Lincoln

WEAPON	TYPOLOGY	POLICING
PISTOL	ASSASSINATION	MANHUNT

FORD'S THEATER, 511 TENTH STREET NORTHWEST

It is difficult to imagine a more turbulent time in American history than April, 1865. After four years of a bloody Civil War that had ravaged the country, killing hundreds of thousands, the Union finally took Richmond, the Confederate capitol, on April 3, after President Jefferson Davis and his army fled. On April 9, Confederate General Robert E. Lee surrendered, effectively ending the war. On April 11, Lincoln gave a celebratory speech, mentioning the impending end of slavery and alluding to a future in which some Black men would even be voting.

In the crowd that day stood John Wilkes Booth. Furious at the notion of anyone but white men voting, he turned to a friend and vowed, "That is the last speech he will ever give."

BELOW Contemporary engravings illustrating the assassination of President Lincoln (above), and the president on his death bed (below).

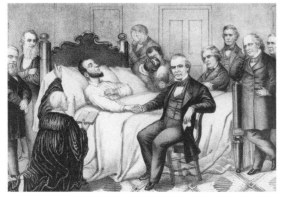

Booth had never joined the Confederate army, but had spent the war years touring the North as an actor, primarily in Shakespearean roles. Some critics felt that he was a genius. But he was not as famous, or as respected, as his brother Edwin, the most acclaimed American actor of the era. Some believe that it was rivalry with his Union-loyalist brother that fueled Booth's rage against Lincoln. Others think that it was racial animosity, or simple disappointment that the South had lost the war. In any case, several smaller motivations coalesced into a visceral hatred of President Lincoln.

Drawing a few others into a conspiracy, Booth initially planned to kidnap the president and and take him to Richmond, where he would be exchanged for thousands of Confederate prisoners. But with the fall of Richmond, the plan fell apart and morphed to an assassination plot. Booth was to kill the president; other conspirators were set to attack Vice President Andrew Johnson and Secretary of State William Seward (Seward was stabbed, but recovered; the assassin scheduled to kill Johnson failed to attack).

On April 14, Booth learned that Lincoln would be attending a performance of "Our American Cousin," a broad comedy, at Ford's Theater, a short carriage ride from the White House. Booth had acted there often enough to know the stagehands, and even sometimes had his mail sent there. He was also familiar enough with the show to know that there would be a big, loud laugh at a line about a "sockdologizing old man trap." Sneaking into the unguarded president's booth, he waited for that line, then fired a fatal shot into Lincoln's head.

After struggling with Major Rathbone, the president's guest, Booth jumped onto the stage and by most accounts shouted, "*Sic Semper Tyranis*," (thus always to tyrants), the state motto of Virginia, before running out the back door to a waiting horse.

The nation, still buzzing from the celebrations that followed Lee's surrender, turned to mourning. Lincoln was given an elaborate cross-country funeral before he was interred in his hometown of Springfield, Illinois.

BELOW, LEFT The box at Ford's Theater where President Lincoln was assassinated, captured the day after the murder. Lincoln was accompanied by his wife, Henry Rathbone, and Rathbone's fiancée Clara Harris.

BELOW, TOP RIGHT The Derringer gun used by John Wilkes Booth to assassinate Abraham Lincoln. Booth shot Lincoln once, the bullet entering his head behind his left ear. He died the following day.

BELOW, BOTTOM RIGHT The horn-handled dagger used by John Wilkes Booth to stab Henry Rathbone in the left forearm, after shooting Abraham Lincoln. Booth then jumped to the stage to make his escape.

But as funeral preparations were put underway and Vice President Andrew Johnson was sworn in as president (an event for which he was reportedly quite drunk), Booth made his escape. Joined by a co-conspirator named David Herold, Booth rode through the night, arriving at the home of Dr. Samuel Mudd in southern Maryland before dawn. Mudd tended to a leg that Booth had broken, either in the jump from Lincoln's box or in his subsequent flight. News had not yet traveled to Mudd's home; Mudd was an enslaver who knew of Booth's earlier kidnapping plot, but was unaware that his friend had just murdered the president. When he learned it from the papers in the morning, he ordered Booth and Herold to leave. The fact that he did not turn them in led to a conspiracy charge for which he was sentenced to life in prison (though he was pardoned by President Johnson in 1869).

Booth hid in Zekiah Swamp for four days, where an accomplice brought him food and news. With help from other supporters, he was able to cross the Potomac and Rappahannock Rivers and make his way into Virginia undetected.

Eventually, Booth and Herold disguised themselves as Confederate soldiers making their way home from their defeat and were sheltering in a barn on a tobacco farm in Port Royal, Virginia, when they were tracked down by Union soldiers. Herold surrendered, but Booth remained in the barn. Soldiers set fire to it to smoke him out, but Booth remained inside until Boston Corbett, a Union troop, fired a bullet that went right through a crack in the barn wall and into Booth's body. His body was taken to a penitentiary burial ground in Washington, D.C., then moved to a family plot in Baltimore four years later. •

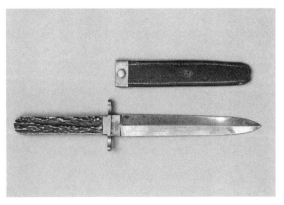

SAMUEL ARNOLD
CONSPIRATOR
LIFE IN
PRISON

LEWIS POWELL
ATTACKED WILLIAM SEWARD
EXECUTED

EDMUND SPANGLER
FORD THEATER STAGEHAND
SIX YEARS OF
HARD LABOR

GEORGE ATZERODT
FAILED ATTACK ON
ANDREW JOHNSON
EXECUTED

JOHN WILKES BOOTH
KILLED ABRAHAM LINCOLN
SHOT

MICHAEL O'LAUGHLEN
CONSPIRATOR
LIFE IN
PRISON

MARY SURRATT
CONSPIRATOR
EXECUTED

JOHN SURRATT
CONSPIRATOR
MISTRIAL

DAVID HEROLD
CONSPIRATOR
EXECUTED

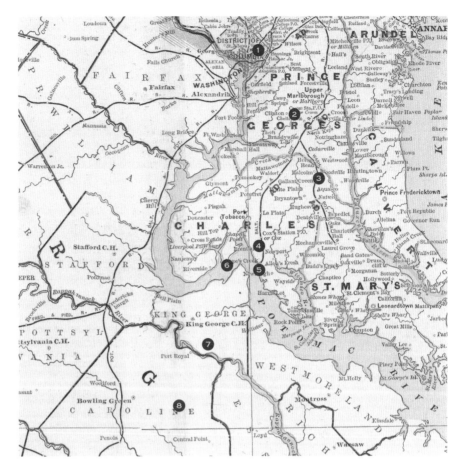

1 2 — APRIL 14

3 — APRIL 15

4 5 — APRIL 16

6 — APRIL 22

7 — APRIL 23

8 — APRIL 24

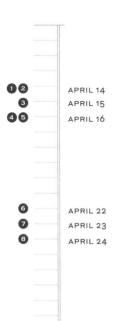

① FORD'S THEATER
The theater in Washington, D.C. where John Wilkes Booth shot Abraham Lincoln.

② SURRATT TAVERN
The home of Mary Surratt, where John Wilkes Booth and David Herold went after the assassination to collect binoculars and rifles.

③ THE HOME OF DR. MUDD
The home of Dr. Samuel Mudd, where John Wilkes Booth received medical attention.

④ THE HOME OF SAMUEL COX
The home of Samuel Cox, who agreed to help John Wilkes Booth and David Herold, but hid them in the woods rather than in his property.

⑤ WOODS
The woods near the home of Samuel Cox, where John Wilkes Booth and David Herold hid between April 16 and 21.

⑥ COL. HUGHES' HOME
The conspirators attempted to cross the Potomac River but instead ended up in Nanjemoy Creek.

⑦ WILLIAM LUCAS'S FARM
After successfully crossing the Potomac River the conspirators hid in the cabin of William Lucas.

⑧ RICHARD GARRETT'S FARM
The conspirators hid at Richard Garrett's farm for two nights before being caught and killed by Union soldiers on April 26.

SURRAT.   BOOTH.   HAROLD.

War Department, Washington, April 20, 1865,

$100,000 REWARD!

THE MURDERER

Of our late beloved President, Abraham Lincoln,

IS STILL AT LARGE.

$50,000 REWARD

Will be paid by this Department for his apprehension, in addition to any reward offered by Municipal Authorities or State Executives.

$25,000 REWARD

Will be paid for the apprehension of JOHN H. SURRATT, one of Booth's Accomplices.

$25,000 REWARD

Will be paid for the apprehension of David C. Harold, another of Booth's accomplices.

LIBERAL REWARDS will be paid for any information that shall conduce to the arrest of either of the above-named criminals, or their accomplices.

All persons harboring or secreting the said persons, or either of them, or aiding or assisting their concealment or escape, will be treated as accomplices in the murder of the President and the attempted assassination of the Secretary of State, and shall be subject to trial before a Military Commission and the punishment of DEATH.

Let the stain of innocent blood be removed from the land by the arrest and punishment of the murderers.

All good citizens are exhorted to aid public justice on this occasion. Every man should consider his own conscience charged with this solemn duty, and rest neither night nor day until it be accomplished.

EDWIN M. STANTON, Secretary of War.

DESCRIPTIONS.—BOOTH is Five Feet 7 or 8 inches high, slender build, high forehead, black hair, black eyes, and wears a heavy black moustache.

JOHN H. SURRAT is about 5 feet, 9 inches. Hair rather thin and dark; eyes rather light; no beard. Would weigh 145 or 150 pounds. Complexion rather pale and clear, with color in his cheeks. Wore light clothes of fine quality. Shoulders square; cheek bones rather prominent; chin narrow; ears projecting at the top; forehead rather low and square, but broad. Parts his hair on the right side; neck rather long. His lips are firmly set. A slim man.

DAVID C. HAROLD is five feet six inches high, hair dark, eyes dark, eyebrows rather heavy, full face, nose short, hand short and fleshy, feet small, instep high, round bodied, naturally quick and active, slightly closes his eyes when looking at a person.

NOTICE.—In addition to the above, State and other authorities have offered rewards amounting to almost one hundred thousand dollars, making an aggregate of about TWO HUNDRED THOUSAND DOLLARS.

OPPOSITE The hanging of Mary Surratt, Lewis Powell, David Herold, and George Atzerodt on July 7, 1865. They were tried by a military tribunal, and the seven-week trial included the testimony of 366 witnesses.

LEFT A wanted poster issued for John Wilkes Booth and two of his accomplices, John Surratt and David Herold (misspelled Harold). Booth and Herold were on the run for twelve days, but John Surratt fled to Canada and then Europe, before being arrested in Egypt in November, 1866. In 1867 he was released after a mistrial.

WASHINGTON, D.C.	*July 1, 1881*

CHARLES GUITEAU
X James Garfield

WEAPON	TYPOLOGY	POLICING
REVOLVER	ASSASSINATION	—

BALTIMORE AND POTOMAC RAILROAD STATION

Charles Guiteau failed his way through life. As a young man, he joined a free love sect called the Oneida Community, but they had to revise their belief that anyone could be in love with anyone else after they met the unloveable Charles. Drifting to Chicago, he worked as a fake preacher and fake lawyer before turning to the last refuge of a scoundrel: politics.

In the 1880 presidential election, congressman James Garfield shocked everyone by becoming the nominee of the Republican party. When Garfield defeated Winfield Scott Hancock for the presidency that November, Charles Guiteau believed that the small handful of speeches he had made supporting Garfield had been the deciding factor and began writing letters and appearing at the White House requesting to be made consul to Paris. This was a job for which he was completely unqualified and Secretary of State James Blaine personally asked Charles to stop bringing it up.

Garfield, by most accounts, was a promising president. A Civil War veteran and still a young man at 49, he was a great orator and a champion of civil rights. There is a good chance that he may have become a memorable leader in what was generally an age of forgettable presidents.

But just a few months into his term, Guiteau trailed the new president to a railway station, stepped up behind him, and shot him twice in the back with an ivory-gripped revolver that he had chosen because he thought it would eventually look good on display in a museum. Garfield was rushed away and Guiteau was captured at once.

In court, Guiteau claimed that it was the doctors, not the bullet, who killed Garfield, and not unreasonably. Garfield lingered for eleven weeks, receiving questionable care, before dying. But the jury found Guiteau guilty and he was hanged in 1882. On the scaffold, he sang a song he had written called "I Am Going to the Lordy." It was even worse than it sounds. •

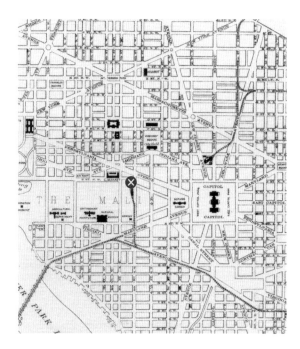

ABOVE An illustration of the revolver, and one of its bullets, used to assassinate James Garfield.

OPPOSITE, TOP A depiction of Charles Guiteau shooting James Garfield at the station.

LEFT The location of the railway station where Charles Guiteau shot James Garfield.

OPPOSITE, BOTTOM James Garfield died eleven weeks after being shot.

ABOVE James Garfield being treated by doctors following the shooting.

ABOVE Charles Guiteau being escorted into court, accused of murder.

ABOVE Charles Guiteau during his trial, which became a media sensation.

ABOVE Charles Guiteau in jail, where he wrote his poem "I am going to the Lordy."

ABOVE The execution of Charles Guiteau, which he apparently attended smiling.

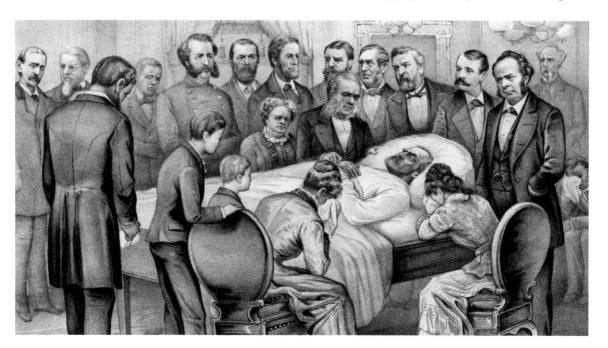

"DEVIL ANSE" HATFIELD   RANDOLPH McCOY

During the 20th century, a reference to the Hatfields and the McCoys could be used to mean any battle between rival factions of hillbillies—the names alone conjure up images of rough-hewn men in overalls, stalking barefoot through the swamp with shotguns pointed at their foes. However, there really was a war between the two families on the Tug Fork of the Big Sandy River, along the Kentucky–West Virginia border, beginning with a murder during the Civil War and extending through the last decades of the 19th century.

William "Devil Anse" Hatfield was the patriarch of a large family and, though he looked very much like a backwoods mountain-man who had just crawled out of a bluegrass murder ballad, he was really a very successful timber merchant. Nearby lived the McCoy family, led by Randolph McCoy, who was not as prosperous as Hatfield, but owned

ABOVE The grave of Calvin Cal McCoy, Randolph McCoy's son, killed in a raid on their home on New Year's Night, 1888. Randolph's daughter Allaphare was also killed.

quite a bit of land. Lucrative moonshine stills probably enriched both families.

Most of the members of each family who served in the Civil War had fought for the Confederacy. But Kentucky and West Virginia were both border states that officially remained loyal to the Union, and Randolph's brother, Asa McCoy, chose to fight for the North. He was mustered out of service in 1864 and shortly after returning home was killed by the Logan Wildcats, a militia group that counted "Devil Anse" Hatfield among its members.

Though the murder could be seen as the start of the feud, most historians see it as more of an isolated incident, one that may have contributed to the animosity, but did not ignite the war itself. The war truly began more than a decade later in 1878, when Randolph McCoy accused Floyd Hatfield of stealing one of his hogs. A witness who appeared in Floyd's favor, and was married into the Hatfield family, was later killed by the McCoys.

In 1882, three of "Devil Anse" Hatfield's brothers fought with three of Randolph McCoy's sons, and Ellison Hatfield was stabbed in the back and shot dead. A group of vengeful Hatfields rounded up the three McCoys, bound them to bushes, and filled them with bullets. To the McCoys' horror, the Hatfields eluded arrest.

By the end of the 1880s, the story of the two families was being retold in major newspapers and the Hatfield–McCoy War became a part of American legend. In 1889, several Hatfields were sentenced to life in prison, and when one of their supporters (possibly the son of Ellison Hatfield) was hanged, thousands of spectators came to watch. By then, the feud had claimed a dozen lives.

After the sentencing in 1891, the feud ended when Aaron Hatfield married Mary McCoy. "Devil Anse" Hatfield found religion (though he continued to make moonshine) and Randolph McCoy became a ferry operator. Though an official truce between the families was not made until 2003, in 1979 descendants of the two came together to compete against one another on the television show *Family Feud*. The Hatfields won. •

ABOVE Tug Fork of Big Sandy River, where much of the war between the Hatfields and the McCoys took place. On the left is West Virginia, and on the right is Kentucky.

THE HATFIELD FAMILY

1 OCK DAMRON
2 ELIAS HATFIELD
3 TROY HATFIELD
4 ROSE HATFIELD
5 JOE HATFIELD
6 CAP HATFIELD
7 W. B. BORDEN
8 TENIS HATFIELD
9 "DEVIL ANSE" HATFIELD
10 LOUVICY HATFIELD
11 WILLIS HATFIELD

THE McCOY FAMILY

1 UNKNOWN
2 UNKNOWN
3 UNKNOWN
4 TOPHER McCOY (POSS.)
5 PHARMER McCOY (POSS.)
6 RANDOLPH McCOY JR. (POSS.)

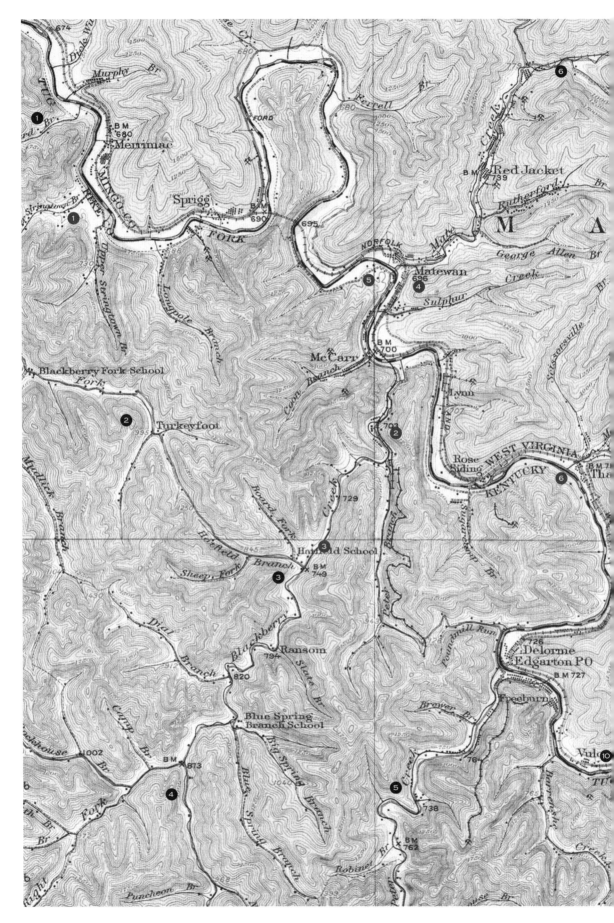

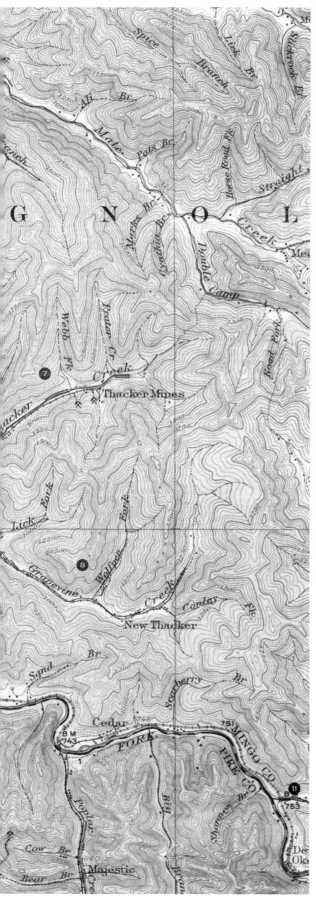

HOMES OF KEY PEOPLE

 ①

BETTY McCOY
The home of Betty McCoy.

②

RANDOLPH McCOY
The home of Randolph McCoy, and scene of the 1888 New Year's Night Massacre.

③

"PREACHER ANSE" HATFIELD
The home of "Preacher Anse" Hatfield.

④

"BAD LIAS" HATFIELD
The home of "Bad Lias" Hatfield.

⑤

ASA HARMON McCOY
The home of Asa Harmon McCoy, killed in 1865 by the Logan Wildcats.

⑥

ELLISON HATFIELD
The home of Ellison Hatfield, killed in a brawl in 1882.

⑦

WILLIAM "DEVIL ANSE" HATFIELD
The home of William "Devil Anse" Hatfield, patriarch of the Hatfield family.

⑧

JOHNSE HATFIELD
The home of Johnse Hatfield.

⑨

CAP HATFIELD
The home of Cap Hatfield, who killed Jeff McCoy in 1886.

⑩

ELIAS HATFIELD
The home of Elias Hatfield.

⑪

VALENTINE HATFIELD
The home of Valentine Hatfield.

PLACES OF INTEREST

①

FLOYD HATFIELD'S HOG PEN
A dispute over the ownership of a hog occurred in c. 1878 when Randolph McCoy claimed one of Floyd Hatfield's hogs was his, claiming that the notches on the pig's ears were McCoy, not Hatfield, marks.

 ②

BLACKBERRY CREEK
The creek was the scene of an election day brawl on August 8, 1882, in which Ellison Hatfield was mortally wounded.

③

WARM HOLLOW
Following the fight Ellison Hatfield was taken to the home of Anderson Ferrel, where he died from his twenty-six stab wounds and one gunshot wound.

 ④

LOG HOUSE SCHOOL
The house where Tolbert, Pharmer, and Randolph McCoy Jr. were held prisoner before being executed by the Hatfields.

⑤

TUG FORK, KENTUCKY SIDE
The location where William "Devil Anse" Hatfield tied Tolbert, Pharmer, and Randolph McCoy Jr. to pawpaw bushes and executed them.

 ⑥

TUG FORK
In 1886, Jeff McCoy killed mail carrier Fred Wolford and was pursued for the crime by Acting Constable Cap Hatfield. Cap and a friend named Tom Wallace shot Jeff while he was on the run on the riverbank.

 ⑦

NEAR JIM VANCE'S HOME
Following the 1888 New Year's Night Massacre a posse rode out to track down the Hatfield group. The posse's first victim was Jim Vance, who was killed in the woods after he refused to be arrested.

 ⑧

GRAPEVINE CREEK
The site of a battle between the Hatfields and the posse. The Hatfields were eventually apprehended, and eight of them were indicted for killing Allaphare McCoy during the New Year's Night Massacre.

HARM DRENTH
×5

WEAPON	TYPOLOGY	POLICING
VARIOUS	PROPERTY CRIME	CRIME SCENE INVESTIGATION

FARM OUTSIDE OF QUIET DELL

Exactly how many people Harm Drenth killed in his basement will never truly be known. When five bodies were dug up in his yard, Drenth refused to answer questions about the other suspected victims, reportedly saying only, "You've got me on five, what good would fifty more do?"

Drenth, also known as Harry Powers, was a used furniture dealer by trade, but it seems that he made a far greater living by marrying wealthy widows, then taking them home to West Virginia to murder them. The killings were said to have been carried out in his own "garage" where he had constructed a veritable dungeon, complete with trap doors and a noose.

In 1931, police were investigating the disappearance of a Park Ridge, Illinois, woman named Asta Eicher, and her three children. After some love letters were traced back to him, Drenth was arrested. Near his home, they found the blood-stained dungeon. Asta and her children were unearthed from a ditch on Drenth's property, along with the body of a 50-year-old woman, Dorothy Lemke, who had been strangled with a belt and buried with it still around her neck. Crowds gathered to watch the property excavated; one man even tried to sell tickets. Photos show large jovial crowds in and around the "garage," including a couple standing inside holding toddlers on their hips.

Though Drenth was suspected of several other disappearances, only those five bodies were uncovered at the property. Authorities saved him from a lynch mob, but held his trial in an opera house in order to accommodate all of the spectators who wanted to watch. Drenth was convicted of murder and given the death penalty. He was hanged in West Virginia State Penitentiary in 1932. He was later the inspiration for "Harry Powell," the murderous preacher in the Davis Grubb novel *Night of the Hunter*, who was played by Robert Mitchum in the classic 1955 film adaptation. •

ABOVE Asta Eicher and her three children, Harry, Annabel, and Greta, all killed by Harm Drenth and discovered buried on his property.

ABOVE Harm Drenth during questioning. He sustained black eyes and bruising after his arrest, allegedly from falling down the stairs.

RIGHT The store in Broad Oaks, Clarksburg, owned by Harm Drenth.

RIGHT Crowds of spectators surrounding Harm Drenth's garage, searched by police during the investigation into the disappearance of Asta Eicher and her children.

RIGHT Crowds of onlookers on Harm Drenth's property. The excavation of the property attracted enormous crowds, eager to see the scene of the gruesome killings.

ABOVE The exterior of Harm Drenth's garage, in which it was believed he killed Dorothy Lemke, as well as Asta Eicher and her children.

ABOVE The interior of Harm Drenth's garage, which was eagerly descended upon by reporters while the property was excavated.

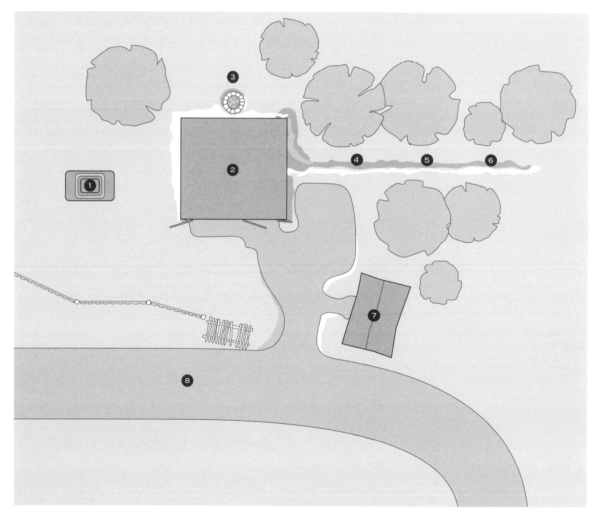

1
CHIMNEY
A ruined chimney in which bones were found.

2
GARAGE
The garage in which the victims were murdered.

3
WELL
An old well found on the property filled with stones.

4
DITCH, LOCATION 1
The place where Dorothy Lemke's body was found.

5
DITCH, LOCATION 2
The place where the bodies of the Eicher children were found.

6
DITCH, LOCATION 3
The place where Asta Eicher's body was found.

7
SHACK
An old shack also on the farm property.

8
DIRT ROAD
The road leading to Quiet Dell, less than a mile away.

ABOVE Harm Drenth being led into his trial.
The trial was held in an opera house due to
the number of spectators.

"A VOLCANIC AND BRUTAL PASSION LIES BENEATH
THE SURFACE OF HIS OUTWARDLY PLEASANT PERSONALITY."

LAWYER BARRETT O'HARA, WHO VISITED HARM DRENTH IN HIS CELL.

BACK PAGE, SHEET MUSIC FOR *THE CRIME AT QUIET DELL*, 1931, FEATURING SCENES FROM THE INVESTIGATION.

FLOYD ALLEN, CLAUDE ALLEN

×5

WEAPON	TYPOLOGY	POLICING
PISTOL	ESCAPE ATTEMPT	MANHUNT

CARROLL COUNTY COURTHOUSE

FLOYD ALLEN · CLAUDE ALLEN

It seems as though no one ever had a nice thing to say about Floyd Allen. Born in Cana, Virginia, in 1856, by the 20th century he was the patriarch of a large southern family. Quick to turn violent when anyone injured his pride, he was involved in several assaults throughout the late 1800s. One judge described him as "Brutal...with...no regard for human life." He was charged with several crimes, but escaped indictment because witnesses were afraid to testify against him. Stories of him beating assault charges through his connections in the community, and of taking revenge on those who brought the charges, were legion.

In 1910, a brawl during a church service saw one of Allen's nephews attacked by a man who had seen the nephew kissing his girlfriend. The nephew and his brother were charged with disorderly conduct and fled to North Carolina. When they were arrested and returned to Virginia, Floyd met the carriage and pistol-whipped the deputy.

After a year of delays and rumors of intimidating witnesses, Floyd Allen was brought to trial for assaulting the deputy and attempting to free his nephews in March, 1912. When the judge sentenced him to a year in prison, Allen said something to the effect of "I ain't a-going." Then the shots broke out.

Exactly who fired first is somewhat disputed, but at some point in the fracas, Allen drew a pistol and began to fire. Then his family, who were present, began to shoot their own weapons. By the end of the shootout, at least fifty shots and been fired; the judge, the sheriff, the jury foreman, a commonwealth's attorney, and a young woman who had testified against Allen had been mortally wounded. Floyd had been shot in the hip and was arrested, but it was months before all of his family could be tracked down and arrested for their role in the shootout. Floyd and his son, Claude, were both electrocuted in prison in 1913. Other family members were sentenced to long prison terms. •

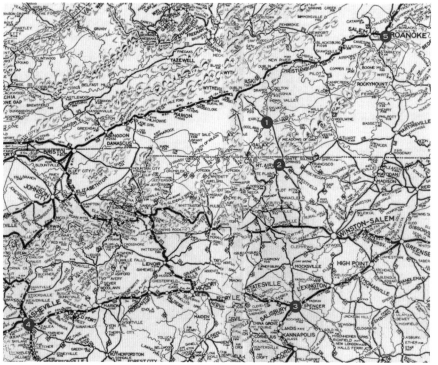

 CARROLL COUNTY COURTHOUSE, HILLSVILLE
The location of the courthouse shootout, in which five people were mortally wounded.

 MOUNT AIRY
On the run, Sidna Allen and Wesley Edwards passed through Mount Airy.

 SALISBURY
Sidna Allen and Wesley Edwards walked to Salisbury, where they purchased train tickets to Asheville.

 ASHEVILLE
From Asheville Sidna Allen and Wesley Edwards went to Des Moines, Iowa.

 ROANOKE
A tip-off allowed detectives to arrest Sidna Allen and Wesley Edwards in Des Moines and take them to Roanoke jail.

RIGHT Sidna Allen and
Wesley Edwards after their
capture by the Baldwin-Felts
Detective Agency, hired to
track down the fugitives
who went on the run
following the shootout.
The detective Billy Baldwin
can be seen in the doorway.

RIGHT The body of Floyd
Allen, who was immediately
captured following the
courthouse shootout, as
he was shot in the hip
and unable to escape.

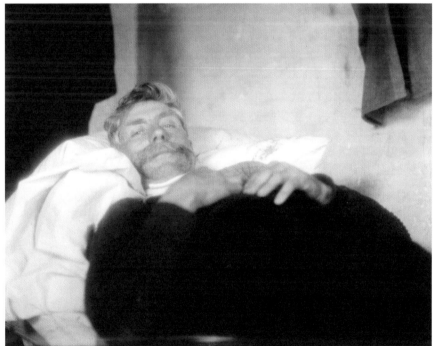

FRIEL ALLEN
FLOYD ALLEN'S NEPHEW
**18 YEARS IN
PRISON**

SIDNA EDWARDS
FLOYD ALLEN'S NEPHEW
**15 YEARS IN
PRISON**

SIDNA ALLEN
FLOYD ALLEN'S BROTHER
**35 YEARS IN
PRISON**

WESLEY EDWARDS
FLOYD ALLEN'S NEPHEW
**27 YEARS IN
PRISON**

UNKNOWN, ATTRIB. LEO FRANK

× Mary Phagan

WEAPON	TYPOLOGY	POLICING
CORD	SEXUAL	FORENSICS

THE NATIONAL PENCIL COMPANY, 37–41 SOUTH FORSYTH STREET

In April 1913, after being laid off from the pencil factory where she worked, 13-year-old Mary Phagan went to the factory to claim her final paycheck, amounting to just over one dollar.

Before dawn the next morning, a night watchman found her body near an incinerator in the factory basement, covered in ash from the dirty floor. Her face was scratched and bruised, and a wrapping cord was tied tightly around her neck. There were signs of sexual assault.

Called to the scene, police found several clues. A door to the alley rigged to open without being unlocked. Bloody fingerprints. A trail of footprints leading to the elevator shaft. And a pair of vaguely coherent notes referencing a "negro boy," which led police to arrest Newt Lee, the night watchman, as their first suspect.

But the evidence was incomplete. This did not usually pose a problem for Georgia police officers who suspected a Black man of murdering a white woman in 1913, but in this case they continued their investigation.

On the first morning of the investigation, the police contacted Leo Frank, who had an office on the second floor of the factory. Frank, a Jewish man who had grown up in New York, said that he was not sure he even knew Mary Phagan, but agreed to view her body at the morgue and to accompany the police around the factory. Though he was not considered a suspect at the time, they noted that he seemed nervous.

In the coming days, the police began to zero in on Frank as their main suspect, and Frank found himself being asked to prove that he had no cuts or wounds on his body, or bloodstains on his clothes. After a coroner's inquest, both Frank and nightwatchman Lee were ordered to be detained.

At the trial, most of the evidence came down to the testimony of Robert Conley, a janitor who claimed that Frank had executed the murder and offered him money to dispose of the body. It was a rather unlikely story on the surface and it changed substantially every time Conley told it, but it satisfied the police and the press, and the public, many of whom believed that Frank was using his connections in the Jewish community to buy the police off. After a messy trial, a jury convicted Frank and sentenced him to hang.

Two years later his sentence was commuted to life in prison due to the evidence against his guilt, but a lynch mob kidnapped him from prison and executed him themselves. Decades later, the story became an anti-semitic blight on the reputation of the South and more evidence emerged suggesting that Conley was the real murderer. Frank was granted a posthumous pardon in 1986. •

ABOVE Reconstruction photographs of the crime. The first two show Mary Phagan in the factory; the second two show her being pushed down a trapdoor and into the basement.

ROBERT CONLEY

LEO FRANK

①
LEO FRANK'S OFFICE
Leo Frank's office on the second floor of the pencil factory.

②
LATHE
Near the lathe in the factory some hair was found by investigators.

③
INCINERATOR
Mary Phagan's body was found in the basement of the factory, near the incinerator.

④
BASEMENT
Mary Phagan's hat and slipper were found near her body.

⑤
ELEVATOR SHAFT
Mary Phagan's parasol was found in the basement, near the elevator shaft.

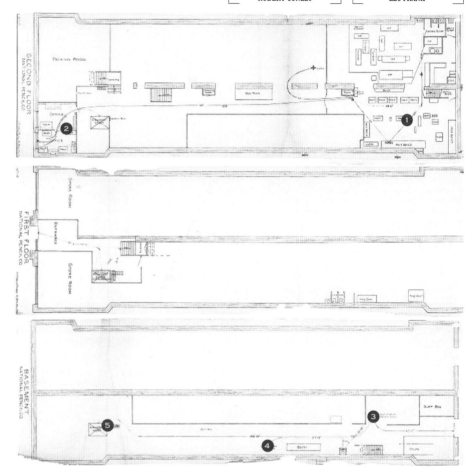

ABOVE These photographs, commissioned by *New York Times* publisher Adolph S. Ochs, attempted to implicate Conley, showing him assaulting and strangling Mary Phagan.

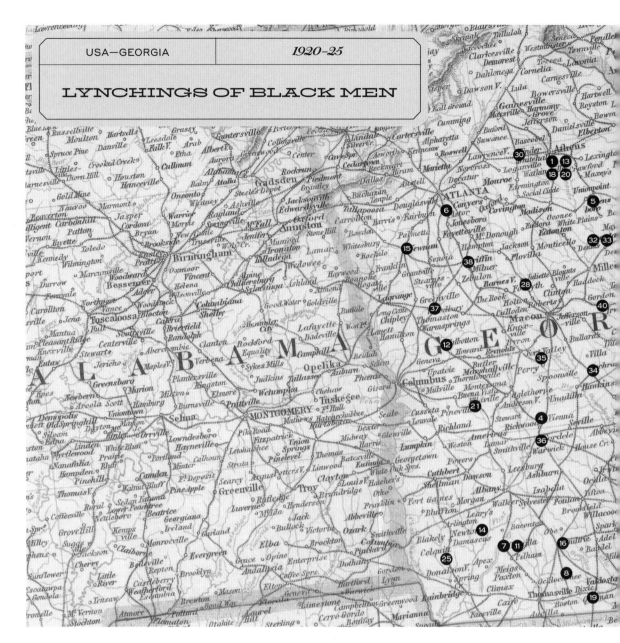

❶ December, 1921
OCONEE COUNTY
✕ GEORGE LOWE

❷ June, 1920
RINCON, EFFINGHAM
COUNTY
✕ PHILIP GAITHERS

❸ August, 1920
EMANUEL COUNTY
✕ JOHN GRANT

❹ September, 1920
DOOLY COUNTY
✕ BOB WHITEHEAD

❺ September, 1920
GREENE COUNTY
✕ FELIX CREMER

❻ September, 1920
FULTON COUNTY
✕ GEORGE KING

❼ November, 1920
MITCHELL COUNTY
✕ CURLEY McKELVEY

❽ November, 1920
PAVO, THOMAS COUNTY
✕ UNKNOWN

❾ November, 1920
DOUGLAS, COFFEE
COUNTY
✕ WILLIAM PERRY

❿ November, 1920
DOUGLAS, COFFEE
COUNTY
✕ WILLIE IVORY

⓫ January, 1921
MITCHELL COUNTY
✕ JAMES ROLAND

⓬ January, 1921
TALBOTTON,
TALBOT COUNTY
✕ SAMUEL WILLIAMS

⓭ February, 1921
OCONEE COUNTY
✕ JOHN LEE
EBERHARDT

⓮ March, 1921
BAKER COUNTY
✕ WILLIAM ANDERSON

⓯ May, 1921
COWETA COUNTY
✕ RAWLS ROSS

⓰ June, 1921
MOULTRIE,
COLQUITT COUNTY
✕ JOHN HENRY
WILLIAMS

⓱ August, 1921
RICHMOND COUNTY
✕ WALKER SMALLEY

⓲ December, 1921
OCONEE COUNTY
✕ GEORGE LOWE

⓳ December, 1921
BROOKS COUNTY
✕ LEE ROBINSON JR.

⓴ December, 1921
OCONEE COUNTY
✕ WES HALE

㉑ February, 1922
ELLAVILLE,
SCHLEY COUNTY
✕ WILLIAM JONES

㉒ March, 1922
HARLEM, COLUMBIA
COUNTY
✕ ALFRED WILLIAMS

㉓ May, 1922
DAVIDSBORO,
WASHINGTON
COUNTY
✕ CHARLES ATKINS

㉔ May, 1922
BRENTWOOD,
WAYNE COUNTY
✕ WILLIAM BYRD

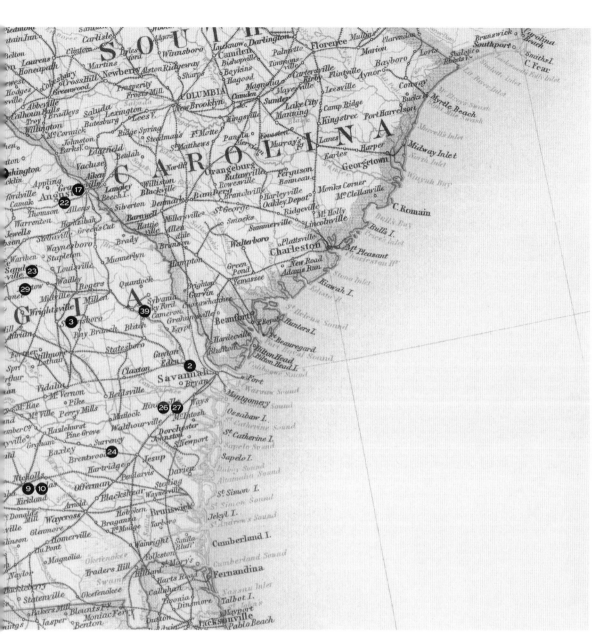

25 July, 1922
COLQUITT,
MILLER COUNTY
✕ JAKE DAVIS

26 July, 1922
LIBERTY COUNTY
✕ JAMES HARVEY

27 July, 1922
LIBERTY COUNTY
✕ JOSEPH JORDAN

28 August, 1922
MONROE COUNTY
✕ JOHN GLOVER

29 September, 1922
WASHINGTON COUNTY
✕ JAMES JOHNSON

30 September, 1922
WINDER, BARROW
COUNTY
✕ JIM REED LONG

31 December, 1922
WILKES COUNTY
✕ **M. B. Burnett**

32 February, 1923
HANCOCK COUNTY
✕ CLINTON CHAMBERS

33 February, 1923
HANCOCK COUNTY
✕ GEORGE BUTTS

34 August, 1923
COCHRAN,
BLECKLEY COUNTY
✕ AARON HARRIS

35 August, 1923
WELLSTON,
HOUSTON COUNTY
✕ LEE GREEN

36 March, 1924
CORDELE, CRISP
COUNTY
✕ JOHN HAYES

37 April, 1924
WOODBURY,
MERIWETHER COUNTY
✕ BEACH THRASH

38 June, 1924
SPALDING COUNTY
✕ MARCUS
WESTMORELAND

39 March, 1925
ROCKY FORD,
SCREVEN COUNTY
✕ ROBERT SMITH

40 September, 1925
WILKINSON COUNTY
✕ WILLIE DIXON

FL—MIAMI	*March 6, 1933*	
GIUSEPPE ZANGARA		
✕ Anton Cermak		
WEAPON HANDGUN	TYPOLOGY ASSASSINATION	POLICING —
BAYFRONT PARK, BISCAYNE BOULEVARD		

In February, 1933, Americans were starting to see a light at the far end of the tunnel. After a few years of economic depression and bad news, Franklin D. Roosevelt had been elected president in a landslide over the incumbent, Herbert Hoover. He promised relief for the ailing farmers and a repeal of Prohibition. Recovery would be slow, but it was coming.

Though his "New Deal" plan has always been branded as socialist by its detractors, it was too conservative for Giuseppe Zangara, an Italian-born bricklayer who had moved to the United States a decade before. In a statement that would become famous, Zangara said, "I have the gun in my hand. I kill kings and presidents first, and next all capitalists."

In February, 1933, Zangara was working odd jobs in Miami, Florida, when President-elect Roosevelt visited the town and gave an impromptu speech. Standing on a folding chair, Zangara pulled a cheap pistol from his pocket, took aim, and fired five bullets. Bystanders grabbed his arm after the first shot, but he managed to hit five people.

Roosevelt was not among the five, but Anton Cermak, the mayor of Chicago who was traveling with him, was not so lucky. Cermak lingered in the hospital for nearly three weeks before succumbing to his wounds. On the way to the hospital, he allegedly said, "I'm glad it was me, not you" to the President-elect. These words are engraved on his Chicago tomb.

Of course, every high-profile assassination generates conspiracy theories. Given that Zangara managed to hit so many people, but not the presumed target, some believed that Cermak was the real target, perhaps in revenge for a recent raid on the remnants of the Capone gang that had nearly killed Capone's successor, Frank "The Enforcer" Nitti.

Zangara was initially sentenced to eighty years in prison for attempted murder (though he defiantly asked the judge to make it a hundred). When Cermak died, the charge was upgraded to murder in the first degree. Zangara pleaded guilty and was executed in the electric chair just over a month after the shooting. His last words were "Go ahead, push the button!" •

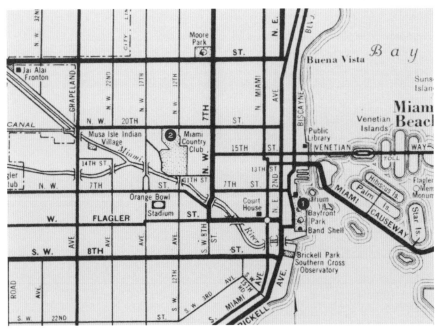

❶ BAYFRONT PARK
The scene of the shooting. Giuseppe Zangara fired five shots, hitting five people.

❷ JACKSON MEMORIAL HOSPITAL
The hospital where Anton Cermak died, after having allegedly said to President Roosevelt, "I am glad it was me, not you."

ABOVE Franklin D. Roosevelt greeting crowds at Bayfront Park, just moments before Giuseppe Zangara fired his shots.

RIGHT Anton Cermak, immediately after the shooting in Bayfront Park. He died from his wounds nearly three weeks later.

RIGHT Giuseppe Zangara in court. He was initially convicted of attempted murder, a conviction upgraded to murder when Anton Cermak died from wounds sustained in the shooting weeks later.

GIUSEPPE ZANGARA IN COURT AFTER BEING FOUND GUILTY
ON FOUR COUNTS OF ATTEMPTED MURDER.

GIUSEPPE ZANGARA READING THE PAPERS
IN HIS PRISON CELL IN MIAMI.

> ## "YOU GIVE ME ELECTRIC CHAIR. I NO AFRAID OF THAT CHAIR!
> ### YOU ONE OF CAPITALISTS. YOU IS CROOK MAN TOO."

GIUSEPPE ZANGARA IN COURT AFTER HE WAS FOUND GUILTY OF MURDER AND SENTENCED TO DEATH.

GIUSEPPE ZANGARA IN HIS PRISON CELL. HE WAS EXECUTED AFTER SPENDING JUST TEN DAYS ON DEATH ROW.

AR—CROOKED CREEK	*November 21, 1912*

ODUS DAVIDSON

✕ Ella Barham

WEAPON	TYPOLOGY	POLICING
SHARP-EDGED TOOL	SEXUAL	FOOTPRINTS
CROOKED CREEK, BOONE COUNTY		

AR—DELAWARE	*March 18, 1913*

JOHN ARTHUR TILLMAN

✕ Amanda Stephans

WEAPON	TYPOLOGY	POLICING
RIFLE	DOMESTIC	BALLISTICS
NEAR DELAWARE, LOGAN COUNTY		

In November, 1912, the dismembered body of 18-year-old Ella Barham was found in Crooked Creek, Arkansas. Posses were formed and stationed along railways, and the sheriff even attempted to use bloodhounds to track the killer. The crime was eventually pinned on a local man, Odus Davidson, who was taken to a jail in another town to save him from being lynched. In court, Davidson was made to step in flour so that his footprints could be compared to those found at the scene of the crime. Some believe that the trial was flawed and that Davidson was framed, but he was convicted and hanged. •

Nineteen-year-old Amanda Stephans disappeared in 1913. A note left on her pillow made it appear as though she had run away to be with her boyfriend, John Arthur Tillman. However, her body, with a bullet hole in the head, was found in a well, and the owners of the well identified Tillman as the man they had seen walking up to it to look inside. Investigators deduced she had been shot using a .22 caliber weapon—Tillman's mother confirmed he had left home with such a weapon on the night of Amanda's disappearance. It eventually transpired that Tillman had shot Amanda when he learned she was pregnant, and he was hanged. •

ABOVE The hanging of Odus Davidson, the last hanging in Boone County before electrocution was introduced.

ABOVE The hanging of John Arthur Tillman, the last person to be hanged in the state of Arkansas.

AR—ELAINE	September 30—October 1, 1919
ELAINE MASSACRE ✕ c. 100	

WEAPON VARIOUS	TYPOLOGY RACIAL	POLICING COLLUSION
ELAINE, PHILLIPS COUNTY		

AR—ST. JAMES	*March 1929*
UNKNOWN ✕ Connie Franklin	

WEAPON VARIOUS	TYPOLOGY TORTURE	POLICING FORENSIC ANTHROPOLOGY
ST. JAMES, STONE COUNTY		

In parts of Elaine County, Arkansas, Black citizens outnumbered white citizens by a ten-to-one ratio in the early 20th century. When the Black farmers began to organize in the hope of getting better treatment from white landowners, rumors circulated that they planned to kill every white person in the area. After shots broke out at a union meeting, violence erupted and Black people were attacked across the county. Federal troops were eventually brought in to end the fighting. The state covered up the massacre, claiming the Black people had been planning an insurrection. •

When he testified at the trial for his own murder, Connie Franklin became known as the "Arkansas Ghost." Franklin was working as a farmhand when he disappeared in 1929. A bloody hat was found and a young woman claimed that Franklin had been about to marry her when he was captured, tortured, and killed by "night riders." A man claiming to be Franklin (though also known as Marion Rogers), alive and well, was found to testify for the defense. Moreover experts were unable to testify that bones and teeth found at the scene of the crime were human and the accused were freed. Whether Connie and Rogers were truly the same man remains in doubt. •

↑ **ABOVE** Official records stated that eleven Black men were killed, but recent estimates place the true toll much higher.

↑ **ABOVE** The trial for the murder of Connie Franklin, at which Connie Franklin testified.

NEW ORLEANS AXE MURDERER
×6

WEAPON	TYPOLOGY	POLICING
RAZOR & AXE	**RANDOM ATTACK**	—

VARIOUS LOCATIONS, NEW ORLEANS

On May 23, 1918, Joseph and Catherine Maggio were sleeping peacefully in the bedroom above their bar-room and grocery store. It was a hot, late spring night in New Orleans, where summer comes early. At some point in the night, an unknown assailant crept into their room and cut both of their throats with a razor. Though this would have killed them both, the killer proceeded to bash in their heads with an axe, then changed into a clean pair of clothes and slipped away unnoticed, leaving the bloody razor in a nearby yard. Money was left in plain sight; this was clearly not a robbery.

The Maggios were only the first victims in a series of grisly murders that rattled New Orleans—a very hard city to rattle—from May, 1918 to October, 1919, during which time a dozen people, mostly Italian-American immigrants, were attacked by an axe-wielding criminal.

The next month, a similar attack was made on grocer Louis Besumer and his girlfriend Harriet Lowe. They were hacked in the head with Besumer's own axe. Remarkably, both survived. Lowe lived long enough to accuse Besumer of being a German spy. She died a few weeks later, and Besumer was brought to trial and acquitted.

Other attacks followed over the course of the next year. In a particularly bizarre twist, in March, 1919, newspapers ran a letter, said to be from the Axeman, claiming that he would strike again the following Tuesday, but would spare any house that was playing jazz music. No murders occurred on the night he named, but it was reportedly a busy night for jazz bands.

Several suspects were named, but no investigations yielded any clues as to the Axeman's identity or motives. Though some believe that similar axe attacks, such as the 1912 murders in Villisca, Iowa (see page 102), may have been committed by the same killer, the New Orleans attacks were over by the end of 1919. New theories are continually proposed, but, with the crimes now more than a century in the past, no new evidence has surfaced. •

BELOW Jake Bird, convicted of killing two women with an axe in 1947, is believed by some to have been the New Orleans Axe Murderer as well.

BELOW Photographs of the houses and back doors of some of the victims, published in the press, in order to suggest a similarity in the homes of the victims.

ABOVE A photograph believed by some to show the Axeman of New Orleans, in the doorway on the right, entering the home of Mike Pepitone.

ABOVE Isolated detail of the suspect in the doorway. The photograph is believed by some to be the work of the French photographer Édouard Martel.

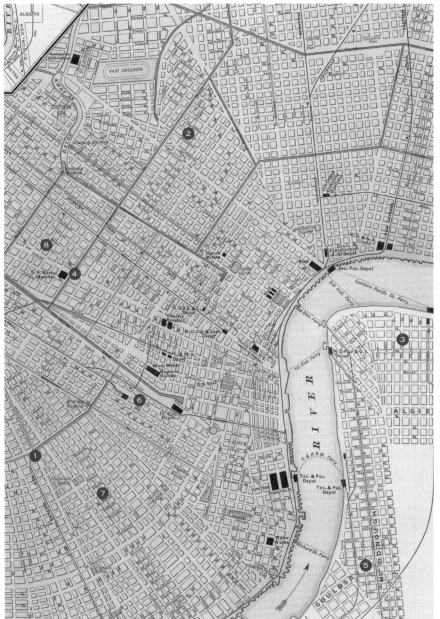

1

CORNER OF UPPERLINE AND MAGNOLIA STREETS
On May 23, 1918, Joseph Maggio and Catherine Maggio were killed.

2

CORNER OF DORGENOIS AND LAHARPE STREETS
On June 27, 1918, Louis Besumer and Harriet Lowe were attacked. Harriet later died.

3

ELMIRA STREET
On August 5, 1918, Anna Schneider was attacked.

4

NEAR TULANE AVENUE AND BROAD STREET
On August 10, 1918, Joseph Romano was killed.

5

CORNER OF JEFFERSON AVENUE AND SECOND STREET
On March 19, 1919, Charles, Rosie, and Mary Cortimiglia were attacked, and Mary died.

6

PRECISE LOCATION UNKNOWN
On August 10, 1919, the grocer Steve Boca was attacked.

7

2128 SECOND STREET
On September 3, 1919, Sarah Laumann was attacked.

8

CORNER OF SOUTH SCOTT AND ULLOA STREETS
On October 27, 1919, Mike Pepitone was killed.

NED CHRISTIE (ATTRIB.)

✕ Daniel Maples

WEAPON FIREARM	TYPOLOGY POLITICAL	POLICING POSSE

NEAR SPRING BRANCH CREEK, NEAR TAHLEQUAH

Ned Christie, also known by his Cherokee name NeDe Wade, was a blacksmith and member of the Cherokee tribal Senate. In 1887, laws were passed that ordered the break-up of many tribal lands, a blatant attempt to destroy Native American culture and force tribe members to assimilate into white society. Christie's opposition to the new laws made him a lot of enemies.

When Christie was falsely accused of the murder of a U.S. Deputy in 1887, he barricaded himself in his house rather than be taken by lawmen, then made his escape when the house was burned down. He reportedly swore that he would never surrender. The government put a $1,000 price on his head and Christie built a double-walled log fort with enough ammunition and provisions to withstand a siege.

In October, 1892, by which point Ned had been a fugitive for five years, a posse was organized for a full-scale assault on the fort, even utilizing a borrowed cannon. On November 3, the fort was blown up with dynamite and a member of the posse shot Christie dead as he tried to flee. They then photographed themselves with his body, and curious spectators were able to take shots of their own when the body was transported to Arkansas, where the posse claimed their reward. Some of the photos of the corpse were even sold as postcards.

More than a generation later, a man admitted to a local paper that he had witnessed the 1887 murder of the deputy, and that it had not been Christie who fired the shot. When asked why he had not spoken up at the time, the man quite reasonably replied that if he claimed that the government was wrong to kill Christie, he would be risking his own neck. Now known to be innocent and assassinated for no real reason, Christie continues to be the subject of movies and biographies, and is memorialized with a plaque in an Oklahoma courthouse. •

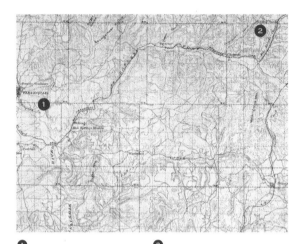

❶ SPRING BRANCH CREEK, NEAR TAHLEQUAH
The approximate location where U.S. Deputy Daniel Maples was shot.

❷ RABBIT TRAP, GOING SNAKE
Ned Christie's home, where he retreated and hid for several years following the murder of Daniel Maples.

RIGHT Photographs of Ned Christie's body, posed with his rifle, were taken and sold.

RIGHT A studio portrait of the posse that attacked Ned Christie's fort in 1892 and shot Christie as he tried to flee.

RIGHT U.S. Marshals posing with the body of Ned Christie, which they have strapped to a door (5). They are Paden Tolbert (1), Captain G. S. White (2), Coon Ratteree (3), Enoch Mills (4), Thomas Johnson (6), Charles Copel (7), and Heck Bruner (8).

RIGHT A photograph of the posse that eventually killed Ned Christie, five years after the murder of Daniel Maples.

WILLIAM HALE
×60

WEAPON	TYPOLOGY	POLICING
VARIOUS	PROPERTY CRIME	B.O.I.

VARIOUS LOCATIONS, OSAGE COUNTY

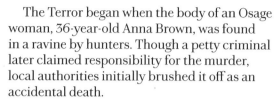

General Phillip Sheridan denied that he ever said his most famous quote, "The only good Indian is a dead Indian." But his record shows that it was a good reflection of his attitude, and it was, in fact, the attitude of much of the United States government for a large portion of American history. To an even greater degree, it was the attitude of much of the American populace. When politicians ordered the removal of tribes, or even large-scale executions, they could claim that their actions were to protect the tribe and get away with it.

Of course, it was often the case that when tribes were removed the fact that they inhabited valuable land was more relevant.

In 1897 oil was discovered in Osage County, Oklahoma, before the territory had become a state. The richness of the land offers one possible motivation for the "Reign of Terror" that occurred in the 20th century, when some estimate that sixty Osage Native Americans were murdered. Others estimate that the number was even higher.

The Terror began when the body of an Osage woman, 36-year-old Anna Brown, was found in a ravine by hunters. Though a petty criminal later claimed responsibility for the murder, local authorities initially brushed it off as an accidental death.

Over the next few years, a number of Osage residents were murdered in a variety of ways, from bombings to shootings to poisoned whiskey, and the rich land that they owned was largely inherited by "guardians" who had been appointed by the government to manage Osage affairs. These "guardians" tended to be rich white men.

The tribe suspected that many of the murders had been ordered by William Hale, a local rancher. Eventually undercover agents from the Bureau of Investigation (the precursor to the F.B.I.) came to the Reservation and acquired enough evidence to arrest Hale. In the end he was convicted of just one killing, that of Anna Brown's cousin Henry Roan, and served eighteen years in prison. •

LEFT Rita Smith and her servant Nettie Brookshire outside their home. Both were killed immediately when a bomb exploded in their residence, and Rita's husband Bill died from his injuries several days later. Investigations revealed that the bomb contained 5 US gallons (19 liters) of nitroglycerin.

OPPOSITE The remains of Rita Smith's house following the explosion in March, 1923, that killed her and her servant Nettie Brookshire. Newspapers at the time described the increasing number of unsolved murders in Osage County as the "Reign of Terror," lasting from 1921 to 1926. Some estimate the Osage death toll to be in the hundreds, though reported numbers are much lower and investigated deaths fewer still.

HENRY ROAN

ANNA BROWN

CHARLES WHITEHORN

LIZZIE Q. KYLE

RITA SMITH

GAS PLANT OSAGE OIL FIELDS

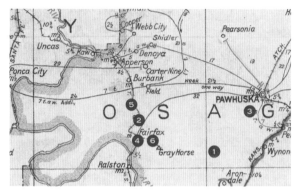

1

OIL FIELDS
The Osage Native Americans became rich from the oil found in their territory.

2

SITE OF BROWN MURDER
On May 27, 1921, Anna Brown was discovered decomposing in a remote ravine.

3

SITE OF WHITEHORN MURDER
Anna Brown's cousin Charles Whitehorn was discovered near Pawhuska on the same day.

4

SITE OF KYLE MURDER
Two months after Brown's murder, her mother Lizzie Q. Kyle was also found dead.

5

SITE OF ROAN MURDER
On February 6, 1923, Henry Roan was found in his car, dead from a shot in the head.

6

SMITH MURDERS
On March 10, 1923, a bomb killed Rita Smith and her servant, Nettie Brookshire.

OK—MARLOW CA—FOLSOM	*April 20, 1931 & September 19, 1937*

ED DAVIS
✕ J. R. Hill ✕ 3

WEAPON	TYPOLOGY	POLICING
SHOTGUN & KNIFE	ESCAPE ATTEMPT	MANHUNT

CORNER OF WEST MAIN STREET AND NORTH SECOND STREET, MARLOW & FOLSOM PRISON, FOLSOM

The Great Depression was a boom time for criminals. Though the era of Wild West outlaws was over and the Prohibition gangsters were dying out, a new generation of lawbreakers took inspiration from both, using the "getaway car," a new term at the time, to revolutionize the world of bank robbing.

Ed Davis grew up committing minor robberies around Oklahoma in the early days of the 20th century. He spent time in reformatories as a teenager, then spent most of his twenties in prison. But life as an inmate failed to reform his character, and a persistent ear infection he contracted while serving time caused him so much constant pain that it may have driven him to madness. It also likely contributed to his hatred for law enforcement officials.

In 1931, he had been out of prison for three years. He happened to be sitting in a car with two other men—both as heavily armed as he was—when the car was approached by two police officers on a routine patrol. The men opened fire on the officers, wounding police chief Ike Veach and killing the officer J. R. Hill instantly. They were all captured after a six-month manhunt, and Davis was convicted of murder and sentenced to life in prison.

He served less than a year before escaping and embarking on a new career robbing banks. He was arrested within weeks, but managed to escape prison yet again and began working with other gangs, including a stint as the getaway driver for the Bailey-Underhill gang. When Bailey was jailed, Davis struck out on his own, robbing banks across Texas. Though the press came to call him "The Fox" for his supposed cleverness, his latest crime spree did not last much longer than his others, and he was serving a life prison sentence in Folsom Prison barely a year after his last escape.

After killing a warden and two prisoners in yet another escape attempt, he was sent to San Quentin State Prison, where he was executed in the gas chamber in 1938. A note found in his cell afterwards read "No regrets for Old Ed. All considered, my conscience is now resting easy." •

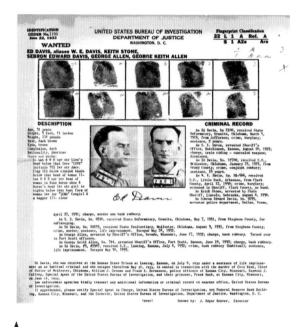

ABOVE The Identification Order for Ed Davis, issued by the Bureau of Investigation, the original name of the F.B.I.

BELOW The corner of West Main Street and North Second Street in Marlow, where J. R. Hill was killed by Ed Davis.

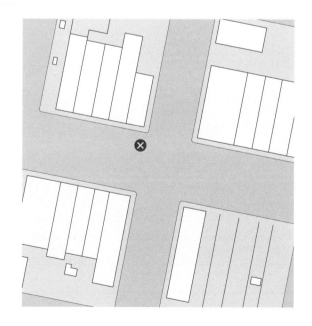

TX—KNICKERBOCKER

TX—KNICKERBOCKER	*December 12, 1895*

THOMAS "BLACK JACK" KETCHUM

✕ John "Jap" Powers

WEAPON	TYPOLOGY	POLICING
FIREARM	PROPERTY CRIME	POSSE

NEAR POWERS'S RANCH, SOUTH OF KNICKERBOCKER

While large cities in the late 1800s often had a number of clubs and hotels frequented by members of competing gangs, the more remote towns had their own dens of iniquity as well. Hole-in-the-Wall Pass in Johnson County, Wyoming, had a log cabin that was frequented by a number of outlaws, including Kid Kurry and Butch Cassidy's Wild Bunch. During his time socializing in the cabin in the 1890s, train robber Tom Ketchum was mistaken for outlaw Will "Black Jack" Christian, and the nickname became his own. As the 20th century approached, "Black Jack" Ketchum's gang became notorious for robbing trains in the west and southwest.

Although he was best known for train robberies, Ketchum had also killed a neighbor, John "Jap" Powers, in Texas in 1895. Word at the time was that Ketchum had shot Powers in a dispute over debts, but he later claimed that Powers's widow had hired him to kill her husband because she had fallen in love with another man.

In July, 1891, members of Ketchum's gang, including his brother, Sam, robbed a train at Twin Mountain, near Folsom, New Mexico. A posse that formed the following day captured several members of the gang and fatally shot Sam. But news traveled slowly to a gang scattered across the territory and Tom Ketchum himself supposedly had not heard the news when he tried to rob the same train at the same location in August. The conductor shot him from the train and he lay bleeding from his wound until the next day, when a posse captured him.

ABOVE The hanging of Tom Ketchum (above), and afterwards, when he had been decapitated due to a too long rope (below).

BELOW Knickerbocker, Texas, where Thomas "Black Jack" Ketchum killed John "Jap" Powers. Following the murder Ketchum fled to Arizona.

For safekeeping, he was taken to Union County, New Mexico, where no citizen had any experience with hangings. There is a trick to execution by rope—if the rope is too short, the death will come by a slow strangulation, but if it is too long, it can result in decapitation. Ketchum's rope was too long. After he said his last words, which were reportedly "Please dig my grave deep; all right, hurry up," the trap door fell and the drop severed his head from his neck. Photographs of the gruesome incident were taken for postcards. •

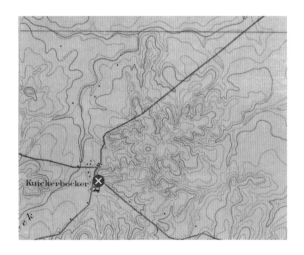

CLYDE BARROW

✕ J. N. Bucher + 12

WEAPON	TYPOLOGY	POLICING
PISTOL	PROPERTY CRIME	AMBUSH

BUCHER'S PAWN SHOP AND FILLING STATION, BETWEEN OLD FORT WORTH ROAD AND THE RAILWAY TRACKS BESIDE PECOS STREET

No one knows whether Clyde Barrow chopped off his own toes, or had another prisoner do it, in order to avoid hard labor in prison. Either way, it is indicative of the lengths Barrow would go to in order to further his own ends.

Clyde Barrow was born into a poor farming family outside of Dallas in 1909. By the time he was a teenager, the family was living in a tent in the Dallas slums. With few options, he fell into a life of crime. As a young man he was frequently arrested for charges ranging from not returning rental cars to possessing stolen turkeys. He was put in Eastham Prison, where he pulled his famous toe-chopping stunt, for stealing a car when he was 21. Friends agreed that something

▲ **ABOVE** The shop owned by J. N. Bucher (above), and a police recreation of the robbery of the shop, in which Bucher was shot and killed by Clyde Barrow (below).

terrible happened to him in prison. After his time there he seemed different. And bent on revenge.

After his release in 1932, he reconnected with Bonnie Parker, an old girlfriend and partner in crime. Together, they embarked on a series of robberies, with Barrow hoping to raise enough money to launch an attack on the prison where he had been incarcerated. Bonnie was caught during a hardware store robbery and did a few months in jail; Barrow remained at large.

While Bonnie was waiting for her trial, Clyde served as the getaway driver when some of his friends—by now gang members—attempted a robbery at a combination filling station and pawn shop in Hillsboro, Texas. Clyde had worked in the shop with a son of the owner, J. N. Bucher, and knew that there was a safe in the back.

Something went wrong in the robbery, and Bucher was shot and killed. The gang escaped but Bucher's wife identified Clyde as one of the shooters, although by some accounts he never left the car. Clyde was now officially a fugitive.

Bonnie reunited with Clyde after a grand jury failed to indict her and she was released. In August, 1932, four months after the Bucher murder, Barrow shot and killed deputy Eugene Moore, the first of nine lawmen that Barrow and his gang would eventually kill.

Over the next two years, Bonnie and Clyde's gang became the terror of the south as they embarked on a spree of robberies. Some members were captured and taken to Eastham Prison in 1933, but early the next year Barrow, likely still traumatized from his time there, orchestrated their breakout. This led the Texas Department of Corrections to bring on former Texas Ranger Frank Hamer, who had killed 53 suspects in his career, to end the gang's reign. After three months of tracking Bonnie and Clyde, Hamer and his men hid in the bushes on a rural route and opened fire into Barrow's passing car, emptying 130 rounds into the vehicle and killing both Parker and Barrow.

The "death car," peppered with bullet holes, was a featured attraction on the carnival circuit for years. •

BELOW, TOP Barrow's partner in crime Bonnie Parker, posing with her pistol in front of a car.

BELOW, CENTER Bonnie Parker and Clyde Barrow's F.B.I. Identification Order.

BELOW, BOTTOM Bullet holes in the V-8 sedan in which Clyde Barrow and Bonnie Parker were killed.

BELOW, TOP Clyde Barrow posing with an assortment of firearms in front of a car.

BELOW, CENTER Clyde Barrow's F.B.I. Identification Order.

BELOW, BOTTOM Clyde Barrow and Bonnie Parker's bodies after they were ambushed and killed.

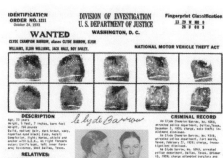

"NEVER GO CROOKED. IT'S FOR THE LOVE OF A MAN
THAT I'M GONNA HAVE TO DIE."

BONNIE PARKER TO GANG MEMBER HENRY METHVIN TWO NIGHTS BEFORE HER DEATH.	A WANTED POSTER FOR BONNIE PARKER AND CLYDE BARROW ISSUED BY THE POLICE DEPARTMENT.

WANTED FOR MURDER
JOPLIN, MISSOURI

F.P.C.29 – MO. 9
26 U 00 6

CLYDE CHAMPION BARROW, age 24, 5'7", 130#, hair dark brown and wavy, eyes hazel, light complexion, home West Dallas, Texas. This man killed Detective Harry McGinnis and Constable J.W. Harryman in this city, April 13, 1933.

BONNIE PARKER   CLYDE BARROW   CLYDE BARROW

This man is dangerous and is known to have committed the following murders: Howard Hall, Sherman, Texas; J.N. Bucher, Hillsboro, Texas; a deputy sheriff at Atoka, Okla; deputy sheriff at West Dallas, Texas; also a man at Belden, Texas.
     The above photos are kodaks taken by Barrow and his companions in various poses, and we believe they are better for identification than regular police pictures.
     Wire or write any information to the

Police Department.

BONNIE PARKER'S HUSBAND ROY THORNTON, AFTER
HEARING THAT SHE AND CLYDE HAD BEEN KILLED.

BONNIE PARKER AND CLYDE BARROW
POSING TOGETHER WITH A RIFLE.

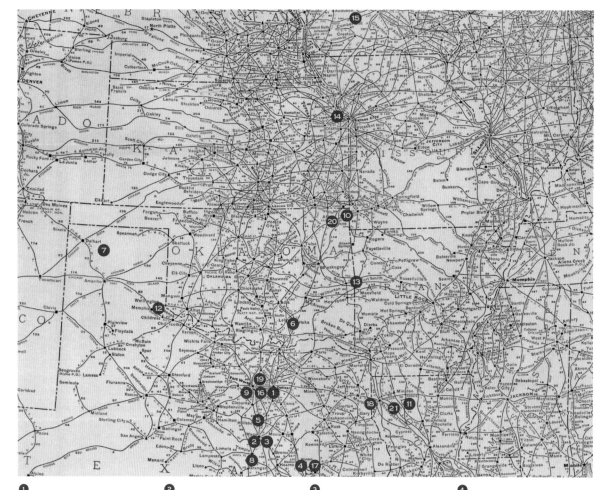

①

JANUARY, 1930,
WEST DALLAS, TX
Bonnie Parker and Clyde
Barrow meet for the first time.

②

FEBRUARY, 1930,
WACO, TX
Clyde is jailed for petty
crimes including robbery.

③

MARCH, 1930,
MCLENNAN COUNTY JAIL, TX
Bonnie helps Clyde escape
from prison.

④

MARCH, 1930, EASTHAM
PRISON FARM, TX
After being captured in Ohio,
Clyde is sent to prison.

⑤

APRIL, 1930,
HILLSBORO, TX
J. N. Bucher is killed during
a robbery.

⑥

AUGUST, 1932,
STRINGTOWN, OK
Lawman Eugene Moore
is killed at a dance.

⑦

OCTOBER, 1932,
SHERMAN, TX
Butcher Howard Hall is killed
during a robbery.

⑧

DECEMBER, 1932,
TEMPLE, TX
Salesman Doyle Johnson is
killed trying to stop a car theft.

⑨

JANUARY, 1933, TARRANT
COUNTY, TX
Deputy Sheriff Malcolm Davis
is killed during a gun battle.

⑩

MARCH, 1933, JOPLIN, MO
Buck Barrow is released
from prison. A month later
two officers die in a gun battle.

⑪

APRIL, 1933, RUSTON, LA
Dillard Darby and Sophia Stone
are kidnapped during a car
theft.

⑫

JUNE, 1933,
WELLINGTON, TX
Bonnie is seriously burned
in a car accident.

⑬

JUNE, 1933, ALMA, AK
Marshal Henry Humphrey
is killed during a shootout.

⑭

JULY, 1933,
PLATTE CITY, MO
The gang is ambushed by
the police.

⑮

JULY, 1933, DEXFIELD PARK,
DEXTER, IO
The police surround the gang
and fatally wound Buck Barrow.

⑯

NOVEMBER, 1933,
SOWERS, TX
Bonnie and Clyde are
ambushed by the police again.

⑰

JANUARY, 1934, EASTHAM
PRISON FARM, TX
Several prisoners are freed
and a prison guard is killed.

⑱

MARCH, 1934,
SHREVEPORT, LA
Clyde steals businessman
Philip Bloomer's car.

⑲

APRIL, 1934,
GRAPEVINE, TX
Two highway officers are
killed.

⑳

APRIL, 1934, COMMERCE, OK
Clyde commandeers a law
officer's car, kills one officer,
and kidnaps another.

㉑

MAY, 1934, BETWEEN
MOUNT LEBANON AND
SAILES, LA
Bonnie and Clyde are
ambushed and killed.

PART FOUR
ALASKA
MONTANA | WYOMING
COLORADO
NEW MEXICO | CALIFORNIA

THE WEST

JESSE MURPHY
FRANK REID
JOHN J. CLAYBOURNE
JAMES J. SMITH
Y. HAGIWARA
CHARLES C. MILLER
THE CAPITOL HILL THUG
EARL DURAND
ALFERD PACKER
BILLY THE KID
THEODORE DURRANT
MADALYNNE OBENCHAIN
ARTHUR BURCH
GORDON STEWART NORTHCOTT
SARAH NORTHCOTT
PERRY COEN
ANTONE NEGRA
ALPHONSE REILLY
GEORGE RYLEY
JOHN GOMEZ
ALBERT DYER

JESSE MURPHY / FRANK REID

✕ Jefferson "Soapy" Smith

WEAPON PISTOL	TYPOLOGY POSSE	POLICING POSSE
JUNEAU WHARF		

The very best con artists never let people know that they have been fooled, or at least not until they are safely out of town.

Jefferson "Soapy" Smith earned his nickname from his success with the "Prize Soap" con, in which he sold bars of soap to large crowds, who believed that some of the bars had large cash prizes in the wrappers. Crowds would buy up the soap and rip open the wrappers. When only a few bars remained and the big prizes had not been won, Smith auctioned these last few bars off for large sums. Naturally, nobody but his confederates ever won anything.

Smith made so much money from this con that he was able to open a saloon and gambling hall in Denver in 1888, and through it he became involved in underworld activities with far higher stakes. In the 1890s, he moved to Skaguay, Alaska, and was soon in control of the town, with the police on his payroll and his saloon known as "the real city hall."

But in 1898, a miner with a bag of gold lost $87 in cash during a three-card monte game with Smith's men. When he refused to pay up, the gang took the gold. Much of the town agreed that the miner had been cheated, and he complained to everyone who would listen, eventually finding enough sympathy from law enforcement in neighboring towns that Smith said that he was willing to return the gold in order to keep things quiet.

This promise, however, was only to keep things calm. When Smith failed to return the gold as promised, a U.S. Commissioner from a nearby town issued warrants to a whole posse, instructing them to bring in Smith and his gang, dead or alive. Hearing that a crowd had formed, Smith made his way to Juneau Wharf, intending to try and calm them down.

The details of what happened in the ensuing shootout are unclear. Some say Smith fired first, others claim that he and one Frank Reid fired in the same instant. Others declare that it was Jesse Murphy, a railway worker, who fired the fatal shot. What is certain is that "Soapy" Smith was shot through the heart. He died instantly. •

ABOVE Jefferson "Soapy" Smith at a bar in a saloon in Skaguay, Alaska. The settlement had grown swiftly into a town in the 1890s due to the discovery of gold in the Klondike Mountains.

ABOVE Jefferson "Soapy" Smith riding a horse. He earned his sobriquet through a con he ran in which people were tricked into buying soap, believing some of the bars contained cash prizes.

1

JEFF SMITH'S PARLOR, SIXTH AVENUE, JUST OFF BROADWAY
Soapy Smith set up his business inside the building.

2

MONDIMEN HOTEL
Where the miner, Stewart, was staying and his poke of gold was originally stored.

3

JUNEAU WHARF
The wharf where the fatal shot was fired and Soapy Smith was killed.

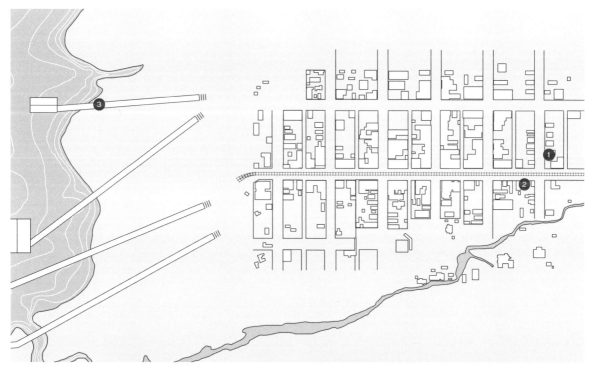

↑ **ABOVE** A crowd of men outside the Skaguay City Hall, captioned "Rounding up Soapy's Gang." Following Smith's death the three gang members who had robbed the miner of his poke of gold received jail sentences.

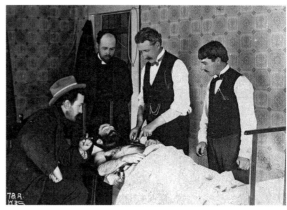

↑ **ABOVE** The body of Jefferson "Soapy" Smith. He was killed on the spot during the shootout on Juneau Wharf, from a bullet to the heart. It is unknown exactly who fired the fatal shot.

MT—MISSOULA	*September 7, 1909*

JOHN J. CLAYBOURNE

✕ Pearl Anderson

WEAPON FIREARM	TYPOLOGY DOMESTIC	POLICING CRIME SCENE INVESTIGATION
285 WEST FRONT STREET		

MT—MELROSE	*April 15, 1912*

JAMES J. SMITH

✕ Clarence Ackaret

WEAPON FIREARM	TYPOLOGY LAND DISPUTE	POLICING SEARCH PARTY
ACKARET'S CABIN		

Missoula's "tenderloin" district was thriving in 1909. One woman who worked there, Pearl Anderson, had moved to Montana from the Seattle area some years before. However, on September 7, 1909, she was found dead in her bedroom by a porter who worked in the saloon where she lived, and who was bringing her a whiskey. A collar discovered at the scene of the crime was found to belong to John J. Claybourne, with whom Pearl had been romantically connected. When confronted with the evidence, Claybourne confessed, telling police that he had been "driven to desperation" by Anderson's jealousy. He was sentenced to life in prison just a week later. •

In 1912, Clarence Ackaret wrote a letter to his parents, saying that he was coming home. He had been leading a solitary life as a trapper and hunter, living in an isolated cabin. But the letter was never sent. Shortly after he finished writing it, he was shot and killed. He had recently been a witness at a hearing in a land contest against one James J. Smith, and Smith had apparently responded by killing Ackaret. Smith then hid Ackaret's body in a well, meaning that it was not until a search party was organized to look for the missing man that Ackaret's body was found. Smith made a desperate run from the law before being caught and convicted. •

↑ **ABOVE** The mugshot taken of John J. Claybourne at Montana Penitentiary.

↑ **ABOVE** The mugshot taken of James J. Smith at Montana Penitentiary.

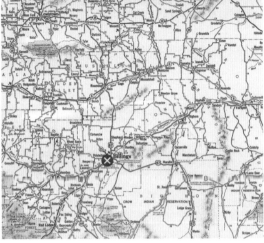

MT—BILLINGS	*December 23, 1912*

Y. HAGIWARA

⨯ H. Sugia

WEAPON	TYPOLOGY	POLICING
FIREARM	DISPUTE	POSTMORTEM

MONTANA COFFEE HOUSE, MINNESOTA AVENUE

MT—KALISPELL	*March 4, 1915*

CHARLES C. MILLER

⨯ Robert J. Benn

WEAPON	TYPOLOGY	POLICING
FIREARM	PROPERTY CRIME	FOOTPRINTS

HOTEL OWNED BY ROBERT J. BENN

In 1912 Y. Hagiwara was working as a cook in a Japanese boarding house in Billings, which catered to railroad workers who had come to work in the mountain states. In the December of that year, he shot and killed a man named H. Sugia at a coffee shop. It seemed the two had some history, with Sugia threatening Hagiwara with knowledge of a past misdemeanor. Hagiwara admitted to the killing, but claimed that he had been acting in self defense, trying to wrestle the gun off Sugia. However an analysis of the bullet's journey through Sugia's body suggested that this was unlikely. Hagiwara was convicted of the murder and sentenced to life in prison •

↑ **ABOVE** The mugshot taken of Y. Hagiwara at Montana Penitentiary.

Hotel-owner Robert J. Benn was found shot through the heart and lying in a pool of blood by one of his hotel porters in the early hours of March 5, 1915. Benn was a well-known and widely popular man in the Great Falls area, and people from across the town joined the hunt for clues. A set of footprints in the snow leading to and from the hotel were traced to Charles C. Miller, a dive bar pianist who police believed ran with a bad crowd. It transpired that Benn had been working late in the hotel bar when Miller had attempted a burglary. When Benn had tried to chase Miller away, Miller had shot him. He was sentenced to life in prison. •

↑ **ABOVE** The mugshot taken of Charles C. Miller at Montana Penitentiary.

UNKNOWN
X Franklin Henry Little

WEAPON	TYPOLOGY	POLICING
NOOSE	POLITICAL	—

MILWAUKEE BRIDGE

In the early 20th century it was strangely common to attribute violence to the Industrial Workers of the World—known as the "Wobblies." Though reports of them engaging in destructive acts were scattered, and often wholly fictional, attributing ill intentions to workers who wanted better treatment has long been a part of America's political D.N.A.

Frank Little, a member of the I.W.W.'s executive board, traveled the country in the 1910s, organizing workers such as lumberjacks and field workers into unions and fighting against employment agencies who were in the habit of conning their recruits out of wages. This was dangerous work: in 1913 he was kidnapped and held at gunpoint by anti-union mercenaries. It was not even the only time in the course of his career that he was kidnapped and threatened with death.

In 1917, he journeyed to Butte, Montana, to help organize mine workers. A mine shaft disaster there had recently cost 168 workers their lives. Little worked to set up picket lines and organize strikes. However, he was weak from a beating he had taken in El Paso, and his vocal criticism of America's entry into World War I made him an even greater target than ever.

On August 1, six masked men broke into the boarding house where Little was staying and kidnapped, then tortured and murdered him.

The atmosphere in Butte had been so tense that when the lynching was announced in the *Butte Miner*, the editors made a point of saying, "This does not mean that any loyal or patriotic citizen can possibly feel any sympathy with the treasonable utterances of Frank Little... a most undesirable citizen [whose] incendiary speeches would have been bad enough in time of peace, and were absolutely inexcusable in time of war."

Little had been tied to the rear bumper of a car and dragged along for some distance, fast enough to destroy his knee caps, before being hanged from a railroad trestle bridge. The *Miner* set the tone for the reaction, condemning the murder but making a point to condemn Little in the process. No one was ever arrested for the crime. •

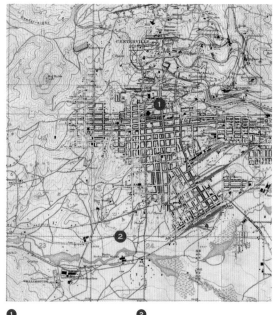

1
NORA BYRNE'S STEEL BLOCK BOARDING HOUSE, 316 NORTH WYOMING STREET
The boarding house where Frank Little was staying, and where he was kidnapped.

2
MILWAUKEE BRIDGE
The approximate location of the bridge from which Frank Little was lynched, after having been dragged behind a car by his kidnappers for some miles.

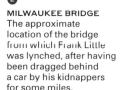

RIGHT One of the smelters of the Anaconda Mining Company in Butte, Montana. Frank Little came to Butte to organize on behalf of the miners who worked there.

RIGHT The ruins of the bridge at the edge of Butte where Frank Little was hanged. His position on World War I, as well as his support for the miners in Butte, had made him many enemies.

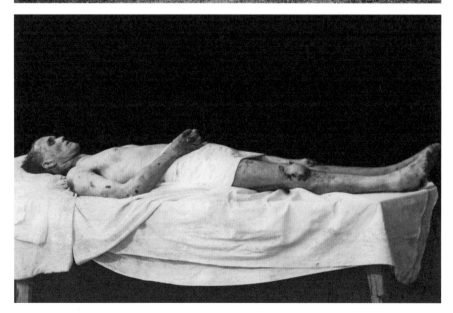

RIGHT Frank Little's body. An autopsy revealed that he had been beaten and dragged behind a car before being hanged from the bridge.

OPPOSITE This note was found pinned to Frank Little's thigh, warning, "Others take notice." It also includes the numbers 3–7–77, a sign used by vigilantes active in the 19th century in Virginia City, and the initials of other union leaders, suggesting that they were the next to be targeted.

FRANK LITTLE
VICTIM OF ANACONDA COPPER COMPANY
THUGS DIED AUG 1 1917 BUTE MONT

ABOVE A photograph of Frank Little. The text below
reads "Frank Little, victim of the Anaconda Copper
Company Thugs. Died Aug.1, 1917, Butte, Montana.

ABOVE The copper smelters of the Anaconda Mining Company in Butte, Montana. Frank Little wanted better safety and higher wages for the company's workers, a position that made him many enemies.

ABOVE This contemporary illustration published in the *Butte Daily Bulletin* suggests the power the Anaconda Mining Company held in Montana. In 1915, the company was the largest copper producer in the world.

ABOVE The funeral procession for Frank Little, attended by thousands of workers, come to pay their respects to the man whose fight for workers' rights had cost him his life.

ABOVE Pallbearers carrying Frank Little's casket. Ribbons on the casket read "martyr for." Frank was viewed as a martyr for the I.W.W. cause.

ABOVE A contemporary cartoon casts the International Workers of the World as a giant, casting aside the rocks of low wages, long hours, militarism, rotten conditions, and the speed-up system.

ABOVE Frank Little's gravestone in Mountain View Cemetery, Butte, which reads "slain by capitalist interest for organizing and inspiring his fellow men."

| MT/WY—BOZEMAN TRAIL | *April 20, 1867* |

UNKNOWN

X John Merin Bozeman

WEAPON	TYPOLOGY	POLICING
PISTOL	VIGILANTE	—

BOZEMAN TRAIL, EXACT LOCATION UNKNOWN

In the days of the Civil War, Chicago was still considered the northwest. The country's population was heavily concentrated on the east coast and the explosive growth of California and the Pacific Coast were decades away. The mountain states were still very much the frontier.

John Merin Bozeman was only in his twenties when he created the Bozeman Trail, which gave miners coming from the east to seek gold in Montana an easier route to follow. But his trail cut through Sioux territory, and deadly fights between would-be settlers and Native American tribes became common.

By 1864, his namesake town of Bozeman, Montana, had been founded, though at first it was little more than six rude shacks and a muddy strip that passed for Main Street. However by April, 1867, the town had grown into a regular settlement.

In that month, Bozeman and a companion, Thomas Cover, were traveling along the Bozeman trail when Bozeman was shot and killed. Returning to town, Cover claimed that Bozeman had been murdered by a group of Native Americans from the Blackfoot Nation. He himself had been shot in the arm.

The story satisfied most people at the time, but Cover's story did not hold up to scrutiny. Bozeman dressed the part of a frontiersman in his buckskin jacket when it was good for business, but the Georgia-born explorer was a southern gambler at heart and had a reputation as a ladies' man with few morals. Some believed that he had been flirting with Cover's wife and that Cover had killed him, shot himself in the arm, and covered up the crime with a story about the Blackfoot.

Recently, historians have uncovered old family stories of a cattle wrangler named Tom Kent who allegedly claimed to have killed Bozeman himself on behalf of the industrialist Nelson Story. None of the theories are entirely satisfactory and it is likely that the truth will never be known. •

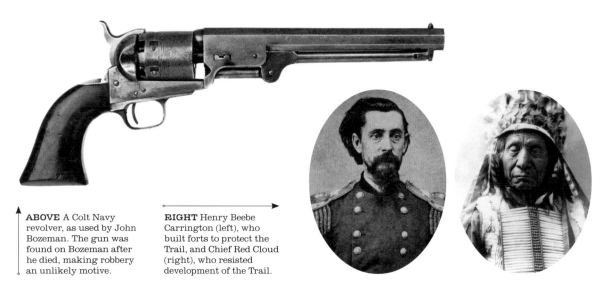

ABOVE A Colt Navy revolver, as used by John Bozeman. The gun was found on Bozeman after he died, making robbery an unlikely motive.

RIGHT Henry Beebe Carrington (left), who built forts to protect the Trail, and Chief Red Cloud (right), who resisted development of the Trail.

VIRGINIA CITY
Virginia City lay at the
western end of the
Bozeman trail.

BOZEMAN
The town named after
John Merian Bozeman,
along the Bozeman trail.

❸
FORT SEDGWICK
Ford Sedgwick lay near
the eastern end of the
Bozeman trail, used by
prospective settlers
traveling west.

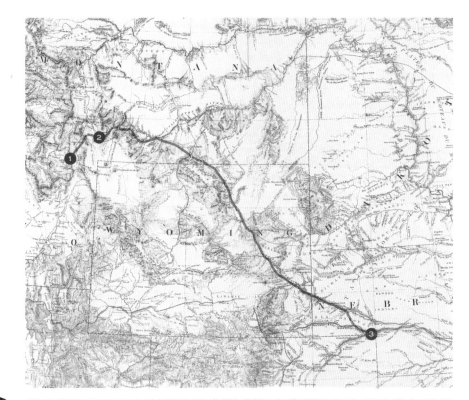

RIGHT A scene in Bozeman,
named after the Bozeman
Trail's founder John
Bozeman.

RIGHT One of the military
forts positioned along the
Bozeman Trail in order
to guide travelers.

EARL DURAND

✕ D. M. Baker ✕ Chuck Lewis
✕ Arthur Argento ✕ Orville Linaberry

WEAPON	TYPOLOGY	POLICING
FIREARM	ESCAPE ATTEMPT	MANHUNT

DURAND FAMILY HOME, POWELL & LITTLE ROCKY CREEK, NEAR THE MOUTH OF CLARK'S FORK CANYON

Earl Durand was a mountain man. Born in 1913, he made a home for himself in the peaks of Wyoming, where he came to be called the "Tarzan of the Tetons." He was a large, shaggy rancher who felt that he was living the outdoor adventure stories that he had read as a boy. People who lived nearby said that he could throw a baseball in the air, take a rifle and shoot four bullets through the ball before it hit the ground. Some claimed he switched to shooting with a bow and arrow as shooting with a rifle was not enough of a challenge.

When the state introduced hunting licenses in 1939, Durand decided to ignore them, and he and a few friends shot four elk near Yellowstone Park without a license. A game warden attempted to arrest them after being tipped off, jumping onto the running board of Durand's moving car. Durand grabbed a rifle, jumped out of the car, and escaped into the dark wilderness.

For a couple of days, Durand wandered the wilds of Wyoming, poaching cattle for meat (leading to newspaper stories claiming that he loved raw meat) while game wardens attempted to follow his tracks. He was quickly captured and taken to jail, but once behind bars, he beat undersheriff Noah Riley over the head with a milk bottle, took his gun, and forced him to drive him 25 miles (40 km) to Durand's parents' home in Powell.

When Deputy Sheriff D. M. Baker and Town Marshall Chuck Lewis tracked Durand to his parents' house, Durand fatally shot both men and made another escape.

With a questionable chain of command, a group of game wardens, sheriffs, deputy sheriffs, and undersheriffs from nearby areas formed a posse, eventually comprising roughly a hundred men. They canvassed the area for tracks in the snow and agreed that if Durand was spotted, they would shoot to kill.

Over the next few days, residents around Powell lived in fear, keeping their doors locked and hoping Durand would not try to hide in their homes. One of the unlucky residents who did get a visit was Herf Graham; Durand came to his home,

◄ **LEFT** Earl Durand, an expert marksman and keen hunter, on horseback. Durand killed four men while on the run from the law, following an arrest for killing elk.

THE POSSE THAT HUNTED EARL DURAND

❶ –

❷ –

❸ JAS CAIN

❹ HENRY SCHMIDTLAGER

❺ HOWLEY KINCADE

❻ G. GREEN ? WHITE

❼ ED WILDER?

❽ DWIGHT KING

❾ CHET CASTLE

❿ PETE SCHULTZ

⓫ –

⓬ –

⓭ SCOTTLUND STROM

⓮ TEX KENNEDY

⓯ –

⓰ –

D. M. BAKER

CHUCK LEWIS

took a rifle, and left a note for Sheriff Blackburn that read, "Of course I know that I'm done for, and when you kill me I suggest you have my head mounted...for the sake of law and order. Your beloved enemy, Earl Durand."

The manhunt extended into Clark's Fork Canyon, where Durand was spotted making a rocky hideout for himself on the side of a cliff. When two men tried to approach him, Durand pleaded with them to stop, then shot both of them dead. When night fell, he took their shoes and weapons and continued his flight.

Days into his escape, with the nation now following the story in the papers, he attempted to rob a bank. With all of the town's police force out searching for him in the wilderness, nowhere close to the bank, it is very likely that he might have been successful. However, in a move that can never be explained, he started firing a gun into the air inside the bank—some thirty or forty shots in all. The noise alerted the townspeople, including a clerk who doubled as a newspaper reporter. He called reports of gunshots in the

bank to his paper and his editor relayed the information to the nearest radio station. By some accounts, it became the first in-progress robbery to be broadcast live on the radio.

Not even realizing Durand was involved, citizens who had heard the gunshots, or the reports of them on the radio, surrounded the bank with firearms of their own. Durand came out of the bank holding one of the clerks as a human shield, but the mob paid no heed to the shield—they opened fire, fatally wounding the clerk in the process.

But when the clerk fell from Durand's arms, the teenager Tipton Cox managed to wound Durand from the doorway of a nearby service station. Durand, knowing he was beaten, crawled bank into the bank, where he put a pistol against his own head and fired. Cox became an instant celebrity and was taken to New York for a radio interview, where he said he planned to study aviation at college. He ended up flying planes in World War II and continued to work in aviation until his death in 2006. •

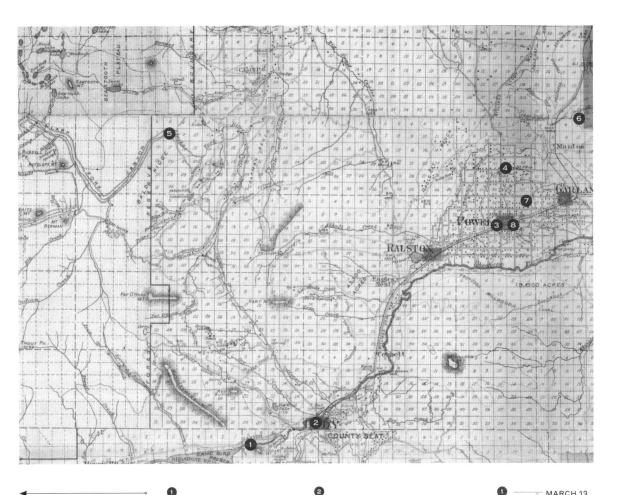

OPPOSITE, TOP The Montana National Guard were called in to aid with the search for Earl Durand. They brought with them a 3-inch trench mortar and a 37-mm howitzer.

OPPOSITE, BOTTOM Members of the posse hunting Earl Durand carrying the bodies of Arthur Argento and Orville Linaberry, who were shot and killed by Durand when they tried to reach him in his hideout in Clark's Fork Canyon.

❶ SHOSHONE RIVER CANYON
The canyon where Earl Durand was arrested by Leonard Morris and Tex Kennedy on March 13.

❸ POWELL
Earl Durand's hometown, where he was followed by D. M. Baker and Chuck Lewis, both of whom he shot and killed.

❺ LITTLE ROCKY CREEK, NEAR THE MOUTH OF CLARK'S FORK CANYON
The canyon where Arthur Argento and Orville Linaberry were shot and killed trying to reach Earl Durand.

❼ NORTHEAST OF POWELL
Earl Durand's parents lived northeast of Powell, and Durand visited them here to pick up some belongings and say goodbye before driving to the bank.

❷ CODY
The town in which Earl Durand was imprisoned before making his escape on March 16.

❹ BITTER CREEK, NEAR POWELL
The creek where Earl Durand hid while the posse searched the surrounding area between March 16 and 21.

❻ NEAR DEAVER
Where Earl Durand drove to in order to fill up with petrol after after commandeering a car.

❽ FIRST NATIONAL BANK, POWELL
Durand entered the bank, robbed it of between $2,000 and $3,000, and then opened fire. After being shot he took his own life.

❶ —————— MARCH 13

❷❸❹ —————— MARCH 16

❺ —————— MARCH 21

❻❼❽ —————— MARCH 24

My Dear Mr Blackburn.

That was one dirty trick for you to jail those 2 boys just because I got away. If you send them over the road I will kill you and that blanckety blank district attorney if I live long enough and possibly can.

Tell King and Kennedy to always carry a pistol. If I ever meet them I will give them a chance for an even draw, something I wont give you if you put up those boys.

Tell that man whose beef I killed that if I live long enough to get back in the mts. that he has nothing to fear from me, I hope I never see him again.

When you get after me better take about 2 o men, for your bodly guard and put braces on their knees.

Of course I know that I am done for and when you kill me I sugest you have my head mounted and hang it up in the court house for the hope of law and order. Your beloved enemy
Earl Durand

P.S. I have notice fing have to the many deputies and armed and I want to state thanks

ABOVE The letter sent by Earl Durand to Sheriff Frank Blackburn, which ends, "Of course I know that I'm done for, and when you kill me I suggest you have my head mounted and hang it up in the courthouse for the sake of law and order. Your beloved enemy, Earl Durand."

RIGHT The First National Bank in Powell, where Earl Durand engaged in a final gunfight with the gathered crowd, before returning inside the bank to kill himself.

RIGHT Bullet holes in the door of the First National Bank in Powell, which Earl Durand robbed at the end of his flight from the law.

RIGHT The body of Earl Durand. In his final gunfight he was shot by the teenager Tipton Cox, before he shot himself in the head.

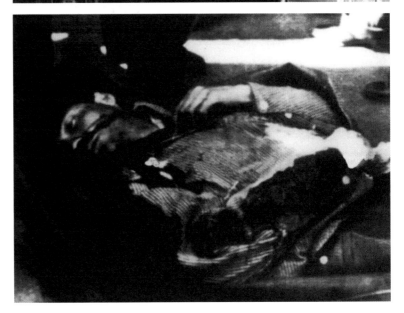

ALFERD PACKER

X Israel Swann + 4

WEAPON	TYPOLOGY	POLICING
HATCHET	PROPERTY CRIME	POSTMORTEM

SAN JUAN MOUNTAINS, EXACT LOCATION UNKNOWN

In 1873, when word came that a huge amount of gold had been discovered in Breckenridge, a group of twenty men left mines in Salt Lake City to try their luck there. They had only gone about 25 miles (40 km) when they encountered Alferd Packer, who said that he knew the San Juan mountains well and offered to join them as a guide.

Later, members of the party described him as lazy, uncooperative, greedy, and completely unable to help them navigate the mountains, having lied about knowing the territory. Just as winter was arriving, the party got lost in the mountains. When they found an encampment of the Tabeguache tribe, Chief Ouray offered to let them stay with the tribe, and share their food supply, until spring, but the party was afraid that all of the gold would be claimed if they did not hurry. Against the chief's advice, six of them resumed the journey after two weeks.

Packer insisted that he knew a quicker route than the directions the chief had given them. They entered the snowy mountains without nearly enough supplies, and with barely enough food to last the projected fourteen days, led by a man who had no idea what he was doing.

Exactly what happened afterwards is still not entirely clear, but it is known that only Packer survived out of the men he led into the snow. When he made his way to civilization months later, he had a convoluted claim that the men had slowly killed one another for meat to keep from starving, until it was only him and Shannon Bell left, whom he had killed in self defense. When the bodies were found though, it appeared that they had all been killed in short order, in the same place. Packer, it seemed, had killed them all in order to both rob and consume them.

Before the authorities could charge Packer, he escaped from the makeshift jail in which he had been placed, and he spent a decade in hiding before being tracked down. When he was finally put to trial, the jury determined that he had murdered Israel Swann first, then killed the others in their sleep. He served eighteen years in jail. •

↑ **ABOVE** A studio portrait of the murderer and cannibal Alferd Packer.

↑ **ABOVE** In 1989 the remains of Alferd Packer's victims were exhumed by researchers specializing in forensic science.

ABOVE Contemporary illustrations showing the site where Alferd Packer murdered his companions (top), Packer cannibalizing his victims (center), and where the victims were eventually buried (bottom).

ABOVE, RIGHT An illustration from *Harper's* of the scene of Alferd Packer's crime.

1 BINGHAM CANYON
The trip began here in the early part of January 1874.

2 GREEN RIVER
The travelers crossed the river here on a raft on January 21.

3 TABEGUACHE CAMP
At the camp Chief Ouray provided the party with some food, around January 25.

4 CHIEF OURAY'S WINTER CAMP
The group remained here from around February 1 to 7.

5 NEAR LAKE SAN CRISTOBAL
Alferd Packer killed five companions here around February 27.

6 LOS PINOS AGENCY
Alferd Packer arrived here alone on around April 1.

7 SAGUACHE
Alferd Packer was jailed here before making his escape and remaining at large for a decade.

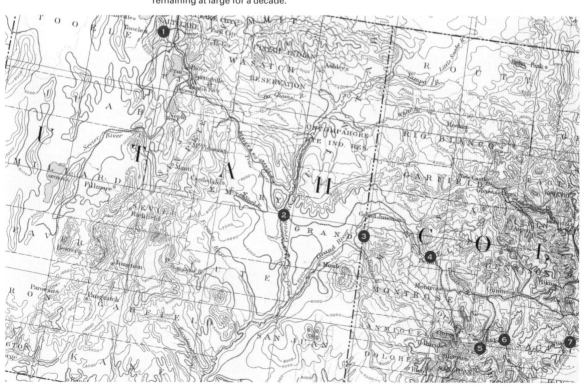

CO—DENVER	1900–01

CAPITOL HILL THUG

× Lillian Bell × Mary Short
× Josephine Unternahrer

WEAPON BLUDGEON	TYPOLOGY RANDOM ATTACK	POLICING —
VARIOUS LOCATIONS, CAPITOL HILL		

Even among the ranks of obscure serial killers, it seems curious that Denver's "Capitol Hill Thug" of 1900–01 has been so thoroughly forgotten today. The murders attributed to him are numerous, and brutal enough that one would expect the spree to survive in the popular imagination. Perhaps it is due to the fact that many of his would-be victims survived the attacks; the "thug" would sneak up on women and hit them on the head with a heavy object, then flee. Most recovered.

On February 22, 1901, 40-year-old Mary Short was found in the Capitol Hill area of Denver, bleeding from her head. She had been attacked with a blunt instrument and died soon after. Two other women were also attacked that night.

These were not the first attacks—in the past several months, eight women had been attacked in the area. Many were women on their way home from church or synagogue services. Denver streets had a reputation for being dangerous and it took some time for anyone to suspect that the first attacks were connected, rather than just run-of-the-mill violence. When they realized there was a "thug" on the loose, police rounded up several small-time crooks and jailed them all, including one man that the police chief insisted was the culprit. But the attacks continued. Throughout the winter of 1900, the police chief announced several times that he had solved the crime, but the attacks always continued.

By the time of the three attacks on February 22, the police had a few clues—witnesses were describing a small man in a long gray Ulster coat and a felt hat, with very light skin and a drooping black mustache. Another February 22 victim, Josephine Unternahrer, lived long enough to describe her attacker as a man with a black mustache. Then a man came forth claiming he had gotten a close-up view of the man who killed Mary Short. On his information, the police pinpointed a man named Alfred Cowan as the Capitol Hill Thug.

But Cowan could not be convicted, and another couple of attacks took place before they abruptly stopped. The crimes were never solved. •

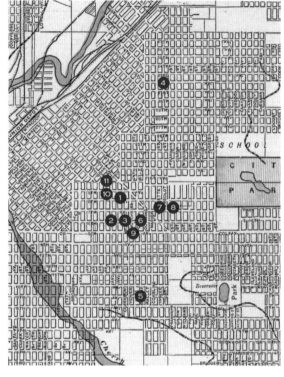

1
1545 PEARL STREET
Elva Jessup was attacked on August 24.

2
16TH & WASHINGTON STREET
Lillian Bell was fatally attacked on August 24.

3
16TH & EMMERSON STREET
Emma Carlson was attacked on September 24.

4
2130 HUMBOLDT STREET
Annie McAtee was attacked on October 5.

5
938 CORONA STREET
Mrs. Dewart Young was attacked on December 22.

6
16TH & OGDEN STREET
Julia Dohr was attacked on January 6.

7
LOCATION APPROX.
Marie Frazier was attacked on February 16.

8
LOCATION APPROX.
Miss Everest was attacked on February 16.

9
16TH & CLARKSON STREET
Mary Short was fatally attacked on February 22.

10
19TH & PENNSYLVANIA STREET
Emma Johnson was attacked on February 22.

11
1950 PENNSYLVANIA STREET
Josephine Unternahrer was fatally attacked on February 22.

UNKNOWN

✕ Al Swearengen

WEAPON	TYPOLOGY	POLICING
BLUNT OBJECT	TARGETED KILLING	—

**NEAR THE DENVER & RIO GRANDE RAILROAD TRACKS
WHERE THEY CROSS ALAMEDA AVENUE**

Though Deadwood, South Dakota, legally belonged to the Lakota Tribe in 1874, once gold was discovered there, it did not take a historian to predict that they would not be able to keep their claim on it for long. Prospectors ignored their territorial rights and swept into the Black Hills, building up the town of Deadwood, which immediately became known for lawlessness (and which, to start with, was an illegal settlement). Wild Bill Hickok was shot dead there in 1876.

In this town of brothels and saloons, perhaps no one had a nastier reputation than Al Swearengen, who first controlled the town's opium trade, then opened the most notorious of all the brothels in the area, the Gem Variety Theater, in 1877. While it did function as a variety theater, in which comedians and musicians fought for stage time against brutal prize fights, the real attraction was the gambling and the women. Some of the women had been lured to the theater by Swearengen with promises of legitimate restaurant jobs, then forced into sex work when they arrived. He treated them roughly, even by the standards of the day.

But the Gem was pulling in thousands of dollars a night and Swearengen, working in a town where the law had very little sway, was able to pay enough people off to keep himself out of trouble.

The Gem was rebuilt after one fire in 1879, but when it burned down again in 1899 Swearengen decided to get out of the business and leave town. In November, 1905, his body was found in the middle of the street in a Denver suburb, a gunshot wound in his head. He had not been robbed, making it appear to be a targeted killing. His twin brother Lemuel had been attacked in a similar manner the previous month, and historians suspect the perpetrator may have been Al's killer, in a case of mistaken identity. But there was never a true suspect and most were happy to let the death go uninvestigated. Stories later spread that Swearengen had died while trying to hop a freight train, which kept interest in finding the killer low. •

ABOVE An exterior and interior view of the Gem Variety Theater in Deadwood, owned by Al Swearengen.

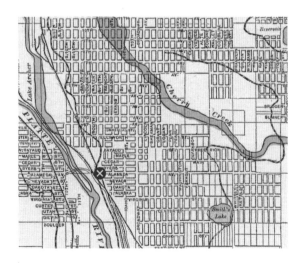

ABOVE The location where Al Swearengen's body was found, near the Denver and Rio Grande railroad tracks.

NM—LINCOLN	*April 1, 1878*

HENRY McCARTY
A.K.A. BILLY THE KID
× William Brady

WEAPON	TYPOLOGY	POLICING
PISTOL	GANG	POSSE

TUNSTALL'S STORE ON MAIN STREET

The lawless days of the Wild West only seem romantic in hindsight. In the 1870s, New Mexico Territory, not yet a state, was a dusty land where the law had little reach. Dry goods companies and cattle ranchers had to fight for survival in the truest sense of the word, recruiting bands of both law men and outlaws to protect their interests from competitors.

In Lincoln County, a relatively new settlement of only a few thousand people, a man named James Dolan had a local monopoly on dry goods and cattle ranching. But when an Englishman named John Tunstall opened a store and ranch of his own in 1876, both stores formed armies to fight for control of the region. The town was not big enough for the both of them.

↑ **ABOVE** Two tintype photographs, believed by some to show Billy the Kid playing croquet with friends.

Dolan's side included Lincoln County Sheriff William Brady. Tunstall's side had both the town constable and a gang of outlaws led by the famous Henry McCarty. Orphaned at 15, McCarty had embarked on a life of robbery and crime in 1875, and that fall began appearing on wanted posters under his more famous nickname, "Billy the Kid."

What should have been a dry battle in the courts over insurance payouts and government contracts turned violent in 1878 when members of Sheriff Brady's posse shot Tunstall dead in cold blood.

Tunstall's murder set off what came to be known as the Lincoln County War. James Dolan, along with his monopoly on dry goods, had most of the territorial law enforcement under his thumb and believed that he was untouchable. Unable to rely on the authorities, Tunstall's enforcers formed an arm—including Billy the Kid—known as the Regulators to avenge his death. A Justice of the Peace deputized the regulators and granted them warrants to arrest the killers, but Sheriff Brady defied their warrants and had them arrested. Upon their release, the Regulators captured and killed a few of Dolan's men.

After a month of violence and anarchy, Brady was asking the territorial governor for help. But on April 1, Billy the Kid and a group of other Regulators hid in the corral behind Tunstall's old store, then ambushed Brady in the middle of the street. The sheriff was shot at least a dozen times and Billy retrieved one of his own rifles, which Brady had confiscated, from the corpse before escaping.

The next few months of 1878 saw Billy and the Regulators engaging in a series of gunfights with the Dolan men, culminating in a three-day shootout. Surrounded, Billy escaped in a haze of pistol fire and made his way out of town to spend the rest of his days as a fugitive.

The Lincoln County War ended much as it had begun, with Dolan controlling most of the business in the area. He was charged with the murder of Tunstall, but was acquitted and even acquired more of Tunstall's property. Victorious, he descended into a haze of alcoholism and died on his ranch in 1898. •

Street scene
Lincoln
N. M.

① MAIN STREET, LINCOLN
Dubbed the "most dangerous street in America," Lincoln Main Street was the center of the War.

② THE COURTHOUSE
Formerly James Dolan & Co., this building became the courthouse.

③ THE WORTLEY HOTEL
William Brady had breakfast at the Wortley shortly before being killed by the Regulators.

④ McSWEEN'S HOUSE
Alexander McSween was a prominent figure in the Lincoln County War.

⑤ LOLA SISNERO'S HOUSE
Following William Brady's assassination Peppin and Matthews ran for cover here.

⑥ BURIAL PLACE
The burial place of Tunstall, McSween, McNab, and Morris.

⑦ TORREON
A short defensive tower, first built for defense against Native Americans.

⑧ FORMER COURTHOUSE
The building used as the courthouse before it moved to James Dolan & Co. [2].

⑨ MONTAÑO STORE
The Montaños were supporters of the Tunstall faction.

⑩ JUAN PATRON'S STORE
Juan Patron was a teacher and supported the Tunstall faction.

⑪ JAIL
Lincoln town's jail.

⑫ ISAAC ELLIS'S STORE
Isaac Ellis was a supporter of the Tunstall faction.

REWARD

($5,000.00)

Reward for the capture, dead or alive, of one Wm. Wright, better known as

"BILLY THE KID"

Age, 18. Height, 5 feet, 3 inches. Weight, 125 lbs. Light hair, blue eyes and even features. He is the leader of the worst band of desperadoes the Territory has ever had to deal with. The above reward will be paid for his capture or positive proof of his death.

JIM DALTON, Sheriff.

DEAD OR ALIVE!
"BILLY THE KID"

OPPOSITE A tintype photograph of Billy the Kid, one of only two confirmed photographs of the infamous outlaw.

RIGHT A wanted poster issued for Billy the Kid, offering a $5,000 reward. He is described as having "light hair, blue eyes and even features."

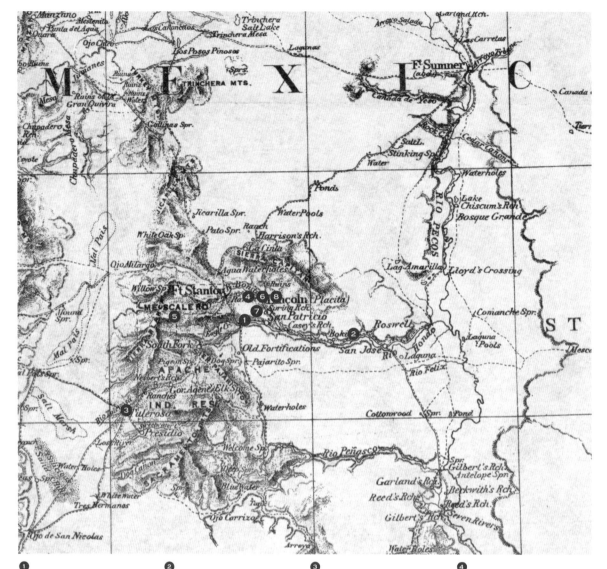

❶
**FEBRUARY 18, 1878,
JOHN TUNSTALL WAS
MURDERED**
Members of Sheriff
William Brady's posse killed
John Tunstall while he and
his ranch hands were herding
his horses back to Lincoln.
Tunstall's murder began the
Lincoln County War, as the
Regulators were formed
to avenge his death.

❷
**MARCH 9, 1878,
BILLY MORTON,
FRANK BAKER, AND
BILL McCLOSKEY
WERE MURDERED**
The Regulators killed Billy
Morton, Frank Baker, and
Bill McCloskey in the
Capitan foothills along
the Blackwater Creek.

❸
**MARCH 9, 1878,
TOM HILL WAS MURDERED**
Two of Tunstall's killers,
Tom Hill and Jesse Evans,
were shot while trying
to rob a sheep drover
near Tularosa.

❹
**APRIL 1, 1878,
WILLIAM BRADY AND
GEORGE HINDMAN WERE
MURDERED**
The Regulators made
ready in the corral behind
Tunstall's store, before
attacking William Brady
and his deputies on
Main Street, Lincoln.

❺
**APRIL 4, 1878,
THE BLAZER'S MILL
GUNFIGHT**
The Regulators headed south-
west from Lincoln, reaching
Blazer's Mill, near Mescalero.
They came across the rancher
Buckshot Roberts, who was
listed on their warrant as one of
Tunstall's killers. In the ensuing
gunfight, the Regulators
mortally wounded Buckshot
Roberts, but in return he killed
Dick Brewer and wounded
John Middleton, Don Scurlock,
George Coe, and Billy the Kid.

❻
**APRIL 29, 1878,
GUNFIGHT AT FRITZ RANCH**
Sheriff George Peppin and
his posse engaged in a
shootout with the Regulators
at the Fritz Ranch. Frank
McNab was killed in the
gunfire, Ab Saunders was
badly wounded, and Frank
Coe was captured.

❼
**JULY 15, 1878,
BATTLE OF LINCOLN**
A large confrontation
between the two forces
occurred when the Regulators
were surrounded in Lincoln,
in the McSween house
and the Ellis store. Opposing
them were James Dolan,
Lawrence Murphy, and the
Seven Rivers cowboys.

❽
**APRIL 28, 1881,
BILLY THE KID ESCAPES
FROM JAIL**
In 1881 the new Sheriff of
Lincoln Pat Garrett arrested
Billy the Kid for the murder
of William Brady and
imprisoned him in Lincoln.
However, one day when
Garrett was out of town,
Billy managed to escape from
the jail. He lived as a fugitive
until July 14, when Garrett
caught up with him and
shot him dead.

THE REGULATORS

JOHN TUNSTALL
THE RANCHER AND STORE OWNER WHOSE DEATH BEGAN THE LINCOLN COUNTY WAR.

BILLY THE KID
THE MOST INFAMOUS CHARACTER OF THE LINCOLN COUNTY WAR, WHO KILLED WILLIAM BRADY.

DICK BREWER
THE COWBOY WHO FORMED THE REGULATORS IN ORDER TO AVENGE JOHN TUNSTALL'S DEATH.

FRANK McNAB
A CATTLE DETECTIVE, AND DICK BREWER'S SECOND-IN-COMMAND IN THE REGULATORS.

AB SAUNDERS
A COWBOY AND GUNMAN, AND A MEMBER OF THE REGULATORS.

FRANK COE
A COWBOY AND GUNMAN, AND A MEMBER OF THE REGULATORS.

GEORGE COE
A COWBOY AND GUNMAN, AND A MEMBER OF THE REGULATORS.

TOM O'FOLLIARD
THE BEST FRIEND OF BILLY THE KID. AFTER THE WAR THEY BECAME RUSTLERS TOGETHER.

ALEXANDER McSWEEN
A PROMINENT FIGURE IN LINCOLN, ACCUSED OF EMBEZZLEMENT BY THE MURPHY-DOLAN FACTION.

SUSAN McSWEEN
THE WIFE OF ALEXANDER McSWEEN. AFTER THE WAR SHE BECAME A PROMINENT CATTLEWOMAN.

THE MURPHY/DOLAN FACTION

JAMES DOLAN
THE LINCOLN BUSINESSMAN WHO HELD A MONOPOLY OVER DRY GOODS AND RANCHING.

LAWRENCE MURPHY
JAMES DOLAN'S BUSINESS PARTNER., AND FOUNDER OF L. G. MURPHY & CO.

WILLIAM BRADY
THE SHERIFF OF LINCOLN COUNTY, UNTIL HE WAS KILLED IN AN AMBUSH BY BILLY THE KID.

JESSE EVANS
THE LEADER OF THE JESSE EVANS GANG, A PROMINENT FORCE IN THE LINCOLN COUNTY WAR.

GEORGE PEPPIN
JOHN COPELAND REPLACED WILLIAM BRADY AS SHERIFF, WHO WAS SOON REPLACED BY GEORGE PEPPIN.

PAT GARRETT
GARRETT WAS ELECTED SHERIFF OF LINCOLN IN 1880 AND EVENTUALLY KILLED BILLY THE KID.

A SELECTION OF THE KEY FIGURES IN THE LINCOLN COUNTY WAR
The Lincoln County War was triggered by the murder of John Tunstall, who had threatened the monopoly on ranching and dry goods held in Lincoln by James Dolan and his associate Lawrence Murphy. The Regulators were formed to avenge the death of Tunstall. Both factions were comprised of both lawmen and outlaws.

THEODORE DURRANT

✕ Blanche Lamont ✕ Minnie Williams

WEAPON	TYPOLOGY	POLICING
VARIOUS	**SEXUAL**	**CRIME SCENE PHOTOGRAPHY**

EMMANUEL BAPTIST CHURCH, BARTLETT STREET

By the early 20th century, the newspaper publisher William Randolph Hearst's name had become synonymous with sensationalistic stories. Some even say that the highly exaggerated stories about the situation in Cuba published in his network of papers pushed the United States into war with Spain. Just a few years before that war, however, he had only owned one paper, *The Examiner* in San Francisco. There, he was able to hone his skill in publishing lurid, highly illustrated stories with tales of a local murderer, Theodore Durrant.

Durrant, a 23-year-old medical student, was the superintendent of a Sunday School at Emmanuel Baptist Church. In 1895, he met a young woman, Blanche Lamont, who had just moved to the Bay Area from Montana. On April 3, they were seen entering the church together. Hours later, Durrant came downstairs, where a practicing organist saw him looking pale and shaky. Blanche was never seen alive again.

Barely a week later, another young parishioner, Minnie Williams, was seen arguing with Durrant outside of the chuch. The next morning, Easter, a woman opened a cupboard in the church to find Minnie's mutilated body inside. A search of the vicinity revealed Blanche Lamont's nude body in the belfry, her head stuck between two boards.

Photographs in newspapers were not yet common, but Hearst published drawings of knives found on the scene and covered entire pages with electrostatic copies of letters Durrant had written. Lurid stories of Durrant killing birds as part of foreplay in brothels began to circulate. *The Examiner* also published important information that would otherwise be since lost, including full transcripts of police interviews with witnesses, and Durrant's own statements. On one morning, Hearst published portraits of Durrant alongside portraits of H. H. Holmes, who was being investigated at the same time (and had also killed a woman named Minnie Williams).

Beyond the rumors in the press, detectives found that a man—identified as Durrant—had tried to pawn a ring owned by Blanche the day after her disappearance. Durrant was convicted of murder and hanged in 1898 at San Quentin Prison, still protesting his innocence. •

BELOW The exterior of Emmanuel Baptist Church, Bartlett Street.

BELOW Bloodstains in the room where Minnie Williams was found.

BELOW The belfry, in which Blanche Lamont's body was found.

MINNIE WILLIAMS   BLANCHE LAMONT

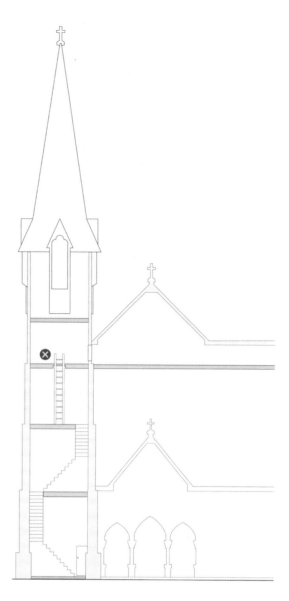

ABOVE A press illustration recreating the murders of Blanche Lamont and Minnie Williams.

BELOW The first floor of the church. Durrant was believed to have entered through the open door on the right.

ABOVE The belfry of Emmanuel Church, where Blanche Lamont's body was found.

BELOW The main auditorium of Emmanuel Church, where Theodore Durrant murdered two women.

CA—LOS ANGELES	*August 5, 1921*

MADALYNNE OBENCHAIN ARTHUR BURCH

× John Belton Kennedy

WEAPON	TYPOLOGY	POLICING
SHOTGUN	DOMESTIC	TIREPRINTS

KENNEDY'S CABIN ON BEVERLY GLEN BOULEVARD

MADALYNNE OBENCHAIN   ARTHUR BURCH

On a hot August night in 1921, George Deering was driving past a cabin in the rustic canyons of Los Angeles when he was flagged down by a sobbing woman who was begging him to stop. A friend of hers, she said, had been badly injured, and she needed help immediately.

George followed the woman, Madalynne Obenchain, to the cabin, where he found the body of John Belton Kennedy, already dead and far beyond help. With no doctor nearby and no telephone available, he drove Obenchain to the nearest police station.

There, she told an odd story: she and John had gone to the cabin to search for a lucky penny she had lost. She had heard a strange noise, followed by two gun shots, in between which she heard John shouting, "Goodnight, Madalynne." She had not thought he needed help because she had not checked on him after hearing the shots.

Madalynne had been trying to marry Kennedy for years, but his mother had not approved, and she had married the attorney Ralph Obenchain instead, to whom she had been officially engaged for years. Even after the marriage, Madalynne carried on an affair with Kennedy, and she and Ralph were separated within three months.

However Kennedy and Madalynne still did not marry, despite continuing a tempestuous love affair. In the meantime Madalynne became reacquainted with a former admirer, named Arthur Burch, who urged her to be with him instead.

Naturally, Madalynne and Arthur were accused of Kennedy's murder. Burch had been seen by his hotel manager carrying something that looked like a shotgun, and his car tires were matched with tireprints found at the scene of the crime. Madalynne's estranged husband Ralph rushed to L.A. to help her, and to star in a movie about their romance. Throughout her trial Madalynne made so many friends that she was referred to as America's most popular murderer.

The case kept Jazz Age Californians on the edge of their seats for over a year. After five sensational trials ended in hung juries, the state turned Madalynne loose. She disappeared from the news and lived a quiet, single life in a small beach community. •

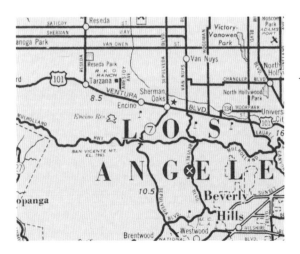

RIGHT John Belton Kennedy, who had a long-term affair with Madalynne Obenchain.

LEFT The location of the cabin on Beverly Glen Boulevard where John Belton Kennedy was killed.

RIGHT Two views of the stairs leading to the cabin on Beverly Glen Boulevard, where the murderer was believed to have hidden.

RIGHT The cabin on Beverly Glen Boulevard, where John Belton Kennedy was found dead. Madalynne Obenchain claimed that they had gone to the cabin to search for a missing lucky penny.

RIGHT A contemporary re-enactment of John Belton Kennedy's murder. The number 1 indicates the couple representing Kennedy and Madalynne Obenchain; the number 2 suggests where the murderer was hiding; and the number 3 indicates the cabin.

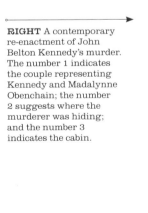

UNKNOWN

✕ William Desmond Taylor

WEAPON	TYPOLOGY	POLICING
PISTOL	UNKNOWN	—

**ALVARADO COURT APARTMENTS,
SOUTH ALVARADO STREET**

In the world of silent films, novelty was the name of the game—even huge hits seldom lasted long in the theaters. This meant studios had to crank out new movies as quickly as possible. As an actor, William Desmond Taylor performed in an average of nine films per year between 1913 and 1915. In 1914, he began directing as well and worked on nearly sixty films over the next eight years, despite a break in the middle to serve in World War I.

The son of a New York society family, named William Cunningham Deane-Tanner, he married actress Ethel May Hamilton on December 7, 1901 with whom he had a daughter a year or so later. Taylor left his wife and child in 1908 and went on the road until 1912, having adventures that remain unrecorded. He emerged in California with a new name, and slipped into the life of an actor and director. He had been in the business for some time before his family in New York became aware of his activities, though when his young daughter wrote to him after seeing him in a movie, he visited her and arranged to make her his heir.

Only months later, in February, 1922, Taylor was found dead in his apartment on Alvarado Street. A doctor announced that Taylor had died of a stomach hemorrhage, then disappeared from the scene without giving his name—which seemed suspicious when Taylor was rolled over to reveal a gunshot wound in his back.

A number of valuables were found on his person, meaning that robbery seemed an unlikely motive. There were multiple murder suspects, from disgruntled former valets to a variety of actresses and girlfriends, including the comedy star Mabel Normand, who, it was whispered, knew that Taylor was trying to put an end to her cocaine use, and Mary Miles Minter, a former child star who had written passionate love letters to Taylor (who, being thirty years her senior, had turned her down), as well as Charlotte Shelby, Minter's mother. The poor investigation of the crime scene, combined with possible corruption in the police, left the case impossible to solve and there was never enough evidence to charge anyone. •

ABOVE A photograph of the interior of William Desmond Taylor's home, with an illustration and arrow indicating where his body was found. When Taylor was rolled over a gunshot wound was discovered in his back.

ABOVE A photograph of the coat that William Desmond Taylor was wearing when he was shot. Gunpowder was found on the coat by the coroner, which indicated that Taylor was shot at close range.

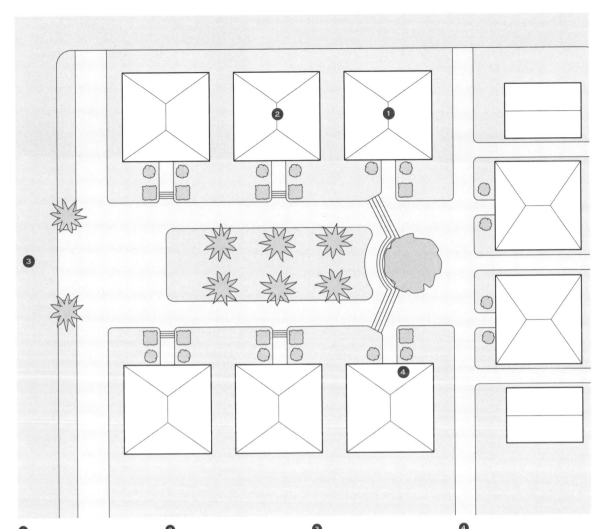

①
WILLIAM DESMOND TAYLOR'S BUNGALOW
The house in which William Desmond Taylor was discovered shot in the back.

②
EDNA PURVIANCE'S BUNGALOW
The house belonging to Taylor's neighbor, leading lady Edna Purviance, one of the first to discover the crime.

③
SOUTH ALVARADO STREET
The street where Mabel Normand parked her car when visiting William Desmond Taylor on the night of the murder.

④
THE McLEANS' BUNGALOW
The house from which Faith McLean, wife of actor Douglas McLean, saw a stocky man leaving Taylor's house on the night of the murder.

— SUSPECTS & WITNESSES —

RUSSO RINALDO
ACCOUNTANT
CONFESSED TO THE MURDER EIGHT YEARS LATER.

J. G. BARRETT
CONVICT
CONFESSED TO THE MURDER SIX YEARS LATER.

OTIS HEFNER
BANDIT
CLAIMED TO HAVE INFORMATION ABOUT THE MURDER.

HARRY FIELDS
—
QUESTIONED BY POLICE DURING INVESTIGATIONS.

EDWARD SANDS
TAYLOR'S VALET
SUSPECTED BUT NEVER ARRESTED DURING INVESTIGATIONS.

HENRY PEAVEY
TAYLOR'S VALET
DISCOVERED TAYLOR'S BODY ON THE MORNING AFTER THE MURDER.

MABEL NORMAND
TAYLOR'S FRIEND
VISITED TAYLOR ON THE NIGHT OF THE MURDER.

MARY MILES MINTER
TAYLOR'S EX-LOVER
A POSSIBLE SUSPECT IN THE INVESTIGATION INTO THE MURDER.

CHARLOTTE SHELBY
MARY'S MOTHER
A POSSIBLE SUSPECT IN THE INVESTIGATION INTO THE MURDER.

MARGARET GIBSON
ACTRESS
CONFESSED TO THE MURDER ON HER DEATHBED.

CA—WINEVILLE	1926–28

GORDON NORTHCOTT SARAH NORTHCOTT
×20

WEAPON	TYPOLOGY	POLICING
AXE	SEXUAL	FORENSIC ANTHROPOLOGY

6330 WINEVILLE AVENUE, JURUPA VALLEY, RIVERSIDE COUNTY

GORDON NORTHCOTT   SARAH NORTHCOTT

When the film industry began to set up shop there in the 1910s, Los Angeles grew very quickly from a town consisting primarily of orange groves to a large metropolis. But farms remained dotted on the outskirts in the 1920s. Gordon Northcott, still just a teenager, convinced his father to buy some land in nearby Wineville (now Mira Loma) in 1924, where he built a chicken ranch.

However the ranch was only a cover for Northcott's true interest, which was abducting, assaulting, and, in many cases, murdering young boys. Authorities eventually believed that he had killed around twenty, occasionally aided by his mother, Sarah Northcott, and nephew.

Wineville was a small town, but nearby Los Angeles provided an almost limitless number of victims. Northcott had likely been operating there for some time by March 10, 1928, when he abducted 9-year old Walter Collins from Pasadena Avenue.

Walter's disappearance became a major news story; his incarcerated father believed that former inmates had kidnapped the boy as part of a revenge scheme. When a boy in Illinois claimed to be Walter, the police chief insisted that Walter's mother take him home, even though she had seen pictures of the boy and insisted it was not her son. The police were under pressure to solve the case and were willing to grasp at straws.

When she brought the boy back, armed with Walter's dental records and other pieces of proof that they had the wrong child, the chief accused her of trying to get rid of her son.

Eventually, a boy named Sanford Clark, a relative of Northcott, told horrifying stories of being forced to watch Collins and other boys being assaulted. He told police that when Northcott was finished with the assaults, he would kill his victims with an axe.

Searching the property, the authorities found pieces of bone in makeshift graves around the ranch, confirming Clark's stories. Northcott had fled, but was arrested in Canada, as was his mother, who confessed to killing Collins herself. She was sentenced to life in prison; Gordon was hanged in 1930. •

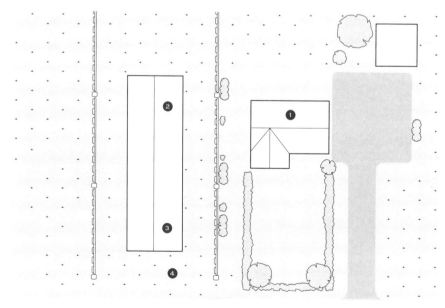

①
THE FARM HOUSE
The main house at Wineville Farm.

②
SITE OF MURDERS
The room in which Sanford Clark claimed that the Winslow brothers were killed.

③
BURIAL SITE
Where Sanford Clark claimed that the Winslow brothers were buried.

④
EVIDENCE DISCOVERED
Charred bones and quicklime were discovered by investigators here.

ALVIN GOTHEA

WALTER COLLINS

LEWIS WINSLOW

NELSON WINSLOW

RIGHT
Investigators searching Gordon Northcott's farm at Wineville.

RIGHT
Investigators who searched Gordon Northcott's property found human remains.

RIGHT
Investigators find a jacket (left) and shoes (right) during their search of Wineville Farm.

RIGHT
Investigators digging for evidence (left) and being escorted around the farm by the murderer Gordon Northcott (right).

> "MY WIFE WOULD GO TO ANY EXTREME,
> NOT EXCEPTING MURDER,
> **TO PLEASE HER SON.**

| CYRUS NORTHCOTT TESTIFYING AGAINST | GORDON STEWART NORTHCOTT'S WRITTEN |
| HIS WIFE, SARAH LOUISE NORTHCOTT. | CONFESSION OF KILLING ALVIN GOTHEA. |

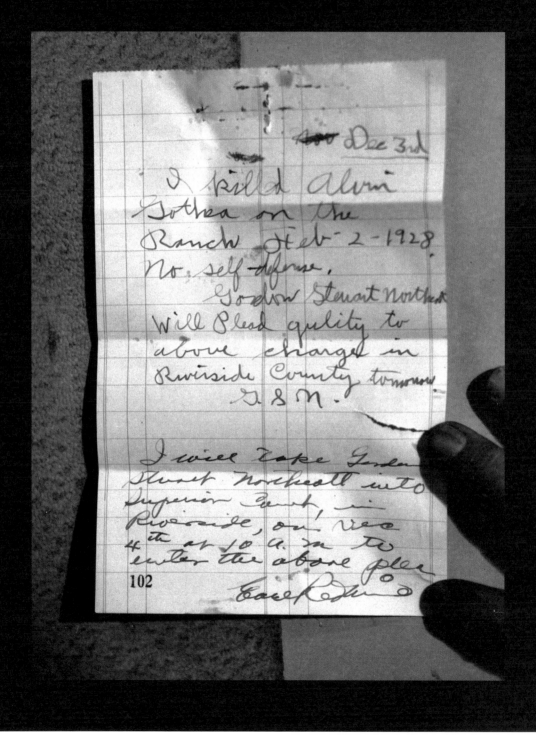

"THOSE SILENT BITS OF EVIDENCE, OF HUMAN BONES AND BLOOD, HAVE SPOKEN **AND CORROBORATED THE TESTIMONY OF LIVING WITNESSES.**"

| ↑ POLICE INVESTIGATORS COMMENTING ON THEIR SEARCH OF WINEVILLE FARM. | SANFORD CLARK EXAMINING EVIDENCE PRESENTED TO HIM BY THE POLICE. ↓ |

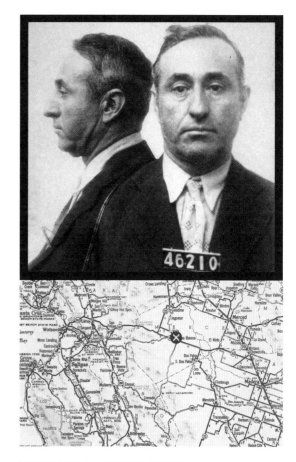

CA—HANFORD	*December 4, 1927*

PERRY COEN
✕ G. Mace Artist ✕ Edna Artist

WEAPON	TYPOLOGY	POLICING
CROWBAR	DOMESTIC	—
HANFORD		

CA—LOS BANOS	*July 24, 1928*

ANTONE NEGRA
✕ Ralph Amabile

WEAPON	TYPOLOGY	POLICING
FIREARM	PROPERTY CRIME	—
SANTA NELLA RANCH, LOS BANOS		

When Isabel Artist's parents were cold towards her boyfriend Perry Coen, with whom she planned to elope, he took matters into his own hands. While the two elder Artists were sleeping, he snuck into their room and bludgeoned both of them to death with a crowbar. Authorities initially arrested Isabel, who was aged just 16, in the belief that she had helped Perry plan the crime, but in the end it was he who was convicted of murder. Following a failed escape attempt in 1928, he was hanged in 1929. •

Cousins (and brothers-in-law) Antone Negra and Ralph Amabile were partners in a sheep business that was operating under a heavy mortgage to a Los Banos bank. Wanting to get out of debt, Negra took out an insurance policy on Amabile's life for $10,000, with a double indemnity clause that would double the payment if he came to a violent end. Negra ensured that he would be paid the sum by shooting his partner in the back. Amabile's body was discovered on a deserted ranch days later and Negra was captured, convicted, and hanged. •

⬆ **ABOVE** The mugshot of Perry Coen, taken at San Quentin Prison.

⬆ **ABOVE** The mugshot of Antone Negra, taken at San Quentin Prison.

CA—LOS ANGELES	*January 8, 1929*

ALPHONSE REILLY
✕ Abraham Sandelman

WEAPON	TYPOLOGY	POLICING
PISTOL	PROPERTY CRIME	—

BEACON SHOE STORE, LOS ANGELES

CA—LIVERMORE	*May 1930*

GEORGE RYLEY
JOHN GOMEZ
✕ George Jones

WEAPON	TYPOLOGY	POLICING
GAS PIPE	PROPERTY CRIME	—

LIVERMORE

After deserting the U.S. Navy, Alphonse Reilly spent time as a straggler and drifter in the midwest, eventually leaving St. Louis and heading to the west coast. While in Los Angeles, he attempted to hold up a shoe store, in the process shooting and killing the owner, Abraham Sandelman. He tried to flee the scene, however after a brief chase he was knocked out by a tailor whose shop he tried to run through. As a deserter, he was released initially to Navy authorities, before being executed in San Quentin prison in 1930. Before his execution, he wrote a note that read, "I went out smiling." •

John Gomez and George Ryley lived near each other in Livermore, and in 1930 they had known each other for years. One night in May they called a taxi together and the driver who arrived was George Jones, an older man who they had also known for several years, well enough to call him "Dad." They also knew that he owned a pool hall. The two conceived a plan to kill George with a gas pipe and then rob his business while it was empty. However they were caught, and after George's attempt to plead insanity failed, they were both executed at San Quentin. •

↑ **ABOVE** The mugshot of Alphonse Reilly, taken at San Quentin Prison.

↑ **ABOVE** The mugshot of George Ryley, taken at San Quentin Prison.

UNKNOWN
✕ Thelma Todd

WEAPON CARBON MONOXIDE	TYPOLOGY DOMESTIC	POLICING AUTOPSY

GARAGE, 17520 REVELLO DRIVE, CASTILLO DEL MAR, PACIFIC PALISADES

In December, 1935, Los Angeles was doing its best to look festive for the holidays—Christmas in a town with no snow. At one party, actress Thelma Todd told her friends, "I'll bet you a dinner that you won't come to my place tomorrow!" The friends laughed and took the bet. But when they called at her house the next day, the butler said Thelma was not home and had not come in the night before. The friends went into the apartment and had dinner anyway, unaware that Miss Todd was lying dead only few hundred feet away.

The next morning, a maid found her body in an automobile parked in a garage: a victim, it seemed, of carbon monoxide poisoning. Coagulated blood stained her mink coat and her silver evening gown. She had been dead for twelve hours.

ABOVE Investigators attending the scene of the crime, the garage belonging to Jewel Carmen, a silent film actress and the ex-wife of Roland West. Thelma Todd was found in her car, apparently killed by carbon monoxide poisoning.

It may have been an accident; some believed that Todd was locked outside by her boyfriend and rushed to the car for warmth. The authorities said it was a suicide. But the engine was not running and there was still fuel in the tank. She had not been in the car for all that long. Her jewelry was still on her body, but there was damage to her lips suggesting that someone had shoved a hose into her mouth. Her friends insisted that it was a murder.

A small-town New England girl, Thelma had been planning to become a teacher when she was spotted by talent scouts during her reign as Miss Massachusetts. Her stunning beauty made her a hit in silent films and her singing voice helped her transition into talkies. She began to act in comedies under the producer Hal Roach and then moved into dramatic roles in early film noir. Over ten years in Hollywood's golden age, she appeared in over a hundred features, sharing the screen with Buster Keaton, the Marx Brothers, and Laurel and Hardy. Though perhaps not a star on the level of a Swanson or a Chaplin, she was well-known enough to have multiple nicknames, including "The Ice Cream Blonde" and "Hot Toddy."

But Tinsel Town could be a dangerous place. In one of early Hollywood's famous brief marriages, she was married from 1932 to 1934 to Pasquale DiCicco, a New York agent who was also a friend of the famed gangster Charles "Lucky" Luciano, with whom Todd was said to have had an affair. She and DiCicco had been seated together at a party days before Thelma's death and had fought very publicly.

Thelma was also running a restaurant with the film director Roland West and he had told her that they were losing money because of their mob payouts. Some believe that Todd was planning to confront the mob. Others point to her romantic attachment to West and wonder if she was planning to confront West's former wife, Jewel Carmen, in whose garage her body was found. But the coroner ruled that it was a suicide and no further investigations were made. The murder—if a murder it was—remains unsolved. •

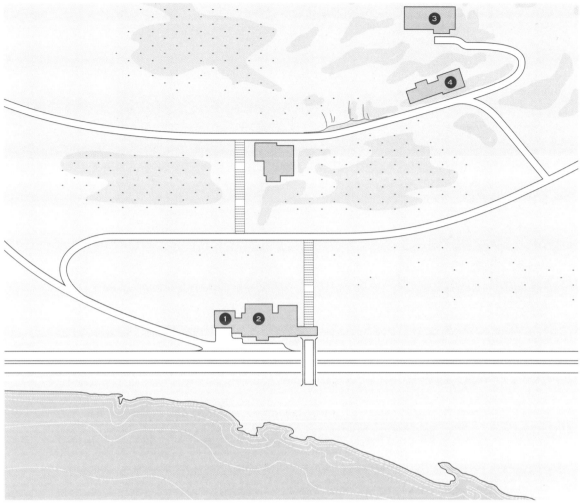

❶
THELMA TODD'S SIDEWALK CAFE, 17575 PACIFIC COAST HIGHWAY
Todd opened her cafe in August 1934. It attracted a diverse clientele of Hollywood celebrities, and many tourists.

❷
THELMA TODD'S HOME
The apartment above the cafe, where Thelma Todd lived, and where her friends ate dinner while she lay dead in Jewel Carmen's garage.

❸
ROLAND WEST'S HOME, 17531 PASETANO ROAD
The home of the director Roland West, who was romantically involved with Todd and a possible suspect in her death.

❹
JEWEL CARMEN'S GARAGE
The garage where Thelma Todd was discovered dead in her car by her maid, Mae Whitehead.

RIGHT Roland West (left), the Hollywood director romantically attached to Thelma Todd, and Jewel Carmen (right), West's ex-wife.

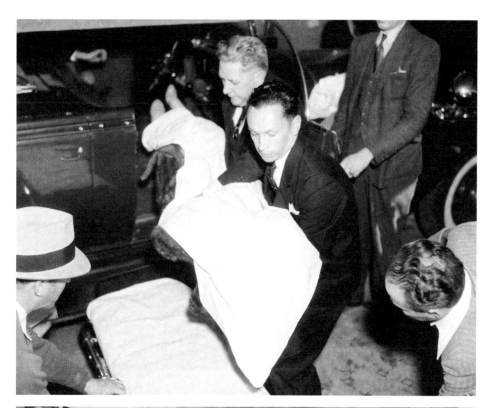

ABOVE, TOP Investigators removing the body of
Thelma Todd from her car, in which she was found
dead in the garage of Jewel Carmen.

ABOVE, BOTTOM Director Roland West grieving for
Thelma Todd on the morning after her death. West was
to become a suspect in the investigation into her death.

ABOVE, TOP Roland West and Harvey Priester, a friend of Todd's, in the audience for the grand jury hearing into the death of Thelma Todd.

ABOVE, BOTTOM Thelma Todd lying in state at the Los Angeles Funeral Chapel. The coroner eventually ruled her death to have been a suicide.

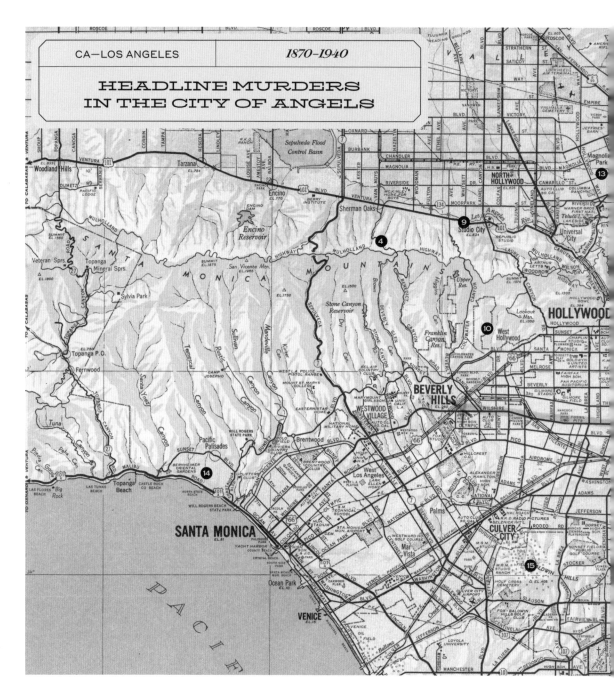

HEADLINE MURDERS
IN THE CITY OF ANGELS

❶ October 24, 1871
CALLE DE LOS NEGROS
MOB
✕ 17–20 CHINESE PEOPLE

❷ January 26, 1906
SOUTH ALVARADO STREET
MORRIS BUCK
✕ CHLOE CANFIELD

❸ June 2, 1920
675 SOUTH CATALINA
STREET
LOUISE PEETE
✕ JACOB C. DENTON

❹ April 5, 1921
BEVERLY GLEN BOULEVARD
MADALYNNE
OBENCHAIN,
ARTHUR BURCH
✕ JOHN BELTON KENNEDY

❺ February 11, 1922
ALVARADO COURT
APARTMENTS, SOUTH
ALVARADO STREET
UNKNOWN
✕ WILLIAM DESMOND
TAYLOR

❻ July 10, 1922
MONTECITO DRIVE
CLARA PHILLIPS
✕ ALBERTA MEADOWS

❼ August 22, 1922
858 NORTH ANDREWS
BOULEVARD [NOW
LAFAYETTE PARK PLACE]
WALBURGA
OESTERREICH
✕ FRED OESTERREICH

❽ December 15, 1927
BELLEVUE ARMS
APARTMENTS
WILLIAM EDWARD
HICKMAN
✕ MARION PARKER

❾ June 18, 1928
12744 VENTURA BOULEVARD
HAZEL GLAB
✕ JOHN GLAB

❿ February 16, 1929
905 LOMA VISTA DRIVE
HUGH PLUNKETT
✕ NED DOHENY

⓫ June 16, 1929
INTERSECTION OF SUNSET
BOULEVARD AND SERRANO
AVENUE
LOIS PANTAGES
✕ JURO (JOE) ROKUMOTO

12 March 24, 1934
THE STERLING ARMS
NELLIE MAY
MADISON
X ERIC MADISON

13 August 4, 1935
VERDUGO ROAD
RATTLESNAKE
JAMES LISENBA
X MARY BUSCH

14 December 16, 1935
17520 REVELLO DRIVE
UNKNOWN
X THELMA TODD

15 June 26, 1937
BALDWIN HILLS
ALBERT DYER
X MADELINE EVERETT
X MELBA EVERETT
X JEANETTE STEPHENS

16 November 9, 1937
VERDUGO VISTA DRIVE
PAUL WRIGHT
X EVELYN WRIGHT
X JOHN BRYANT KIMMEL

17 December 10, 1938
THE ROAD FROM MOUNT
WILSON, NEAR PASADENA
LAUREL CRAWFORD
X RUTH CRAWFORD
X ALICE CRAWFORD
X HELEN CRAWFORD
X PAUL CRAWFORD
X RALPH BARNETT

CA—LOS ANGELES	*June 26, 1937*

ALBERT DYER

✕ Madeline Everett ✕ Melba Everett
✕ Jeanette Stephens

WEAPON	TYPOLOGY	POLICING
STRANGULATION	SEXUAL	CRIME SCENE INVESTIGATION

DITCH, BEAN FIELD, INGLEWOOD

In the summer of 1937, four boy scouts joined a statewide search for three young girls—two sisters and their playmate—who had gone on a picnic two days before and had never returned home. It was the scouts who came across the body of one of the girls in a gully 2 miles (3 km) from the road; her neck was tied tightly with clothesline and her body showed signs of sexual assault. The other two girls were found in a similar condition in bushes several feet away.

As a crowd gathered, one of the volunteer policemen asked a man to refrain from smoking out of respect. The man was 32-year-old Albert Dyer—the man who had murdered the three girls.

As a traffic guard at the local elementary school, he had known the girls slightly. The way he behaved at the crime scene aroused the suspicion of the police and he quickly joined a growing list of suspects, which initially included a man who liked to show children in the park how to tie knots.

As various suspects were interviewed, the police were able to quickly ascertain that Dyer was the killer. They rushed him out of town to avoid the growing lynch mobs, but when he refused to confess, they threatened to take him back and leave him to the mob. At that, Dyer broke and told the officers how he had lured the girls into the woods on the pretense of catching rabbits, then killed them, then prayed over their bodies. He had sexually assaulted at least one of the bodies; some accounts say it was more than one of them.

Later, wild inconsistencies were noticed in Dyer's confessions, leading some to suspect that police had forced a confession out of the wrong man. But the jury had no doubts. He was tried, convicted of murder, and sentenced to die. He was hanged at San Quentin prison. •

ABOVE A mounted search party organized to look for the missing girls, who were eventually found by boy scouts in the Baldwin Hills.

ABOVE The Chief of Investigation for the District Attorney's office, Eugene Williams (second from left, back row), discussing the case with his colleagues.

MADELINE EVERETT

MELBA EVERETT

JEANETTE STEPHENS

❶ DITCH, LOCATION 1
The location at which Jeanette Stephens's body was found.

❷ DITCH, LOCATION 2
The location at which Madeline Everett's body was found.

❸ DITCH, LOCATION 3
The location at which the girls' shoes were found.

❹ DITCH, LOCATION 4
The location at which Melba Everett's body was found.

❺ TEST OIL WELL
The location at which a green car was sighted prior to the murders.

ABOVE Albert Dyer posing after having his fingerprints taken by the police. He was arrested for the murder of Madeline and Melba Everett and Jeanette Stephens.

ABOVE The clothes and shoes belonging to the three victims, which were found during the investigation into their murder.

MURDERER	ENVIRONMENT	GENDER	WEAPON	TYPOLOGY	PROFILE
BAKER, Frankie	Urban	Female	PISTOL	DOMESTIC	Single
BARNES, Iva	Urban	Female	KNIFE	DOMESTIC	Single
BARROW, Clyde	Rural	Male	PISTOL	PROPERTY CRIME	Serial
BENDER FAMILY	Rural	Male & Female	KNIFE & HAMMER	PROPERTY CRIME	Serial
BLUMENFELD, Isadore	Urban	Male	SUBMACHINE GUN	POLITICAL	Single
BOOTH, John Wilkes	Urban	Male	PISTOL	ASSASSINATION	Single
BORDEN, Lizzie	Urban	Female	AXE	DOMESTIC	Single
BROTHERS, Leo Vincent	Urban	Male	FIREARM	GANG	Single
BURCH, Arthur*	Rural	Male	SHOTGUN	DOMESTIC	Single
CAPITOL HILL THUG	Urban	—	BLUDGEON	RANDOM ATTACK	Serial
CAPONE, Al (attrib.)	Urban	Male	FIREARM	GANG	Single
CARTER, Frank	Urban	Male	PISTOL	RANDOM ATTACK	Serial
CHICAGO OUTFIT	Urban	Male	FIREARM	GANG	Single
CHICAGO OUTFIT	Urban	Male	FIREARM	GANG	Single
CHRISTIE, Ned (attrib.)	Rural	Male	FIREARM	POLITICAL	Single
CLARK HYDE, Bennett	Urban	Male	POISON	PROPERTY CRIME	Single
CLAYBOURNE, John J.	Urban	Male	FIREARM	DOMESTIC	Single
CLEVELAND TORSO MURDERER	Urban	—	SHARP OBJECT	RANDOM ATTACK	Serial
COEN, Perry	Urban	Male	CROWBAR	DOMESTIC	Single
CREAM, Thomas Neill	Urban	Male	STRYCHNINE	DOMESTIC	Serial
CZOLGOSZ, Leon	Urban	Male	PISTOL	ASSASSINATION	Single
DAVIDSON, Odus	Rural	Male	SHARP-EGDED TOOL	SEXUAL	Single
DAVIS SING, Alice	Urban	Female	KNIFE	DOMESTIC	Single
DAVIS, Ed	Urban	Male	SHOTGUN & KNIFE	ESCAPE ATTEMPT	Single
DECKER, Calvin A.	Urban	Male	SHOTGUN	DOMESTIC	Single
DINSMORE, Frank	Rural	Male	FIREARM	DOMESTIC	Single
DRENTH, Harm	Rural	Male	VARIOUS	PROPERTY CRIME	Serial
DURAND, Earl	Rural	Male	FIREARM	ESCAPE ATTEMPT	Serial
DURRANT, Theodore	Urban	Male	VARIOUS	SEXUAL	Serial
DYER, Albert	Rural	Male	STRANGULATION	SEXUAL	Single
ELAINE MASSACRE	Urban & Rural	—	VARIOUS	RACIAL	Serial
FLOYD, Allen*	Urban	Male	PISTOL	ESCAPE ATTEMPT	Single
FLOYD, Claude*	Urban	Male	PISTOL	ESCAPE ATTEMPT	Single
FORD, Robert	Urban	Male	PISTOL	REWARD	Single
FRANK, Leo (attrib.)	Urban	—	CORD	SEXUAL	Single
GALLEANISTS	Urban	—	BOMB	BOMBING	Single
GILLIS, Lester a.k.a. Baby Face Nelson	Rural	Male	FIREARM	GANG	Serial
GLENN YOUNG, Seth	Urban	Male	FIREARM	POLITICAL	Single

POLICING	RESULT	SENTENCE	YEAR	LOCATION	PAGE	
—	Acquitted	—	1899	St. Louis, MO	110	
—	Acquitted	—	1916	Chicago, IL	79	
Ambush	Killed	—	1932	Hillsboro, TX	160	
Manhunt	Not Found	—	1871–73	Cherryville, KS	114	
Police Line-up	Acquitted	—	1935	Minneapolis, MN	100	
Manhunt	Killed	—	1865	Washington, D.C.	122	
Crime Scene Photography	Acquitted	—	1892	Fall River, MA	24	
—	Guilty	Imprisoned	1930	Chicago, IL	91	
Tireprints	Mistrial	—	1921	Los Angeles, CA	196	
—	Not Found	—	1900–01	Denver, CO	186	
Raids	Not Convicted	—	1926	Cicero, IL	86	
—	Guilty	Executed	1927	Omaha, NE	113	
—	Not Convicted	—	1926	Chicago, IL	90	
—	Not Convicted	—	1929	Chicago, IL	91	
Posse	Killed	—	1887	Spring Branch Creek, OK	154	
Toxicology	Guilty	Overturned	1909	Kansas City, MO	103	
Crime Scene Investigation	Guilty	Imprisoned	1909	Missoula, MT	170	
Polygraph	Not Found	—	1935–39	Cleveland, OH	66	
—	Guilty	Executed	1927	Hanford, CA	204	
Toxicology	Guilty	Executed	1881	Chicago, IL	76	
Psychiatry	Guilty	Executed	1901	Buffalo, NY	36	
Footprints	Guilty	Executed	1912	Crooked Creek, AR	150	
—	Acquitted	—	1913	Chicago, IL	79	
Manhunt	Guilty	Executed	1931 & 1937	Marlow, OK & Folsom, CA	158	
Crime Scene Photography	Acquitted	—	1915	New York City, NY	39	
—	Guilty	Imprisoned	1899	Odessa, NE	112	
Crime Scene Investigation	Guilty	Executed	1931	Quiet Dell, WV	134	
Manhunt	Killed	—	1939	Powell, WYO	178	
Crime Scene Photography	Guilty	Executed	1895	San Francisco, CA	194	
Crime Scene Investigation	Guilty	Executed	1937	Los Angeles, CA	212	
Collusion	Cover Up	—	1919	Elaine, AR	151	
Manhunt	Guilty	Executed	1912	Hillsville, VA	140	
Manhunt	Guilty	Executed	1912	Hillsville, VA	140	
Reward	Pardon	—	1882	St. Joseph, MO	104	
Forensics	Guilty, pardoned	Lynched	1913	Atlanta, GA	142	
Bomb Reconstruction	Not Found	—	1920	New York City, NY	40	
F.B.I.	Killed	—	1934	Mantowish, WI & Barrington, IL	92	
—	Killed	—	1925	Herrin, IL	84	

CRIMINOLOGY MATRIX [2/3]
PERTAINING TO EVERY MURDER EXAMINED IN THIS BOOK

MURDERER	ENVIRONMENT	GENDER	WEAPON	TYPOLOGY	PROFILE
GOMEZ, John*	Urban	Male	GAS PIPE	PROPERTY CRIME	Single
GUITEAU, Charles	Urban	Male	REVOLVER	ASSASSINATION	Single
GUNNESS, Belle	Rural	Female	VARIOUS	PROPERTY CRIME	Serial
HAGIWARA, Y.	Urban	Male	FIREARM	DISPUTE	Single
HALE, William	Rural	Male	VARIOUS	PROPERTY CRIME	Serial
HALLIDAY, Lizzie	Rural	Female	FIREARM & SCISSORS	MENTAL ILLNESS	Serial
HATFIELDS	Rural	Male	KNIVES & GUNS	FEUD	Serial
HAUPTMANN, Richard	Rural	Male	THERMOS BOTTLE	KIDNAPPING	Single
HAYDEN, Herbert	Rural	Male	JACKNIFE & ARSENIC	DOMESTIC	Single
HOLMES, Henry Howard	Urban	Male	CHLOROFORM & POISON	PROPERTY CRIME	Serial
HUTCHINSON, Nannie	Rural	Female	KNIFE	DOMESTIC	Single
KETCHUM, Thomas "Black Jack"	Rural	Male	FIREARM	PROPERTY CRIME	Single
LEOPOLD, Nathan*	Urban	Male	CHISEL	THRILL KILL	Single
LOEB, Richard*	Urban	Male	CHISEL	THRILL KILL	Single
"LUCKY" LUCIANO, Charles	Urban	Male	PISTOL	GANG	Single
McCARTY, Henry a.k.a. Billy the Kid	Rural	Male	PISTOL	GANG	Single
McCOYS	Rural	Male	KNIVES & GUNS	FEUD	Serial
McLEOD, Lucille	Urban	Female	PISTOL	DOMESTIC	Single
MILLER, Charles C.	Urban	Male	FIREARM	PROPERTY CRIME	Single
MURPHY, Jesse / REID, Frank	Rural	Male	PISTOL	POSSE	Single
MUSSO, Lena	Urban	Female	PISTOL	DOMESTIC	Single
NACK, Augusta*	Urban	Female	PISTOL	DOMESTIC	Single
NEGRA, Antone	Rural	Male	FIREARM	PROPERTY CRIME	Single
NEW ORLEANS AXE MURDERER	Urban	—	RAZOR & AXE	RANDOM ATTACK	Serial
NOAKES, Elmo	Rural	Male	SUFFOCATION & GUN	DOMESTIC	Single
NORTH SIDE GANG	Urban	Male	FIREARM	GANG	Single
NORTHCOTT, Gordon*	Rural	Male	AXE	SEXUAL	Serial
NORTHCOTT, Sarah*	Rural	Female	AXE	SEXUAL	Serial
OBENCHAIN, Madalynne*	Rural	Female	SHOTGUN	DOMESTIC	Single
PACKER, Alferd	Rural	Male	HATCHET	PROPERTY CRIME	Single
PETRILLO, Herman*	Urban	Male	POISON	CONTRACT	Serial
PETRILLO, Paul*	Urban	Male	POISON	CONTRACT	Serial

POLICING	RESULT	SENTENCE	YEAR	LOCATION	PAGE	
—	Guilty	Executed	1930	Livermore, CA	205	
—	Guilty	Executed	1881	Washington, D.C.	128	
Postmortem Identification	Suicide	—	1884–1908	La Porte, IN	72	
Postmortem	Guilty	Imprisoned	1912	Billings, MT	171	
B.O.I.	Guilty	Imprisoned	1921–26	Osage County, OK	156	
Property Search	Guilty	Life in Hospital	1891 & 1906	Mamakating & Beacon, NY	33	
—	—	—	1878–89	Big Sandy River, KY/WV	130	
Marked Bills	Guilty	Executed	1932	Mercer County, NJ	50	
Toxicology	Mistrial	—	1878	Rockland, CT	28	
Pinkerton Detectives	Guilty	Executed	1894	Philadelphia, PA	56	
Footprints	Guilty	Imprisoned	1903	Bostwick, NE	112	
Posse	Guilty	Executed	1895	Knickerbocker, TX	159	
Forensics	Guilty	Imprisoned	1924	Chicago, IL	80	
Forensics	Guilty	Imprisoned	1924	Chicago, IL	80	
—	Not Convicted	—	1931	New York City, NY	46	
Posse	Arrested, escaped, killed	—	1878	Lincoln, NM	188	
—	—	—	1878–89	Big Sandy River, KY/WV	130	
—	Acquitted	—	1906	Chicago, IL	78	
Footprints	Guilty	Imprisoned	1915	Kalispell, MT	171	
Posse	Not Tried	—	1898	Skaguay, AK	168	
—	Acquitted	—	1912	Chicago, IL	78	
Postmortem Identification	Guilty	Imprisoned	1897	New York City, NY	34	
—	Guilty	Executed	1928	Los Banos, CA	204	
—	Not Found	—	1918–19	New Orleans, LA	152	
Forensics	Suicide	—	1934	Pine Grove Furnace & Duncansville, PA	60	
—	Not Convicted	—	1928	Chicago, IL	90	
Forensic Anthropology	Guilty	Executed	1926–28	Los Angeles, CA	200	
Forensic Anthropology	Guilty	Imprisoned	1926–28	Los Angeles, CA	200	
Tireprints	Mistrial	—	1921	Los Angeles, CA	196	
Postmortem	Guilty	Imprisoned	1874	San Juan Mountains, CO	184	
Double Agent	Guilty	Executed	1938	Philadelphia, PA	62	
Double Agent	Guilty	Executed	1938	Philadelphia, PA	62	

CRIMINOLOGY MATRIX [3/3]

PERTAINING TO EVERY MURDER EXAMINED IN THIS BOOK

MURDERER	ENVIRONMENT	GENDER	WEAPON	TYPOLOGY	PROFILE
POMEROY, Jesse	Urban & Rural	Male	MULTIPLE	RANDOM ATTACK	Serial
REILLY, Alphonse	Urban	Male	PISTOL	PROPERTY CRIME	Single
RYLEY, George*	Urban	Male	GAS PIPE	PROPERTY CRIME	Single
SMETAK, Adolph	Rural	Male	HAMMER	DOMESTIC	Single
SMITH, James J.	Rural	Male	FIREARM	LAND DISPUTE	Single
THOMAS, Ora	Urban	Male	FIREARM	POLITICAL	Single
THORN, Martin*	Urban	Male	PISTOL	DOMESTIC	Single
TILLMAN, John Arthur	Rural	Male	RIFLE	DOMESTIC	Single
UNKNOWN	Urban	—	—	GANG	Single
UNKNOWN	Urban	—	IRON BAR	PROPERTY CRIME	Single
UNKNOWN	Urban	—	KNIFE	RANDOM ATTACK	Serial
UNKNOWN	Urban	—	KNIFE	GANG	Serial
UNKNOWN	Urban	—	REVOLVER	GANG	Single
UNKNOWN	Rural	—	AXE	RANDOM ATTACK	Serial
UNKNOWN	Rural	—	VARIOUS	TORTURE	Single
UNKNOWN	Rural	—	NOOSE	POLITICAL	Single
UNKNOWN	Rural	—	PISTOL	VIGILANTE	Single
UNKNOWN	Urban	—	BLUNT OBJECT	TARGETED KILLING	Single
UNKNOWN	Urban	—	PISTOL	UNKNOWN	Single
UNKNOWN	Urban	—	CARBON MONOXIDE	DOMESTIC	Single
WALLACE-WALKUP, Minnie	Urban	Female	POISON	PROPERTY CRIME	Serial
WILLWORD, Albert	Urban	Male	PISTOL	DOMESTIC	Single
ZANGARA, Giuseppe	Urban	Male	HANDGUN	ASSASSINATION	Single

POLICING	RESULT	SENTENCE	YEAR	LOCATION	PAGE	
Footprints	Arrested	Imprisoned	1874	Boston, MA	22	
—	Guilty	Executed	1929	Los Angeles, CA	205	
—	Guilty	Executed	1930	Livermore, CA	205	
—	Guilty	Imprisoned	1925	Prague, NE	113	
Search Party	Guilty	Imprisoned	1912	Melrose, MT	170	
—	Killed	—	1925	Herrin, IL	84	
Postmortem Identification	Guilty	Executed	1897	New York City, NY	34	
Ballistics	Guilty	Executed	1913	Logan County, AR	150	
—	Not Found	—	1933	Pawtuxet Village, RI	30	
Crime Scene Investigation	Not Found	—	1870	New York City, NY	32	
Crime Scene Photography	Not Found	—	1915	New York City, NY	38	
Crime Scene Photography	Not Found	—	1915	New York City, NY	39	
—	Not Found	—	1928	New York City, NY	44	
Postmortem	Not Found	—	1912	Villisca, IA	102	
Forensic Anthropology	Acquitted	—	1929	St. James, AR	151	
—	Not Found	—	1917	Butte, MT	172	
—	Not Found	—	1867	Bozeman Trail, MO	176	
—	Not Found	—	1905	Denver, CO	187	
—	Not Found	—	1922	Los Angeles, CA	198	
Autopsy	Not Found	—	1935	Los Angeles, CA	206	
Toxicology	Not Convicted	—	1885	Emporia, KS	118	
Crime Scene Photography	Guilty	Not known	1914	New York City, NY	38	
—	Guilty	Executed	1933	Miami, FL	146	

FURTHER READING

WRITER	TITLE	PUBLISHER
ADLER, JEFFREY S.	FIRST IN VIOLENCE, DEEPEST IN DIRT: HOMICIDE IN CHICAGO, 1875–1920	CAMBRIDGE, MA: HARVARD UNIVERSITY PRESS, 2006
BINDER, JOHN J.	AL CAPONE'S BEER WARS: A COMPLETE HISTORY OF ORGANIZED CRIME IN CHICAGO DURING PROHIBITION	AMHERST, NY: PROMETHEUS BOOKS, 2017
CANTER, DAVID	CRIMINAL SHADOWS: INSIDE THE MIND OF THE SERIAL KILLER	LONDON: HARPERCOLLINS, 1994
COLE, SIMON A.	SUSPECT IDENTITIES: A HISTORY OF FINGERPRINTING AND CRIMINAL IDENTIFICATION	CAMBRIDGE, MA: HARVARD UNIVERSITY PRESS, 2001
DICKIE, JOHN	COSA NOSTRA: A HISTORY OF THE SICILIAN MAFIA	LONDON: HODDER, 2004
FULTON, MAURICE GARLAND	HISTORY OF THE LINCOLN COUNTY WAR	TUCSON, AZ: UNIVERSITY OF ARIZONA PRESS, 1969
GARDNER, LLOYD C.	THE CASE THAT NEVER DIES: THE LINDBERGH KIDNAPPING	NEW BRUNSWICK, NJ: RUTGERS UNIVERSITY PRESS, 2004
GRANN, DAVID	KILLERS OF THE FLOWER MOON: THE OSAGE MURDERS AND THE BIRTH OF THE F.B.I.	NEW YORK, NY: DOUBLEDAY, 2017
KAUTE, WILFRIED	MURDER IN THE CITY: NEW YORK, 1910–1920	NEW YORK, NY: MACMILLAN, 2017
LANE, ROGER	MURDER IN AMERICA: A HISTORY	COLUMBUS, OH: OHIO STATE UNIVERSITY PRESS, 1997
McCRERY, NIGEL	SILENT WITNESSES: THE STORY OF FORENSIC SCIENCE	LONDON: RANDOM HOUSE, 2013
PERRY, DOUGLAS	GIRLS OF MURDER CITY: FAME, LUST, AND THE BEAUTIFUL KILLERS WHO INSPIRED *CHICAGO*	NEW YORK, NY: PENGUIN BOOKS, 2011
RENNER, JOAN	THE FIRST WITH THE LATEST!: AGGIE UNDERWOOD, THE *LOS ANGELES HERALD*, AND THE SORDID CRIMES OF A CITY	LOS ANGELES, CA: PHOTO FRIENDS OF THE LOS ANGELES PUBLIC LIBRARY, 2015
REPPETTO, THOMAS	AMERICAN POLICE: A HISTORY 1845–1945	NEW YORK, NY: ENIGMA BOOKS, 2010
ROTH, RANDOLPH	AMERICAN HOMICIDE	CAMBRIDGE, MA: BELKNAP PRESS OF HARVARD UNIVERSITY PRESS, 2009
RUSHDY, ASHRAF H. A.	AMERICAN LYNCHING	NEW HAVEN, CT: YALE UNIVERSITY PRESS, 2012
RUSSO, GUS	THE OUTFIT: THE ROLE OF CHICAGO'S UNDERWORLD IN THE SHAPING OF MODERN AMERICA	NEW YORK, NY: BLOOMSBURY, 2002
WALLIS, BRIAN	WEEGEE: MURDER IS MY BUSINESS	MUNICH: PRESTEL, 2013
WEINER, TIM	ENEMIES: A HISTORY OF THE F.B.I.	LONDON; NEW YORK, NY: RANDOM HOUSE, 2011
WILHELM, ROBERT	THE BLOODY CENTURY: TRUE TALES OF MURDER IN 19TH CENTURY AMERICA	BOSTON, MA: NIGHTSTICK PRESS, 2014
WHITAKER, ROBERT	ON THE LAPS OF GODS: THE RED SUMMER OF 1919 AND THE STRUGGLE FOR JUSTICE THAT REMADE A NATION	NEW YORK, NY: THREE RIVERS PRESS, 2009

SOURCES OF ILLUSTRATIONS

Every effort has been made to locate and credit copyright holders of the material reproduced in this book. The author and publisher apologize for any omissions or errors, which can be corrected in future editions.

Unless otherwise indicated, all maps are David Rumsey Map Collection, www.davidrumsey.com.

a= above, c= centre, b= below, l= left, r=right

1, Los Angeles Herald Examiner Photo Collection, Los Angles Public Library, **2–6**, Bettmann via Getty Images, **8**, Library of Congress, Washington, D.C. , **9**, Hugo J. von Hagen, *Reading Character from Handwriting* (1902), **9**, Bettmann via Getty Images, **11–2**, Library of Congress, Washington, D.C. , **13**, Courtesy of the F.B.I, **14 a**, National Institute of Standards and Technology Digital Archives, Gaithersburg, MD 20899, **14 b**, Smithsonian Institution Archives, Accession 90-105, Science Service Records, Image No. SIA2007-0458, **16–7**, International Center of Photography via Getty Images, **18 l**, **18c**, New York Daily News Archive via Getty Images, **18 r**, ullstein bild Dtl. via Getty Images, **19 l**, New York Daily News Archive via Getty Images, **19 c**, Irving Haberman/IH Images via Getty Images, **19 r**, Bettmann via Getty Images, **20–1**, Bettmann via Getty Images, **22 a**, Library of Congress, Washington, D.C., **22 br**, *Frank Leslie's Illustrated Newspaper*, 9 May 1874, **23 a**, Library of Congress, Washington, D.C. , **23 cl**, **cr**, **b**, Courtesy of the Boston Public Library, Leslie Jones Collection, **24 a**, Private Collection, **24 cl**, Edwin H. Porter, *The Fall River Tragedy* (1893), **24 bl**, Bettmann via Getty Images, **24 c**, **cr**, **br**, Fall River Historical Society, **25 a**, Private Collection, **27 a**, The Picture Art Collection / Alamy Stock Photo, **27 ac**, Balfore Archive Images / Alamy Stock Photo, **27 bc**, **b**, The Picture Art Collection / Alamy Stock Photo, **28–9**, *The Rev. Herbert H. Hayden; an autobiography* (1880), **30**, Private Collection, **31 cl**, **b**, Courtesy of the Boston Public Library, Leslie Jones Collection, **31 cr**, Sueddeutsche Zeitung Photo / Alamy Stock Photo, **32**, British Newspaper Archive, **33 a**, *Oshkosh Daily Northwestern*, 1 October 1906, **33 br**, "Mrs Halliday's Murders", *The Illustrated American*, 7 October 1893, **33 bl**, Library of Congress, Washington, D.C. , **34–5**, Library of Congress, Washington, D.C. , **36 a**, L. Vernon Briggs, *The Manner of Man That Kills* (1921), **36 r**, DEA / A. DAGLI ORTI via Getty Images, **37 a**, Niday Picture Library / Alamy Stock Photo, **37 cl**, Universal Images Group via Getty Images, **37 ccl**, The Montifraulo Collection via Getty Images, **37 ccr**, The Picture Art Collection / Alamy Stock Photo, **37 cr**, PhotoQuest via Getty Images, **37 bl**, Everett Collection Historical / Alamy Stock Photo, **37 br**, RGB Ventures / SuperStock / Alamy Stock Photo, **38 al**, **ar**, **39 al**, **ar**, Courtesy Municipal Archives, City of New York, **40–3**, Library of Congress, Washington, D.C. , **44**, FPG via Getty Images, **45 al**, Transcendental Graphics via Getty Images, **45 ar**, Christian Cipollini collection, **45 c**, **b**, New York Daily News Archive via Getty Images, **46 al**, Santi Visalli via Getty Images, **46 ar** , Bettmann via Getty Images, **46 b**, From The New York Public Library, Map Div. 19-130, **47 a**, New York Daily News Archive via Getty Images, **47 cl**, Bettmann via Getty Images, **47 cr**, Granger/Shutterstock, **47 bl**, **blc**, Granger Historical Picture Archive / Alamy Stock Photo, **47 bc**, Science History Images / Alamy Stock Photo, **47 brc**, Archive PL / Alamy Stock Photo, **47 br**, Everett Collection Historical / Alamy Stock Photo, **48–9**, Slim Aarons / Stringer via Getty Images, **50 al**, Hulton Archive / Stringer, **50 ar**, Mondadori Portfolio via Getty Images, **50 b**, **51**, Bettmann via Getty Images, **52 al**, Perry-Castañeda Library, Map Collection University of Texas Libraries, **52 cl**, **c**, Bettmann via Getty Images, **52 cr**, Hulton Archive via Getty Images, **52 bl**, Bettmann via Getty Images, **52 bc**, New York Daily News Archive via Getty Images, **52 br**, **53 a**, Bettmann via Getty Images, **53 c**, George Rinhart via Getty Images, **53 b**, Imagno via Getty Images, **54**, **55 a**, **b**, Bettmann via Getty Images, **56 al**, *The Holmes-Pitezel Case* (1896), **56 ar**, **57 l**, Library of Congress, Washington, D.C. , **57 c**, *The Holmes-Pitezel Case* (1896), **57 b**, Chicago Tribune Historical Photos/TCA, **58–9**, Information from Philadelphia police arrest reports, see Roger Lane, *Murder in America: A History* (Columbus: Ohio State University Press, 1997) **60 al**, Robert and Elmo Noakes, c. 1918, **60 ar**, **cl**, **cr**, Private Collection, **61**, Private Collection, **62–3**, Philadelphia Police Department, **64–5**, Bettmann via Getty Images, **66 a**, **b**, Michael Schwartz Library, Cleveland State University, **67 a**, The Cleveland Police Historical Society, Inc., **67 cl**, **bl**, Michael Schwartz Library, Cleveland State University, **67 cr**, **br**, The Cleveland Police Historical Society, Inc., **69 a**, **b**, Bettmann via Getty Images, **70–1**, Michael Schwartz Library, Cleveland State University, **72**, The LaPorte County Historical Society and Museum, **73–4**, The LaPorte County Historical Society and Museum, **76 a**, © McCord Museum, Montreal, Canada, 2007, **76 bl**, Private Collection, **77a**, McGill University Archives, PL007815, **77 b**, Science Museum / Science and Society Picture Library, **78 al**, **ar**, **79 al**, **ar**, DN-0004287, DN-0060221, DN-0061102, DN-0067181, Chicago Daily News collection, Chicago History Museum, **80 al**, **ar**, Topical Press Agency / Stringer via Getty Images, **80 c**, New York Daily News via Getty Images, **80 b**, Bettmann via Getty Images, **81 a**, Rolls Press/ Popperfoto via Getty Images, **81 cl**, **cr**, New York Daily News via Getty Images, **81 b**, Topical Press Agency / Stringer via Getty Images, **82**, Courtesy of McCormick Library of Special Collections and University Archives, Northwestern University: Harold S. Hulbert Papers., **83 a**, Chicago History Museum via Getty Images, **83 cl**, **cr**, **bl**, **br**, New York Daily News via Getty Images, **84**, **85 a**, *Life and Exploits of Seth Glenn Young* (c. 1925), **85 c**, **b**, Marion Illinois History Preservation, **86 l**, IanDagnall Computing / Alamy Stock Photo, **86 r**, ullstein bild Dtl. via Getty Images, **87**, Chicago History Museum via Getty Images, **90 l**, Chicago History Museum via Getty Images, **90 r**, New York Daily News Archive via Getty Images, **91 l**, Bettmann via Getty Images, **91 r**, Chicago History Museum via Getty Images, **92**, Everett Collection Historical / Alamy Stock Photo, **93–4**, Courtesy of the F.B.I, **95 al**, CPC Collection / Alamy Stock Photo, **95 ar**, Photo courtesy of Morphy Auctions, www.morphyauctions.com, **95 b**, Courtesy of the F.B.I, **96 l**, Private Collection, **96 r**, **97 a**, Bettmann via Getty Images, **97 b**, Tribune Content Agency LLC / Alamy Stock Photo, **98**, Hulton Archive / Stringer via Getty Images, **99**, Courtesy RMY Auctions, **100 l**, Private Collection, **100 r**, Library of Congress, Washington, D.C. , **101**, Courtesy Minnesota Historical Society, 68643, **102**, Library of Congress, Washington, D.C., **103**, Missouri Valley Special Collections, Kansas City Public Library, **104 al**, Granger Historical Picture Archive / Alamy Stock Photo, **104 ar**, Library of Congress, Washington, D.C. , **105 a**, **c**, Lordprice Collection / Alamy Stock Photo, **105 b**, Library of Congress, Washington, D.C. , **106**, Pictorial Press Ltd / Alamy Stock Photo, **107**, Historic Collection / Alamy Stock Photo, **108 al**, **ac**, **al**, **acl**, **acc**, **cl**, **c**, **cr**, **bcr**, **bcl**, **bl**, **bc**, *The Life Times and Treacherous Death of Jess James* (1882), **108 acr**, **bcc**, **br**, *Illustrated Lives and Adventures of Frank and Jesse James* (1882), **110 a**, St. Louis Mercantile Library at the University of Missouri-St. Louis, **111**, *The Saga of Frankie and Johnnie* (1930), **112 al**, **ar**, **113 al**, **ar**, History Nebraska, [RG2418.PH0-003741], **114 a**, Courtesy of the Historical Cherryvale Museum, Inc., **114 b**, Private Collection, **115 al**, Charles Wesley Alexander, *The Five Fiends* (1874), **115 ar**, John T. James, *The Benders of Kansas* (1913), **115 a**, **c**, **b**, **116**, Kansas Historical Society, **118**, **119 a**, Library of Congress, Washington, D.C. , **119 br**, DN-0062543, Chicago Daily News Collection, Chicago History Museum, **120–1**, Bettmann via Getty Images, **122 al**, Library of Congress, Washington, D.C. , **122 ar**, Pictorial Press Ltd / Alamy Stock Photo, **122 c**, Library of Congress, Washington, D.C. , **122 b**, From The New York Public Library, b13476047, **123 l**, Science History Images / Alamy Stock Photo, **123 ar**, **br**, **124 al**, **ac**, **ar**, **cl**, **c**, **cr**, **bc**, **br**, Library of Congress, Washington, D.C. , **124 bl**, Alamy Stock Photo, **125 cl**, Library of Congress, Washington, D.C. , **125 ccl**, Tom Williams via Getty Images, **125 ccr**, **cr**, Courtesy of the Maryland Historical Trust, **125 bl**, **bcr**, Osborn Oldroyd, *The assassination of Abraham Lincoln* (1901), **125 bcl**, Private Collection, **125 br**, Private Collection, **126–7**, Library of Congress, Washington, D.C. , **128 a**, **bl**, Library of Congress, Washington, D.C. , **128 br**, Bettmann via Getty Images, **129 a**, Photo 12 via Getty Images, **129 cl**, **ccl**, **cc**, DEA / BIBLIOTECA AMBROSIANA via Getty Images, **129 ccr**, Kean Collection via Getty Images, **129 cr**, Universal History Archive via Getty Images, **129 b**, Education Images via Getty Images, **130 al**, West Virginia and Regional History Collection WVU Libraries, **130 ar**, Private Collection, **130 b**, Time Life Pictures via Getty Images, **131 a**, Time Life Pictures via Getty Images, **131 c**, Kentucky Historical Society, **131 b**, Corbis Historical via Getty Images, **132–3**, Perry-Castañeda Library, Map Collection University of Texas Libraries, **134 a**, Uncredited/ AP/Shutterstock, **134 bl**, *Marysville Journal-Tribune*, 31 August 1931, **134 br**, Uncredited/AP/Shutterstock, **135 a**, Private Collection, **135 c**, **b**, **136 al**, West Virginia and Regional History Collection WVU Libraries, **136 ar**, Private Collection, **137**, AP Shutterstock, **138–9**, West Virginia State Archives, **140**, Courtesy of the Library of Virginia, **141 a**, Courtesy of the Virginia Room, Roanoke Public Libraries, **141 c**, Library of Congress, Washington, D.C. , **141 b**, Courtesy of the Library of Virginia, **142 a**, **143 al**, **c**, Leofrank.org, **143 ar**, Library of Congress, Washington, D.C. , **142–3 b**, From The New York Public Library, Crime scene reconstructions comissioned by Adolph S. Ochs, **144–5**, Mapped information from the Monroe Work Today Dataset Compilation, as shown at www.plaintalk history.com/monroeandflorencework **146**, **147 a**, Bettmann via Getty Images, **147 c**, Imagno via Getty Images, **147 b**, Bettmann via Getty Images, **148**, Chicago History Museum via Getty Images, **149**, Bettmann via Getty Images, **150 al**, Private Collection, **150 ar**, Arthur Tillman hanging, G3897, Arkansas State Archives, **151 al**, Elaine massacre, G1595.11, Arkansas State Archives, **151 ar**, Private Collection, **152 bl**, Washington State Archives, **152 br**, *Times-Picayune*, 1919, **153 al**, **ar**, Private Collection, **154 al**, Private Collection, **154 ar**, *Tahlequah Daily Press*, **154 c**, Perry-Castañeda Library, Map Collection University of Texas Libraries, **154 b**, UALR Center for Arkansas History and Culture, **155 a**, Oklahoma Historical Society Photograph Collection, ark:/67531/metadc228900, **155 a**, UALR Center for Arkansas History and Culture, **155 c**, Oklahoma Historical Society Photograph Collection, ark:/67531/ metadc1620616, **156**, Courtesy of the F.B.I, **157 al**, Bettmann via Getty Images, **157 alc**, Courtesy of the F.B.I, **157 ac**, **acr**, **ar**, Bettmann via Getty Images, **157 cla**, Oklahoma Historical Society Photograph Collection, ark:/67531/ metadc1622145, **157 clb**, Courtesy of the F.B.I, **157 cr**, Private Collection, **158 a**, California Prison and Correctional Records, **158 c**, Image Courtesy of Waddington's Auctioneers and Appraisers, Toronto, **159 a**, Kansas State Historical Society, **159 ac**, Denver Public Library Special Collections, **159 bc**, Heritage Auctions, HA.com, **159 b**, Perry-Castañeda Library, Map Collection University of Texas Libraries, **160 al**, Archive PL / Alamy Stock Photo, **160 ar**, Private Collection, **161 al**, **ar**, Popperfoto via Getty Images, **161 cl**, **cr**, Courtesy of the F.B.I, **161 bl**, Bettmann via Getty Images, **161 br**, AP/Shutterstock, **162**, Everett/ Shutterstock, **163**, **165**, Library of Congress, Washington, D.C. , **166–7**, Los Angeles Times Photographic Archive, Library Special Collections, Charles E. Young Research Library, UCLA, **168 a**, **bl**, **169 al**, Library of Congress, Washington, D.C. , **168 br**, **169 ar**, **bl**, Alaska State Library, ASL-P226-068, ASL-P226-090, ASL-P226-087, **169 br**, History and Art Collection / Alamy Stock Photo, **170 al**, Prisoner description sheet, John E. Clayborne. Montana State Prison Records, 1869-1974. RS 197. Box 45 Folder 5. Montana Historical Society Research Center, Archives, Helena, Montana., **170 ar**, Prisoner description sheet, James J. Smith. Montana State Prison Records, 1869-1974. RS 197. Box 53 Folder 4. Montana Historical Society Research Center, Archives, Helena, Montana., **171 al**, Prisoner description sheet, Y. Hagiwara. Montana State Prison Records, 1869-1874. RS 197. Box 48 Folder 1. Montana Historical Society Research Center, Archives, Helena, Montana., **171 ar**, Prisoner description sheet, Charles C. Miller. Montana State Prison Records, 1869-1974. RS 197. Box 51 Folder 1. Montana Historical Society Research Center, Archives, Helena, Montana., **172 a**, University of Michigan Library (Joseph A. Labadie Collection, Special Collections Research Center), **172 c**, Perry-Castañeda Library, Map Collection University of Texas Libraries, **172 b**, George Tompkins, *The Truth About Butte*, 1917. Publications and Ephemera from the Montana Historical Society. PAM 3208. Montana Historical Society Research Center, Archives, Helena, Montana., **173 a**, Private Collection, **173 c**, Andrew Lichtenstein via Getty Images, **173 b**, **174**, University of Michigan Library (Joseph A. Labadie Collection, Special Collections Research Center), **175 al**, Everett Collection Inc / Alamy Stock Photo, **175 ar**, *Butte Daily Bulletin*, 2 October 1920, **175 cl**, Walter P. Reuther Library, **175 cr**, Private Collection, **175 bl**, George Rinhart via Getty Images, **175 br**, Private Collection, **176 a**, Courtesy of the Museum of the Rockies, Bozeman, MT, **177 bc**, Courtesy of PBA Galleries, **176 bl**, Private Collection, **176 br**, Library of Congress, Washington, D.C. , **177 c**, Montana State University Libraries, **178 b**, *The photographic history of the Civil War* (1911), **178 a**, Homesteader Museum, **178 b**, **al**, **ar**, **b**, **a**, **b**, Park County Archives, **181**, Yellowstone National Park Map & Park County, Wyoming State Archives Map Case Collection, **182**, Park County Archives, **183 a**, Hulton Deutsch via Getty Images, **183 c**, **b**, Park County Archives, **184 a**, **bl**, Everett Collection Historical / Alamy Stock Photo, **184 br**, Courtesy of Grant Houston, **185 ala**, **alb**, Granger Historical Picture Archive / Alamy Stock Photo, **185 alc**, Chris Hellier / Alamy Stock Photo, **185 ar**, *Harper's Weekly*, October 17 1874, **186 a**, Private Collection, **187**, Private Collection, **188 al**, Private Collection, **188 ar**, William Brady (1825-1878), Lincoln County Sheriff shot by Billy the Kid, ca. 1870s, Courtesy of the Palace of the Governors Photo Archives (NMHM/DCA), 105103a, **188 b**, Courtesy of Kagins.com, **189 a**, Group on street across from courthouse, Lincoln, New Mexico, 1910?, Courtesy of the Palace of the Governors Photo Archives (NMHM/DCA), 105474, **189 b**, *A Study of the Outlaw* (1907), **190**, Private Collection, **191**, Fototeca Storica Nazionale via Getty Images, **192**, Library of Congress, Washington, D.C., **193 al**, **alc**, **ac**, **bcl**, **bccl**, Private Collection, **193 ar**, Heritage Auctions, HA.com, **193 acl**, John Hodges, Mr. and Mrs. Frank Coe (Helena Anne Tully Coe and Benjamin Franklin Coe), Durango, Colorado, 1881, Courtesy of the Palace of the Governors Photo Archives (NMHM/DCA), 105075, **193 accl**, Photo courtesy of the US National Park Service, Historic Photograph Collection, **193 acc**, Tom O'Folliard, 1878?, Courtesy of the Palace of the Governors Photo Archives (NMHM/DCA), 104721, **193 accr**, **acr**, **bl**, *A Study of the Outlaw* (1907), **193 bcc**, William Brady (1825-1878), Lincoln County Sheriff shot by Billy the Kid, ca. 1870s, Courtesy of the Palace of the Governors Photo Archives (NMHM/DCA), 105103a, **193 bccr**, Unidentified couple (man is possibly Jesse Evans), woman holding pistol, New Mexico, 1870?, Courtesy of the Palace of the Governors Photo Archives (NMHM/DCA), HP.1992.21.50, **193 bcr**, Private Collection, **194**, **195 al**, **ar**, **bl**, **br**, *Report of the trial of William Henry Theodore Durrant* (1899), **195 cl**, Library of Congress, Washington, D.C. , **196 al**, **ar**, Los Angeles Times Photographic Archive, Library Special Collections, Charles E. Young Research Library, UCLA, **196 br**, Private Collection, **197 al**, **ar**, **c**, **b**, Los Angeles Times Photographic Archive, Library Special Collections, Charles E. Young Research Library, UCLA, **198 a**, Bettmann via Getty Images, **198 br**, Private Collection, **198 bl**, USC Digital Library. Los Angeles Examiner Photographs Collection, **199 bl**, Bettmann via Getty Images, **199 bcl**, **bc**, Library of Congress, Washington, D.C. , **199 bcr**, University of Southern California via Getty Images, **199 br**, Everett Collection Inc / Alamy Stock Photo, **200**, Los Angeles Times Photographic Archive, Library Special Collections, Charles E. Young Research Library, UCLA, **201 aa**, Private Collection, **201 al**, **ar**, **acl**, **acr**, **bcl**, **bcr**, Los Angeles Times Photographic Archive, Library Special Collections, Charles E. Young Research Library, UCLA, **201 bl**, **br**, Private Collection, **202**, Los Angeles Times Photographic Archive, Library Special Collections, Charles E. Young Research Library, UCLA, **203**, Los Angeles Herald Examiner Photo Collection, Los Angeles Public Library, **204 al**, **ar**, **205 al**, **ar**, UC Berkeley, Bancroft Library, **206 a**, The Print Collector / Alamy Stock Photo, **206 b**, UC Berkeley, Bancroft Library, **207 bl**, Everett Collection Inc / Alamy Stock Photo, **207 br**, Zuri Swimmer / Alamy Stock Photo, **208**, Bettmann via Getty Images, **209 a**, Los Angeles Daily News Negatives, Library Special Collections, Charles E. Young Research Library, UCLA , **209 b**, Bettmann via Getty Images, **210–1**, Private Collection, **212 a**, Los Angeles Herald Examiner Photo Collection, Los Angeles Public Library, **212 bl**, **br**, **213 bl**, **br**, Los Angeles Daily News Negatives, Library Special Collections, Charles E. Young Research Library, UCLA, **213 al**, Private Collection, **224**, Michael Schwartz Library, Cleveland State University

ACKNOWLEDGMENTS

The author would like to thank Mandy, Leyla, Patti, and Ben from the Effing Collective, and the Mysterians, all of whom helped keep me focused in an out-of-focus year. Also my agent, Adrienne, and the other cemetery regulars around Chicago and New York.

Tristan de Lancey, Jane Laing, Isabel Jessop, Phoebe Lindsley and Sadie Butler at Thames & Hudson.

WITH 764 ILLUSTRATIONS

OPPOSITE The eyes of a victim of the Cleveland Torso Murderer, who decapitated many of their victims.

PAGE 1 The eyes of Albert Dyer, who killed three girls in Inglewood, LA, in 1937.

PAGE 2 The infamous image of Joe "the boss" Masseria after he was killed, with an ace of spades in hand. Masseria was playing cards before he was shot, but it is likely the card was placed in his hand by reporters after his death.

PAGE 4 The body of the editor Howard Guilford slumped in his car, after he was shot on his way to work in 1934.

COVER Higgins, Belden & Co., *Centre Township, Laporte County, Indiana*, 1874

FRONT The body of Joe "the boss" Masseria, killed in 1934 by men in the employ of Charles "Lucky" Luciano.

BACK, ABOVE LEFT The victim of a murder in New York City in 1916.

BACK, ABOVE RIGHT The mugshot of Lester Gillis, a.k.a. Baby Face Nelson.

BACK, BELOW Investigators removing the remains of a victim of the Cleveland Torso Murderer from Lake Erie.

ABOUT THE AUTHOR

Adam Selzer is an author and researcher specializing in the secret side of history, rescuing long-lost stories from microfilm reels, tracing urban legends to their sources, and uncovering the criminal underworld. He has been a tour guide in New York and Chicago, and has written over twenty books. Titles include multiple works of crime history, including *H. H. Holmes: The True History of the White City Devil*, *Mysterious Chicago* and *The Ghosts of Chicago*.

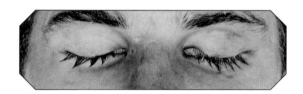

First published in the United Kingdom in 2021 by Thames & Hudson Ltd, 181A High Holborn, London WC1V 7QX

First published in the United States of America in 2021 by Thames & Hudson Inc., 500 Fifth Avenue, New York, New York 10110

Murder Maps USA © 2021 Thames & Hudson Ltd, London

Text © 2021 Adam Selzer

For image copyright information, see page 221

Designed by Anil Aykan at Barnbrook

Illustrations by Adrian Cartwright at Planet Illustration

British Library Cataloguing-in-Publication Data A catalogue record for this book is available from the British Library

Library of Congress Control Number 2021934165

ISBN 978-0-500-25259-8

Printed and bound in China by C&C Offset Printing Co. Ltd

Be the first to know about our new releases, exclusive content and author events by visiting
thamesandhudson.com
thamesandhudsonusa.com
thamesandhudson.com.au